12/21

Bruce A. Ragsdale, Federal Judicial Center

The Trial of Chicago Seven

e-artnow 2021

Bruce A. Ragsdale, Federal Judicial Center

The Trial of Chicago Seven

e-artnow, 2021
Contact: info@e-artnow.org

ISBN 978-80-273-4194-8

Contents

The Chicago Conspiracy Trial: A Short Narrative   11

The Judicial Process: A Chronology   27

The Federal Courts and Their Jurisdiction   39

Legal Questions Before the Federal Courts   43

Legal Arguments in Court   53

Biographies   57

Media Coverage and Public Debates   95

Historical Documents   99

The Official Trial Transcript – The Crucial Parts   125

The Chicago Conspiracy Trial: A Short Narrative

The trial of political activists accused of inciting riots during the Democratic National Convention of 1968 attracted national attention and exposed the depths of political and cultural divisions at a crucial moment in the nation's history. The trial of the "Chicago Seven" became a defining event in public debates about the Vietnam War, the student protest movement, and the fairness of the federal judicial process.

The defendants and their lawyers used the courtroom as a platform for a broad critique of American society and an almost anarchic challenge to the legitimacy of governmental authority. The judge in the case displayed open contempt for the defendants, and his own unorthodox behavior threatened public confidence in the judiciary. The nearly five-month long trial illustrated the contentious and often theatrical nature of public affairs during the late 1960s and early 1970s.

Table of Contents

Planning for the Democratic National Convention of 1968

In the fall of 1967, the Democratic Party decided to hold its 1968 national convention and the expected renomination of President Lyndon Johnson in Chicago. Mayor Richard Daley promised his city would be free of the civil disorders that had broken out in major cities in recent summers. By the summer of 1968, the prospects for a smooth convention had vanished. Johnson, in the face of growing protests against the Vietnam War and alter assessing the surprising strength of Eugene McCarthy's campaign for President, withdrew in March from the race for the nomination. The assassination of Martin Luther King in April provoked devastating urban riots in Chicago and other cities. The assassination of Robert Kennedy in June further shocked the nation and complicated the race for the Democratic nomination. The spring of 1968 had also brought the Tet offensive against American forces in Vietnam and unprecedented student protests on university campuses. By August, many Americans believed the nation was in the midst of a profound political and cultural crisis.

Organizing protests at the Democratic convention

In the fall of 1967, members of the National Mobilization Committee to End the War in Vietnam proposed a massive anti-war demonstration to coincide with the expected renomination of President Johnson in Chicago. The National Mobilization Committee was directed by David Dellinger, a long-time pacifist, who had organized the march on the Pentagon in October 1967. In early 1968, the National Mobilization opened a Chicago office directed by Rennie Davis and Tom Hayden, who were leading political organizers and former leaders of Students for a Democratic Society.

A small group of cultural radicals, including Jerry Rubin, who helped Dellinger organize the march on the Pentagon, and Abbie Hoffman, an organizer of political theater events, planned a "Festival of Life" to counter the Democratic "Convention of Death." Rubin and Hoffman dubbed themselves the Yippie movement, later explained as an acronym for the Youth International Party. They planned outdoor concerts, nonviolent self-defense classes, guerrilla theater, and a "nude-in" on a Chicago beach.

In March, representatives of various left-wing and radical student groups met in Lake Villa, Illinois, to discuss coordination of the protests and demonstrations planned for the Democratic convention. Tom Hayden and Rennie Davis drafted a proposal for various protests of the Vietnam War and social injustice, culminating with a mock funeral march to the convention hall on the night Johnson was to be renominated. The Lake Villa proposal advised that "the campaign should not plan violence and disruption against the Democratic National Convention. It should be nonviolent and legal." The National Mobilization Committee sought permits for the proposed march, and the Yippie leaders applied for permits to sleep in the city parks, but in negotiations that continued to the week of the convention, the Daley administration refused almost all permit requests.

Confrontations in Chicago

On the eve of the convention, Mayor Daley, citing intelligence reports of potential violence, put the 12,000 members of the Chicago Police Department on twelve-hour shifts and called for the governor to activate the National Guard. The U.S. Army placed 6,000 troops in position to protect the city during the convention. Both the police and the demonstrators organized workshops for training in the event of violence. The estimated number of demonstrators who came to Chicago during convention week was about 10,000, dramatically less than earlier predictions, but the police were determined to present a show of force and to enforce the 11:00 p.m. curfew in the parks.

Beginning on Sunday, August 25, the police and demonstrators clashed in city parks where many of the protests were staged and where visiting demonstrators hoped to sleep. For three nights, the aggressive police sweep through Lincoln Park was met with the demonstrators' taunting and occasional rocks. With tear gas and clubbings, the police forced demonstrators out of the park and into commercial areas, where demonstrators smashed windows. Police repeatedly targeted journalists and destroyed their cameras.

Violence escalated on the afternoon of August 28, when police at the week's largest rally charged through the crowd in Grant Park to prevent a man from lowering a U.S. flag. Many in the crowd met the police charge with a volley of rocks and improvised missiles. After some measure of peace returned, David Dellinger attempted to negotiate a permit to march to the convention hall. When the city denied the permit and demonstrators attempted to regroup in front of one of the convention delegates' hotels, police lost control of the crowd and violently attempted to clear a street intersection. Television cameras recorded indiscriminate police brutality while demonstrators chanted "The whole world is watching." Inside the convention hall that night, Senator Abraham Ribicoff of Connecticut condemned the "Gestapo tactics on the streets of Chicago," while Mayor Daley, in full view of television cameras, shouted obscenities and anti-Semitic slurs at the senator. Hubert Humphrey won the presidential nomination that night, but the nationally broadcast images of police violence and of Daley's tirade became the lasting memories of the convention.

Investigating the violence

The violence surrounding one of the essential rites of American democracy deepened the widespread perception that the nation faced a political and cultural crisis in 1968. The city of Chicago, the U.S. Department of Justice, the House Committee on Un-American Activities, and the presidentially appointed National Commission on the Causes and Prevention of Violence all responded with investigations of the violence. Within days, the Daley administration issued the first report, blaming the violence on "outside agitators," described as "revolutionaries" who came to Chicago "for the avowed purpose of a hostile confrontation with law enforcement." The chair of the House Un-American Activities subcommittee, Richard Ichord, suspected communist involvement in the demonstrations, but his hearings devolved into a bizarre preview of the conspiracy trial when a shirtless, barefooted Jerry Rubin burst into the hearing room with a bandolier of bullets and a toy gun. In December 1968, the report of the National Commission on the Causes and Prevention of Violence labeled the disturbances in Chicago a "police riot" and presented evidence of "unrestrained and indiscriminate police violence on many occasions." The commission's Walker Report, named after its chair Daniel Walker, acknowledged that demonstrators had provoked the police and responded with violence of their own, but it found that the "vast majority of the demonstrators were intent on expressing by peaceful means their dissent."

On September 9, 1968, three days after release of the Daley report, Chief Judge William J. Campbell of the U.S. District Court for the Northern District of Illinois convened a grand jury to investigate whether the organizers of the demonstrations had violated federal law and whether any police officers had interfered with the civil rights of the protestors. The Department of Justice report, however, found no grounds for prosecution of demonstrators, and Attorney General Ramsey Clark asked the U.S. attorney in Chicago to investigate possible civil rights violations by Chicago police.

Indictment

John Mitchell, the new U.S. Attorney General appointed by President Nixon following his inauguration in January 1969, worked with the U.S. attorney's office in Chicago to strengthen draft indictments of demonstrators, and Department of Justice officials asked U.S. Attorney Thomas Foran, a political ally of Mayor Daley, to remain in office and direct the prosecution. On March 20, 1969, the grand jury indicted eight demonstrators and eight policemen. Seven policemen were charged with assaulting demonstrators and the eighth policeman was charged with perjury.

The indicted demonstrators, soon known as the "Chicago Eight," were charged with conspiring to use interstate commerce with intent to incite a riot. Six of the defendants-David Dellinger, Rennie Davis, Tom Hayden, Abbie Hoffman, Jerry Rubin, and Bobby Seale of the Black Panther Party-were also charged with crossing state lines with the intent to incite a riot. The other two defendants, academics John Froines and Lee Weiner, were charged with teaching demonstrators how to construct incendiary devices that would be used in civil disturbances. If convicted of all charges, each of the defendants faced up to ten years in prison. The case entered the court record as *United States v. Dellinger et al.* These were the first prosecutions under the anti-riot provisions of the Civil Rights Act of 1968.

It was an unlikely group to engage in conspiracy. Dellinger, at 54, had been active in pacifist movements for years before the rise of the student protests of the 1960s. Hayden and Davis were skilled organizers with focused political goals, and they had never been interested in the street theater and cultural radicalism of Hoffman and Rubin. John Froines and Lee Weiner were only marginally involved in the planning for the demonstrations, and their participation during the convention differed little from that of hundreds of others. The unlikeliest conspirator was Bobby Seale, who had never met some of the defendants until they were together in the courtroom and who had appeared in Chicago briefly for a couple of speeches during the convention. Seale was one of the founders of the Black Panther Party, which federal and state prosecutors had recently targeted in numerous prosecutions around the country.

The eight were linked less by common action or common political goals than by a shared radical critique of U.S. government and society. Rennie Davis thought the government "lumped together all the strands of dissent in the sixties," and Tom Hayden concluded that the government had "decided to put radicalism on trial." On the witness stand, Abbie Hoffman dismissed the idea of any conspiracy among the eight defendants, adding, "we couldn't even agree on lunch."

Judge and jury

The randomly assigned judge, Julius Jennings Hoffman, became as much of a symbol as any of the defendants. Judge Hoffman's imperious manner and apparent bias against the defendants inflamed tensions in what would have been a confrontational trial under any circumstances. At 73, Hoffman had been on the federal bench since his appointment by Eisenhower in 1953, and lawyers in Chicago described him as a judge who usually sided with the government attorneys. Judge Hoffman was proud of the efficiency with which he managed cases, and from the first encounters with the defense attorneys, he was determined to show that he would exercise strong control over the case. When four of the attorneys serving the defense during the pretrial proceedings withdrew from the case before the start of the trial, Hoffman held them in contempt, ordered their arrest, and had two of them jailed. A nationwide protest of prominent lawyers convinced Judge Hoffman to relent and accept the new defense team of William Kunstler and Leonard Weinglass. Throughout the trial, Kunstler and Weinglass aggressively challenged Judge Hoffman's procedural rulings, which almost uniformly affirmed the motions of the prosecution.

In his examination of prospective jurors, Hoffman ignored all but one of the questions submitted by the defense attorneys and never asked potential jurors about pretrial publicity or about their attitudes toward student radicals or the Vietnam War. The jury of ten women and two men was selected in a day. Within a week, Hoffman learned that the homes of two jurors had received identical letters saying that the Black Panthers were watching them. After one of those two jurors acknowledged that she could not be impartial in light of the threat, the judge replaced her with an alternate juror and sequestered the remaining jurors for the duration of the trial. Seale denied any Black Panther involvement with the letters.

A mistrial for Bobby Seale

Conflict over the defense attorneys reemerged when Bobby Seale refused to be represented by anyone other than Charles Garry, who originally agreed to represent the defendants but remained in California because of an illness. Judge Hoffman refused Seale's subsequent request to represent himself, and Seale responded with a barrage of courtroom denunciations of the judge as a "pig," a "fascist," and a "racist." When the prosecuting attorney accused Seale of encouraging Black Panthers in the courtroom to defend him, the proceedings degenerated into worse shouting matches. Seale condemned the judge for keeping a picture of the slave owner George Washington above the bench, and Hoffman then followed through on his repeated warning to restrain Seale. In what provided for many the indelible image of the trial, Judge Hoffman ordered U.S. marshals to bind and gag Seale before his appearances in the courtroom. Hoffman allowed Seale in court without restraints the following week, but when Seale argued for his right to cross-examine a witness, Judge Hoffman sentenced him to four years in prison for contempt of court and declared a mistrial in the prosecution of Seale. The Chicago Eight were now the Chicago Seven.

The government's case

Seale's attempts to cross-examine witnesses came as the government presented its case against the defendants. Led by Thomas Foran and Assistant U.S. Attorney Richard Schultz, the government prosecutors relied primarily on the testimony of undercover policemen and informers. Police officer Robert Pierson described how he let his hair grow, rented a motorcycle, and dressed in biker clothes for convention week. He testified that he heard Abbie Hoffman say that the demonstrators would break windows if the police pushed them out of Lincoln Park for a second night, and that Rubin, Seale, and Davis had urged crowds to resist the police or to employ violence. William Frapolly, another policeman, told the court how he enrolled in an Illinois college, grew sideburns and a goatee, and then joined Students for a Democratic Society, the National Mobilization Committee, and other peace groups. Frapolly testified that he had attended various planning meetings and that he had heard nearly all of the defendants state their intention to incite confrontations with the police and to pro-mote other civil disturbances. He also testified that Wiener and Froines had openly discussed the use of incendiary devices and chemical bombs. The government called 53 witnesses, most of whom recounted similar encounters with the defendants.

The defense strategy

The defendants and their attorneys went well beyond the rebuttal of the criminal charges and sought to portray the proceedings as a political trial rather than a criminal prosecution. In their legal arguments, in their courtroom behavior, and in their numerous public appearances, they challenged the legitimacy of the court and the judge as well as the substance of the indictment. The trial became for the defense an opportunity to portray the dissent movement that had converged on Chicago for the Democratic Convention.

The defense called more than 100 witnesses, many of them participants or by-standers in the clashes between the police and the demonstrators. The jury heard repeated testimony about unprovoked police violence and the extensive injuries among the demonstrators. Well-known writers and performers, including Allen Ginsberg, William Styron, Dick Gregory, Norman Mailer, Arlo Guthrie, and Judy Collins, testified to the peaceful intent of the defendants. The judge denied the request to subpoena President Johnson. Mayor Daley appeared as a defense witness but said little as the judge upheld the government's objection to most of the defense questions.

Abbie Hoffman and Rennie Davis were the only defendants to testify. Abbie Hoffman described himself as a resident of the Woodstock Nation and an orphan of America, and he offered a lengthy narrative of his involvement in politics and the origins of the Yippie movement. Davis recounted his role in the organization of the demonstrations and his encounters with the police during the convention. On cross-examination, the government attorneys attempted to establish that use of the words "revolution" and "battle" constituted incitements to riot, but the exchanges with the defendants made clear how difficult it was to connect demonstrators' rhetoric with the violence in Chicago.

Procedural disputes

Much of the trial was consumed by arguments over procedure. Even before the trial started, Judge Hoffman granted only thirty days for pretrial motions rather than the six months requested by the defense. The judge denied the defense attorneys' access to government evidence obtained without a warrant and barred the defense from submitting the Lake Villa document in which Hayden and Davis set out their nonviolent strategy. Judge Hoffman prohibited former Attorney General Ramsey Clark from testifying about his opposition to prosecution of demonstrators, and Hoffman sharply limited the defense lawyers' ability to question Mayor Daley. Frequently the trial was interrupted by arguments over seemingly petty questions: Could the defendants distribute birthday cake in the courtroom? Could the defendants use the public restrooms, or should they be limited to the facilities in the holding rooms? Could the musician witnesses sing the songs they performed at demonstrations, or was the judge correct in insisting that they recite lyrics?

Court theater

For the public that followed the trial in the daily media, the substantive arguments and procedural questions were overshadowed by the intentionally subversive behavior of the defendants and the high-handed dramatics of the judge. Jerry Rubin pleaded not guilty with a raised fist. When introduced to the jury, Abbie Hoffman blew them a kiss (and Judge Hoffman ordered them to "disregard that kiss"). The defendants often refused to rise when so instructed. On the day of the Moratorium to End the War in Vietnam, the defendants draped a Viet Cong flag over the defense table. Throughout the trial various defendants called out obscenities and labeled the judge and prosecutors liars or Gestapo officers. In the most theatrical display of contempt for judicial authority, Abbie Hoffman and Jerry Rubin entered the courtroom in judicial robes and then flung them to the floor and stomped on them.

Judge Hoffman was all too easily provoked by the antics of the defendants, and his own instinct for the theatrical added to the carnival atmosphere. By all accounts, his exaggerated reading of the indictment left the jury with no doubt about his opinion of the defendants' guilt. He returned the defendants' name calling and publicly referred to Weinglass as a "wild man." Reporters described his "mimicking" voice as he read the Seale contempt convictions. Judge Hoffman defended himself against personal insults from the defendants, such as when he answered Seale's cry of "racist!" with an account of his pro-civil rights decisions. The defendants believed Judge Hoffman intentionally mispronounced their names, such as when he repeatedly called Dellinger "Dillinger."

Contempt and a verdict

For all the apparent anarchy in courtroom, Judge Hoffman issued no contempt orders until the argument phase closed. Then, while the jury deliberated, the judge cited the defendants and their lawyers for 159 counts of criminal contempt and sentenced them to prison terms ranging from less than three months for Lee Weiner to more than four years for Kunstler. Some of the convictions were for courtroom outbursts and profanities, many were for laughter, and others were based on the refusal of a defendant to rise as the judge entered or left the courtroom. The lawyers' were repeatedly convicted of contempt for persisting in offering motions or challenging a ruling of the judge. The disparities in the sentences surprised many courtroom observers. Abbie Hoffman received a much shorter sentence for the cited instances of sarcasm and personal insults than Tom Hayden received for his challenges to the judge's procedural decisions.

After five days of deliberation, the jury on February 19 acquitted all seven defendants of conspiracy and acquitted Froines and Weiner on all charges. The jury found the five defendants (other than Froines and Weiner) guilty of traveling between states with the intent to incite a riot. Judge Hoffman imposed the maximum sentence of five years in prison on each of the defendants found guilty.

In a separate proceeding in the Northern District of Illinois, a jury acquitted seven of the eight indicted policemen. The case against the eighth was dropped.

Appeals

The defendants and their attorneys appealed to the U.S. Court of Appeals for the Seventh Circuit for a reversal of the criminal convictions and the contempt citations. They argued that the anti-riot provisions of the Civil Rights Act were unconstitutional, that Judge Hoffman's prejudice against the defendants made a fair trial impossible, that they had been denied the right to present a full defense and that they had been denied the right to an impartial jury. They argued that the judge should not have waited until the end of the trial to issue contempt orders and that the conduct cited did not legally constitute contempt. They also argued that the excessive sentences for contempt violated the requirement for a jury trial in any proceeding resulting in greater than six months imprisonment.

On November 21, 1972, an appeals court panel of Judges Thomas E. Fairchild, Wilbur J. Pell, and Walter J. Cummings unanimously overturned the defendants' criminal convictions. The court of appeals found that Judge Hoffman had erred in not asking potential jurors about political and cultural attitudes or about exposure to pretrial publicity, that he had improperly excluded evidence and testimony, and that his failure to notify the defense of his communications with the jury was ground for reversal. In unsparing language, the court of appeals censured Judge Hoffman and the government attorneys for their open hostility toward the defendants and their failure to fulfill "the standards of our system of justice." Their demeanor alone, the court concluded, was sufficient reason to reverse the conviction. The reversal left open the government's option of retrying each of the defendants individually, and the court of appeals reviewed the evidence that it believed a jury might find sufficient for conviction. In January 1973, the U.S. Department of Justice announced that it would not pursue any further prosecution. Only Judge Pell found the Anti-Riot Act to be unconstitutional, so that statute stood.

On May 11, 1972, in a separate proceeding, the same panel of judges on the court of appeals had declared some of the contempt charges against the lawyers to be legally insufficient, and the court reversed all other contempt convictions, which were remanded for retrial before another judge. Judge Edward T. Gignoux, of the U.S. District Court for Maine, was assigned by Chief Justice Warren Burger to preside at the retrial that began in October 1973. The government reduced the number of contempt charges and thereby avoided the requirement of the court of appeals that any defendant subject to more than six months' imprisonment be tried before a jury. Gignoux convicted Dellinger, Hoffman, Rubin, and Kunstler of a total of thirteen contempt charges, but the judge rejected the U.S. attorney's argument that "substantial jail sentences" were necessary to protect the judicial process and deter others of such misbehavior. Gignoux thought that the behavior of the defendants and their lawyers could not be considered "apart from the conduct of the trial judge and prosecutors. Each reacted to provocation by the other, and the tensions generated during four and a half months of so acrimonious a trial cannot be ignored." He was satisfied that the judgment alone preserved the integrity of the trial process.

Legacy

The judicial rebuke of Judge Hoffman prompted only minor notice in the national media that had so closely followed the trial. In many ways the cultural and political moment that defined the trial had passed by the fall of 1972. Even the judges of the U.S. court of appeals felt the need to remind readers of their opinion of how divided the country had been in 1968. The killings at Kent State University in May 1970 had changed forever the youth protest movement, which lost much of its political focus. Left-wing political groups like the Students for a Democratic Society had since splintered, leaving older leaders like Tom Hayden permanently alienated from the increasingly violent agenda of groups like the Weather Underground. The federal government again relied on the Anti-Riot Act to bring charges against anti-war protestors at the Mayday demonstration in 1971, when Abbie Hoffman, John Froines, and Rennie Davis were among those arrested, but the U.S. Court of Appeals for the District of Columbia Circuit blocked most of the prosecutions, and the same court in 1973 found that the mass arrests of nearly 8,000 demonstrators had violated the Fourth Amendment of the Constitution. The Chicago trial had established no precedent for use of the Anti-Riot Act against political demonstrators. The trial of the Chicago Seven lived on less as a legal milestone than as a cultural marker of dissident youth culture in the 1960s and the political divisions surrounding the Vietnam War.

The Judicial Process: A Chronology

September 9, 1968

Grand jury convened in the U.S. District Court for the Northern District of Illinois to investigate whether any demonstrators violated federal law and whether Chicago police officers violated the civil rights of demonstrators.

March 20, 1969

Grand jury in the U.S. District Court for the Northern District of Illinois indicted eight persons on charges of conspiracy to travel in interstate commerce with the intent to incite riots in Chicago. Six of the defendants were indicted on individual charges of traveling in interstate commerce with the intent to incite a riot, in violation of the Anti-Riot Act. On the same day, the grand jury indicted seven Chicago police officers on charges of depriving individuals of their civil rights and an eighth police officer of perjury before the grand jury.

April 9, 1969

Defendants in the conspiracy case were arraigned in the district court and pleaded not guilty.

September 24, 1969

Start of the conspiracy trial.

November 5, 1969

Judge Julius Hoffman declared a mistrial in the prosecution of Bobby Seale and severed his case from the remaining seven defendants. Hoffman also convicted Seale on sixteen counts of contempt and sentenced him to four years in prison.

February 14,1970

Judge Julius Hoffman convicted the seven defendants and their two attorneys of a total of 159 charges of criminal contempt for behavior throughout the trial.

February 19,1970

The jury acquitted all defendants of the conspiracy charge and defendants Froines and Wiener of all charges. The jury found the other five defendants guilty of violating the Anti-Riot Act.

May 11, 1972

The U.S. Court of Appeals for the Seventh Circuit reversed most of the contempt convictions, dismissed others, and remanded the remaining contempt charges for retrial by another judge in the district court. On the same day, the U.S. Court of Appeals for the Seventh Circuit, in a separate opinion, dismissed four counts of contempt against Bobby Seale and remanded the remaining twelve contempt specifications against Seale for retrial by another judge.

November 21, 1972

The U.S. Court of Appeals for the Seventh Circuit reversed the convictions of the five defendants on the charge of intent to incite a riot, and the court of appeals remanded the cases to the district court for retrial at the discretion of the government.

January 4, 1973

Attorney General Richard Kleindienst announced that the government would not retry any of the defendants on the charge of intent to incite a riot.

December 6, 1973

Edward Gignoux, sitting by assignment in the District Court for the Northern District of Illinois at the retrial of the contempt charges, dismissed all contempt charges against two of the defendants and attorney Leonard Weinglass, and convicted three of the defendants and attorney William Kunstler of a total of thirteen contempt charges. Gignoux did not impose any further jail sentence.

The Federal Courts and Their Jurisdiction

Table of Contents

U.S. District Court for the Northern District of Illinois

The Chicago Eight, later Seven, were indicted in the U.S. District Court for the Northern District of Illinois on charges of conspiracy to incite riots and on individual charges of intent to incite riots or to promote the use of incendiary devices. The court's chief judge, William Campbell, presided over the grand jury investigation. Campbell was randomly selected as the trial judge following the grand jury's indictment, but he recused himself because of his familiarity with the evidence presented to the grand jury. Then Judge Julius Hoffman was randomly selected to preside over the trial.

When the defendants appealed their convictions on criminal contempt, all of the district court's active judges, except for Judge Hoffman, petitioned the U.S. Court of Appeals for the Seventh Circuit for permission to file a brief supporting the broad authority and discretion of a trial judge to punish contempt. The court of appeals denied permission, saying that it would be almost impossible for the district judges to avoid the appearance of supporting one side in the dispute over Judge Hoffman's contempt charges. More than two years later, the U.S. court of appeals reversed the contempt convictions and remanded them for retrial by another judge in the district court. At the request of the chief judge of the court of appeals, Chief Justice Warren Burger designated Judge Edward Gignoux, of the U.S. District Court of Maine, to serve on temporary assignment as the judge of the retrial of the contempt charges. Gignoux presided over the trial that ended on December 6, 1973, with the conviction of three defendants and one of their attorneys on thirteen counts of contempt.

The district courts were established by the Congress in the Judiciary Act of 1789, and they serve as the trial courts in each of the judicial districts of the federal judiciary. The U.S. District Court for the Northern District of Illinois was established in 1855, when Congress divided Illinois into two judicial districts. Illinois was subsequently divided into three judicial districts, but the Northern District has always included Chicago. The court's jurisdiction over the Chicago conspiracy trial was based on federal laws making it a crime to travel across state lines with the intent to incite riots and on laws making it a crime to demonstrate the use or manufacture of explosives that might be used to disrupt commerce.

U.S. Court of Appeals for the Seventh Circuit

The five defendants found guilty in the Chicago conspiracy trial appealed their convictions to the U.S. Court of Appeals for the Seventh Circuit. All seven defendants and their two attorneys also appealed their contempt convictions to the same court. A panel of three judges, Walter Cummings, Thomas Fairchild, and Wilbur Pell, heard arguments in both appeals. On May 11, 1972, in an opinion written by Judge Cummings, the panel reversed the contempt convictions of all of the defendants and remanded the contempt charges to the district court for retrial. The panel dismissed some of the contempt convictions of attorneys Kunstler and Weinglass and reversed the attorneys' other convictions, which were also remanded to the district court. On November 21, 1972, in an opinion written by Judge Fairchild, the panel reversed the convictions on the charge of violating the Anti-Riot Act and remanded the individual cases to the district court for retrial at the discretion of the government attorneys. By a 2-1 vote, the court upheld the constitutionality of the Anti-Riot Act, and Judge Pell wrote a dissenting opinion explaining why he thought the act was unconstitutional.

The U.S. Court of Appeals for the Seventh Circuit heard various other cases related to the conspiracy trial. In the fall of 1969, the court of appeals upheld a district judge's decision rejecting the National Mobilization Committee's motion for a court order halting the grand jury investigation of the demonstrators and for an order declaring the Anti-Riot Act unconstitutional. In May 1972, the court of appeals dismissed four of Bobby Seale's contempt convictions, reversed the other twelve, and remanded the remaining charges to the district court for retrial before another judge. The court of appeals rejected the appeal of the three defendants and attorney William Kunstler, who had been found guilty of contempt in the retrial conducted by Judge Gignoux. In 1981, following release of information about private communications between Judge Hoffman and the U.S. attorney during the original trial, the court of appeals upheld Judge Gignoux's decision not to reverse the contempt convictions.

The U.S. courts of appeals were established by the Congress in 1891. A court of appeals in each of the regional judicial circuits was established to hear appeals from the federal trial courts, and the decisions of the courts of appeals are final in many categories of cases. The Seventh Circuit consists of Illinois, Indiana, and Wisconsin, and the Seventh Circuit court of appeals has always met in Chicago.

Legal Questions Before the Federal Courts

Table of Contents

1. Were the seven defendants guilty of engaging in a conspiracy to incite a riot?

No, said the jury in the district court trial.

The indictment described a conspiracy of the eight defendants, eighteen unindicted coconspirators, and other unknown persons, who traveled in interstate commerce with the intent to incite a riot and to commit overt acts to promote and carry out the riot, all in violation of a recent statute passed by Congress in response to the urban riots of the mid-1960s. The defendants were also accused of conspiring to teach the manufacture and use of incendiary devices and to interfere with the official duties of firemen and law enforcement officers. The indictment specified meetings at which various defendants planned the demonstrations and confrontations with law enforcement officers. The indictment also listed speeches and meetings that allegedly constituted the overt acts required for conviction under the Anti-Riot Act.

The government prosecutors argued that the defendants shared a "tacit understanding" of their common goal of provoking a riot, although the eight never met as one group. The defense attorneys described the conspiracy charge as absurd on the face of it, and directed most of their arguments to disproving the charges of intent to incite a riot.

2. Did the defendants violate the Anti-Riot Act by using interstate commerce with the intent to incite a riot and by committing at least one overt act to promote a riot?

The jury found five defendants guilty of the charge. The U.S. court of appeals reversed that decision because of errors by the trial judge but found that some of the evidence might be sufficient for conviction if the government chose to retry the five persons in individual trials.

The indictment charged David Dellinger, Rennie Davis, Tom Hayden, Abbie Hoffman, Jerry Rubin, and Bobby Seale with individual violations of the Anti-Riot Act. The indictment specified evidence of intent prior to interstate travel and evidence of overt acts by which each of the six defendants incited a riot during the convention week in Chicago. Seale's case was separated from the others by Judge Hoffman, and the remaining five defendants charged with intent to incite a riot were found guilty by the jury.

The U.S. Court of Appeals for the Seventh Circuit reversed the convictions, but concluded that the evidence presented for each defendant might reasonably be interpreted by a jury as proof of guilt. In their detailed review of the evidence against each defendant, the three judges who heard the appeal found that the evidence of overt acts of inciting a riot was clearer than the evidence of an earlier intent to incite a riot. One of the judges did not find any reasonable evidence of earlier intent in the case of Dellinger. The court of appeals judges did not conclude that any of the defendants was guilty, only that a jury might determine guilt or innocence based on the evidence presented at the original trial.

The court of appeals left for the government the option to retry any or all of the defendants, but the court commented on several issues that were likely to arise in a new trial. The court of appeals dismissed the defendants' claim that the testimony of undercover policemen violated their constitutional rights, and it denied that defendants had a right to address the jury. In a decision that may have convinced the government not to retry, the court of appeals, citing a recent Supreme Court decision, said that in any further proceedings, the defendants had a right to review logs of the government's electronic surveillance of them and a right to a hearing to determine if evidence obtained through that surveillance violated the defendants' constitutional rights.

On January 4, 1973, Attorney General Richard Kleindienst announced that the government would not retry any of the defendants on the charge of intent to incite a riot.

3. Were John Froines and Lee Weiner guilty of instructing demonstrators in the manufacture and use of incendiary devices?

No, the jury found Froines and Weiner not guilty of the charge.

The indictment charged Froines and Weiner with teaching people how to make and use an incendiary device and with the intent to incite civil disorder and to disrupt interstate commerce through the use of such devices. The U.S. attorneys called on undercover policemen for testimony that Froines and Weiner had discussed plans to use flares as weapons, to purchase chemicals for stink bombs, and to make Molotov cocktails for firebombing the parking garage under Grant Park. On cross-examination, the principal government witness admitted that he heard Froines say he didn't know how to make a Molotov cocktail. In their closing arguments, both defense attorneys challenged the credibility of the testimony about the Grant Park garage and emphasized that police never found any physical evidence of firebombs or materials to be used in the manufacture of bombs.

4. Was the Anti-Riot Act of 1968 unconstitutional?

No, the U.S. Court of Appeals for the Seventh Circuit, in a 2-1 decision, decided that the act did not violate the Constitution.

In their appeal, the defendants challenged the constitutionality of the Anti-Riot Act under which they had been convicted. Judges Thomas Fairchild and Walter Cummings found that the act was not so vague or so broad as to be unconstitutional, although they found that the case raised difficult questions. The judges were satisfied that the act required a sufficiently close relationship between speech and action that demonstrated intent to incite a riot. The act's requirement of "an overt act" in support of inciting a riot was enough to prevent the act from suppressing or "chilling" speech protected by the Constitution.

Judge Wilbur Pell dissented from the majority opinion, and wrote that the Anti-Riot Act was an unconstitutional restriction on free speech. Pell, a recent Nixon appointee, found that the act did not distinguish between speech that advocated violence and speech that was directly related to the incitement of violence. The advocacy of "an idea or expression of belief" could not be limited under the Constitution.

In the fall of 1968, lawyers for the National Mobilization Committee had challenged the constitutionality of the Anti-Riot Act in their suit asking for a court order to halt the grand jury inquiry into the demonstrations. On November 1, 1968, Judge Abraham Marovitz of the district court for the Northern District of Illinois dismissed the suit, and the U.S. Court of Appeals for the Seventh Circuit agreed that the challenge to the statute did not raise sufficient constitutional questions.

5. Were the defendants and their attorneys guilty of criminal contempt?

Judge Hoffman convicted the seven defendants and their two attorneys of 157 counts of criminal contempt. The U.S. Court of Appeals for the Seventh Circuit dismissed some of the charges against the attorneys and reversed all other convictions, which the appellate court sent back to the district court for retrial before a different judge. In the new trial, Judge Edward Gignoux found three of the defendants and one of their attorneys guilty of a combined total of thirteen contempts.

The U.S. court of appeals reversed all of the defendants' contempt convictions and remanded them to the district court for retrial. The court of appeals dismissed some of the contempt convictions of attorneys Kunstler and Weinglass because their actions involved legitimate efforts to defend their clients; the remaining attorney convictions were remanded for new trials. The court of appeals also ruled that any defendant subject to more than six months' imprisonment on the contempt charges would be entitled to a trial by jury.

The court of appeals cited recent Supreme Court decisions that restricted a district judge's authority to issue contempt convictions at the conclusion of a trial if the allegedly contemptuous behavior involved personal insults that would likely create bias in the judge. By the time of the hearings on the Chicago Seven appeals, the government attorneys conceded that the defendants' convictions should be retried before another judge in the district court, and the government's decision to drop many of the charges eliminated the need for any jury trials.

Judge Edward Gignoux presided over the retrial of the fifty-two remaining contempt charges. Gignoux quickly dismissed two charges and acquitted the defendants of twenty-four others, including all of those pending against John Froines and Lee Weiner. Following a trial of more than four weeks, Gignoux's decision on the remaining specifications rested on the criteria that the court of appeals had prescribed for determining guilt: the contemptuous behavior must have occurred in the court or close enough to obstruct the proceedings; the conduct must have violated the expected behavior in a courtroom; the individual must have intended to disrupt the court proceedings; and the conduct must have resulted in an obstruction of the courtroom.

Gignoux found David Dellinger guilty of seven contempt charges, most involving repeated insults directed at the judge while the jury was present. Jerry Rubin and Abbie Hoffman were found guilty of two charges each, including their appearance in the courtroom in judicial robes. William Kunstler was guilty of two contempt charges for extended attacks on the judge that resulted in a significant disruption in the courtroom. Gignoux imposed no jail time for any of the contempt convictions.

6. Did the jury selection process protect the defendants' right to a fair trial?

No. The U.S. Court of Appeals for the Seventh Circuit found that the district judge was in error for failing to ask potential jurors about their exposure to pretrial publicity. The court of appeals also found that the district judge should have asked potential jurors about their attitudes toward the Vietnam War, the counterculture, and the Chicago police.

The defendants claimed that the "perfunctory" jury selection, completed in one day, did not solicit the information necessary to make reasoned challenges to jurors. Judge Hoffman asked the defense to submit questions for jurors, but he asked jurors only one question from the defense list. The defense submitted many questions about attitudes toward the Vietnam War, student dissent, and hippie culture. The defense also suggested that the judge ask if the potential jurors knew who Janis Joplin and Jimi Hendrix were, if their daughters wore "brassieres all the time," and if they considered "marihuana habit-forming." The court of appeals considered some of the defense questions "inappropriate," but the court also said that public opinion at the time of the trial was so divided over the Vietnam War and the rise of the counterculture that the judge had an obligation to ask jurors about their views. "We do not believe that a prospective juror is so alert to his own prejudices," that the district court can rely on a general question about the ability to be fair. The defense must be able to ask specific questions about potential prejudices of a juror. The court of appeals decision said that in a case with "widespread publicity about highly dramatic events," the district judge must ask about the impact of pretrial publicity even if, as in this trial, the defense had not raised the issue during the selection of the jury.

The court of appeals did not accept the defendants' other argument that the reliance on voter lists for the selection of grand jury members created a biased grand jury. The court found that the reliance on voter lists underrepresented young people, but that the age imbalance was not so pronounced as to produce a biased grand jury.

7. Did Judge Hoffman unfairly restrict the defense's right to submit evidence and call witnesses?

Yes. The U.S. court of appeals determined that Judge Hoffman had erred in his decision to exclude certain evidence and witnesses for the defense.

The defense attorneys asked to submit various documents as evidence of their claim that the defendants had always intended to engage in peaceful demonstrations at the Democratic National Convention. Judge Hoffman excluded these memos and magazine interviews on the grounds that they were self-serving declarations of the defendants. The court of appeals rejected any blanket rule excluding allegedly self-serving evidence. According to the court of appeals, that standard for evidence was rooted in the long-abandoned rule that defendants in criminal trials could not testify on their own behalf. The court of appeals called special attention to the Lake Villa document drafted by Tom Hayden and Rennie Davis for an organizational meeting in March 1968. It was up to the jury, not the judge, to determine if the Lake Villa policy of nonviolence represented the intentions of the organizers.

The court of appeals also found that Judge Hoffman was wrong to sustain the prosecutors' objection to all expert witnesses called by the defense. The court of appeals supported a trial judge's broad discretion in determining the suitability of witnesses, but Hoffman had been mistaken to exclude the witnesses called to testify about crowd control and law enforcement. The court of appeals determined that these witnesses might have helped the jury assess the defense allegation that police had provoked the violence. The court of appeals upheld Judge Hoffman's decision to exclude expert witnesses who would have testified about racism and social injustice.

The court of appeals found that Judge Hoffman should have allowed former Attorney General Ramsey Clark to testify before the jury. Clark's testimony about a phone call to Mayor Daley in support of permits for the demonstrators would have provided important perspective on the defense claim that the defendants sincerely tried to obtain legal permits.

8. Did the attitude and demeanor of Judge Hoffman and the government attorneys violate the defendants' right to a fair trial?

Yes. The U.S. Court of Appeals of the Seventh Circuit found that the demeanor of the judge and the government attorneys was sufficient reason to reverse the convictions.

The court of appeals found that from the opening of the trial, the district judge made clear his "deprecatory and often antagonistic attitude toward the defense." Judge Hoffman had consistently made sarcastic and gratuitous criticisms of the defense attorneys. The appeals court was especially disturbed that Judge Hoffman had denigrated the defense's key argument that the Daley administration and the Chicago police deliberately provoked the demonstrators. Judge Hoffman's most serious offense, according to the court of appeals, was to make these caustic remarks in front of the jury.

On procedural questions, Judge Hoffman consistently ruled against the defense, and he failed to restrain the U.S. attorney's personal attacks on the defendants. The court of appeals considered U.S. Attorney Thomas Foran's closing arguments, with their emphasis on dress and appearance and references to "evil men" and "violent anarchists," beyond all standards of acceptable behavior. The court of appeals acknowledged the disruptive behavior of the defendants, but that behavior did not justify a disregard of "the high standards for the conduct of judges and prosecutors." "A defendant ought not to be rewarded for success in baiting the judge and the prosecutor."

Legal Arguments in Court

The attorneys for the U.S. government

U.S. Attorney Thomas Foran and Assistant U.S. Attorney Richard Schultz argued that:

1. The seven (originally eight) defendants conspired to provoke government violence against the demonstrators at the Democratic National Convention in Chicago. The prosecutors acknowledged that the defendants had never met as a group, but seven had met in smaller groups to devise their strategy and to coordinate demonstrators' resistance to the police. The testimony of government witnesses established a "tacit understanding" among the defendants and a mutual understanding of the goals of the conspiracy.
2. The defendants intended to incite violence by attracting to Chicago very large crowds to participate in ostensibly peaceful protests of the Vietnam War and social injustice. The defendants incited the demonstrators against the police, the National Guard, and the Army, and the defendants orchestrated confrontations with the intent of provoking law enforcement officers to respond with violence.
3. The defendants privately and in small gatherings, before and during the week of the convention, described their goals of disruption and confrontation, and their goal of inciting not only riots in Chicago, but a popular uprising against the government. The government attorneys cited the defendants' rhetoric about hoping to "smash the city," bringing "the United States military machinery to a halt," and creating the "first steps towards the revolution" as proof that the seven organizers jointly planned to incite violence in Chicago during the Democratic Convention.
4. At least six of the original defendants crossed state lines with the intent to incite violence and thus violated the anti-riot provisions of the Civil Rights Act of 1968.
5. Froines and Weiner discussed the manufacture and possible uses of incendiary devices during the convention.

The attorneys for the defendants

William Kunstler and Leonard Weinglass, attorneys for the seven defendants, rejected a strategy that focused closely on disproving the charges in the indictment. Rather, they emphasized that this was, in their view, more of a political trial than a criminal prosecution. The defense called many witnesses to rebut the testimony of the undercover police, but their goal was always to establish the peaceable intent of the defendants and to expose the political motivation of the prosecution. In their opening and closing arguments, the defense attorneys argued that:

1. The U.S. and Chicago governments engaged in a conspiracy to prevent demonstrations against the Vietnam War and related issues. Kunstler argued that "the police of this city embarked on an organized conspiracy of berserk brutal action against these demonstrators."
2. The prosecution witnesses, who were almost all government employees or informants paid by the government, could not offer impartial or credible testimony. The defense asked the jury to consider why the government had called no by-standers as witnesses of the violence during the convention.
3. The indictment, and particularly the conspiracy charge, was on the face of it absurd. The charges in the indictment implied that seven veterans of the peace movement suddenly rejected their long-standing beliefs and embraced a violent strategy sure to result in their imprisonment.
4. A large number of witnesses, including prominent politicians and entertainers who performed at the protest rallies, testified that they had heard no incitements to violence during the planning and staging of rallies surrounding the convention; nor had they witnessed any diversionary tactics designed to provoke police violence.
5. The indictment represented an assault on First Amendment rights. With their frequent reference to the American Revolution and the Founders, the defense attorneys placed the defendants' activities in Chicago in an American tradition of popular defense of liberties.

Biographies

Table of Contents

The judges

Julius Jennings Hoffman (1895-1983)

Presiding judge at the Chicago conspiracy trial

Judge Julius J. Hoffman
Courtesy of Bettman/Corbis.

Judge Julius Hoffman earned as much notoriety for his management of the Chicago conspiracy case as the defendants did for their disruptive behavior. Hoffman was born in Chicago and received his law degree from Northwestern University. He entered private practice in Chicago in 1915 and served as general counsel of the Brunswick-Balke-Collender Company (later the Brunswick Corporation) from 1936-1944. Hoffman was elected judge of the Cook County Superior Court in 1947 and was nominated in 1953 by President Eisenhower to the U.S. District Court for the Northern District of Illinois. By the time of the Chicago conspiracy trial, Hoffman was known for his efficient courtroom. Hoffman was randomly assigned to the case after Chief Judge William Campbell recused himself because of his exposure to the evidence presented to the grand jury investigation over which he presided.

As the trial progressed, Hoffman was unrelenting in his opposition to the defense and in his support for the government attorneys. He rejected the defense motion requesting six months for the preparation of pretrial motions, and he accepted the prosecutions' recommendation of one month; he ordered the arrest of attorneys who assisted in the pre-trial proceedings but who withdrew before the start of the trial; he refused to incorporate all but one of the questions submitted by the defense for prospective jurors; he disregarded Bobby Seale's repeated complaints that he was not being represented by an attorney of his own choice; he rejected crucial evidence of the defendants' intent, and he barred witnesses, like Ramsey Clark, who were prepared to testify to the defendants' intent to abide by the law; he failed to reveal to the defense his communications with the jury as it deliberated; and he delayed issuing any contempt citations until completion of the trial. Many of Judge Hoffman's individual rulings were well within the authority of a district judge, but the cumulative impact, combined with his undisguised disdain for the defendants and their attorneys, set him up for an unusually personal censure from the U.S. Court of Appeals for the Seventh Circuit. That court, in an opinion written by Judge Thomas Fairchild and reversing the criminal convictions, found that "the district judge's deprecatory and often antagonistic attitude toward the defense is evident in the record from the very beginning." Judge Hoffman's order that Seale be bound and gagged brought even greater condemnation from the press and Judge Edward Gignoux, who described the incident as an "appalling spectacle."

Judge Hoffman was not without supporters. On the day after he convicted Bobby Seale of contempt, Judge Hoffman entered the dining room of a private club for his daily lunch and received a standing ovation from the other guests. When the defendants appealed their contempt convictions, Judge Hoffman's colleagues on the district court tried to submit a brief in support of his authority to issue the criminal contempt convictions. During the course of the trial, Judge Hoffman received hundreds of supportive letters from the public. The defendants themselves had mixed feelings about Judge Hoffman, despite their angry, profanity-laden confrontations with him in court, and some later acknowledged that he often made them laugh.

After the close of the trial, Judge Hoffman left for his home in Florida, but he was soon invited by President Nixon to attend the national prayer breakfast at the White House, and the Gridiron Club honored Hoffman at its annual dinner in Washington. He assumed a reduced caseload in 1972, and served on the court until his death. In an interview in 1982, Judge Hoffman said "I did nothing in that trial I am not proud of, I presided with dignity. When I felt I had to be firm, I was firm."

William Joseph Campbell (1905-1988)

Chief judge of the U.S. District Court for the Northern District of Illinois

Judge William J. Campbell
Courtesy of the Seventh Circuit Library.

On September 9, 1968, three days after the Daley administration released its report blaming the violence at the Democratic National Convention on outside agitators, Chief Judge William

Campbell of the Northern District of Illinois convened a grand jury to investigate the demonstrators' possible violation of the federal anti-riot law and the police's possible infringement of civil rights. During the convention, Campbell had refused to restrain the police from interfering with reporters. Following release of the Walker Report that attributed much of the violence to the police, Campbell publicly questioned the motivation for release of the report before it was presented to the grand jury, and he suggested that the grand jury might investigate whether the release of the report was an attempt to influence the same grand jury's investigation of the convention violence. After the grand jury indicted eight demonstrators and eight policemen, the court's random assignment procedure originally selected Campbell as the judge for the trial of the eight defendants, but Campbell recused himself because of his detailed knowledge of the evidence presented to the grand jury. As chief judge of the court during the conspiracy trial, Campbell had authority over the rules regulating media access, and he prohibited cameras and sound equipment from public areas of the courthouse.

Campbell was appointed to the U.S. District Court for the Northern District of Illinois by President Franklin Roosevelt in 1940. Campbell was born in Chicago and received his law degree from Loyola University. He served as U.S. attorney for the Northern District of Illinois for two years before his appointment to the district court. Campbell assumed a reduced caseload in March 1970, but he continued to serve as a senior judge until his death.

Edward T. Gignoux (1916-1988)

U.S. district judge for the District of Maine

Judge Edward T. Gignoux
Garbrecht Law Library, University of Maine School of Law.

Chief Justice Warren Burger assigned Edward Gignoux to be the judge for the retrial of the contempt charges against the defendants and their attorneys. In its reversal of the contempt convictions issued by Judge Hoffman, the U.S. Court of Appeals for the Seventh Circuit cited a recent Supreme Court opinion as authority for requiring a different judge to preside over any retrial of the contempt charges that the government attorneys might choose to pursue. By law, the Chief Justice of the United States may assign a district judge to preside in a district in another judicial circuit if the chief judge of the other circuit specifies a need. (No judge in the Seventh Circuit, which encompasses Illinois, Indiana, and Wisconsin, wanted to preside in the retrial.)

In his personal demeanor and his style of case management, the highly respected Gignoux proved to be the very opposite of Judge Hoffman. Years later, even William Kunstler offered a backhanded compliment. Gignoux, he said, "was a dangerous man. He makes the system look good." Gignoux presided at a trial with no jury because the government attorneys dropped enough contempt charges so that none of the defendants was subject to more than six months' imprisonment if convicted on all counts. Acting Attorney General Robert Bork recommended not retrying the contempts, but the U.S. attorney in Chicago, James Thompson, thought it was important to pursue some of the charges. Gignoux found three of the defendants and attorney William Kunstler guilty of a total of thirteen contempt charges, but Gignoux refused to impose further jail time on any of them. Gignoux's written decision concluded with an eloquent statement on the need for proper courtroom decorum and civility to ensure that citizens can defend their civil liberties.

Gignoux was born in Portland, Maine, and graduated from Harvard College and the Harvard Law School. He was appointed to the U.S. District Court for the District of Maine by President Eisenhower in 1957. Gignoux again served by assignment to another district in 1983 when he presided at the bribery trial of Alcee Hastings, a federal judge in the Southern District of Florida.

Walter Joseph Cummings (1916-1999)

Judge Walter J. Cummings
Courtesy of the Seventh Circuit Library.

Walter Cummings was appointed to the U.S. Court of Appeals for the Seventh Circuit by President Johnson in 1966, and he served on the court until his death. Cummings was the author of the court's opinion of May 11, 1972, *In re David Dellinger* et al., which overturned the contempt convictions of the defendants and remanded most of the charges for retrial by a different judge. The opinion ordered that any defendant facing contempt charges subject to more than six months' imprisonment would be entitled to a jury trial. Cummings also authored the court's opinion in *United States v. Bobby G. Seale*, in which the appeals court reversed the contempt convictions of Bobby Seale and remanded for retrial most of those charges, minus four that the court decided were not based on behavior that obstructed the trial.

Cummings graduated from Yale University in 1937 and from the Harvard Law School in 1940. He then served as an attorney in the Department of Justice for six years, including a term as assistant solicitor general. He later served as the solicitor general from 1952-1953, the youngest person to hold that position. Before joining the court of appeals, Cummings was in private practice in Chicago for twenty years, during which time he served as president of the Seventh Circuit Bar Association.

Thomas Edward Fairchild (1912-2007)

Judge Thomas E. Fairchild
Courtesy of the Seventh Circuit Library.

Thomas Fairchild was appointed to the U.S. Court of Appeals for the Seventh Circuit by President Johnson in 1966, and he served until his death in 2007, after taking a reduced caseload in 1981. Fairchild wrote the court's opinion of November 1972 in *United States v. David T. Dellinger et al.*, the appeal of the five defendants who had been convicted on the charges of inciting a riot. The court found several grounds for reversal of the convictions, and Fairchild's opinion censured Judge Julius Hoffman and the government attorneys for their openly critical remarks about the defendants and their attorneys.

Fairchild received his law degree from the University of Wisconsin in 1938, and he worked in private practice before serving as the state attorney general, the U.S. attorney for the Western District of Wisconsin, and as a justice of the Wisconsin Supreme Court. Fairchild was an unsuccessful candidate for the U.S. Senate in 1950 and again in 1952, when he challenged incumbent Senator Joseph McCarthy.

Wilbur Frank Pell, Jr. (1915-2000)

Judge Wilbur F. Pell, Jr.
Courtesy of the Seventh Circuit Library.

Wilbur Pell was the most recently appointed of the three judges who heard the appeals associated with the Chicago conspiracy trial. Pell had joined the court in April 1970 following his appointment by President Nixon. In a dissent from the majority opinion of the court on the appeal of the convictions on the charge of incitement to riot, in *United States v. David T. Dellinger et al.*, Pell argued that the Anti-Riot Act was an unconstitutional infringement of free speech.

Pell graduated from the Harvard Law School in 1940 and practiced law in his native Indiana for many years. He also served as an FBI agent and as deputy attorney general of Indiana.

The defendants

Rennie Davis (1941-)

Rennie Davis
Courtesy of Bettman/Corbis.

Rennie Davis, an early member of the Students for a Democratic Society and a veteran organizer, grew up in Virginia, the son of John C. Davis, chairman of President Truman's Council of Economic Advisers. Rennie Davis attended Oberlin College and graduate school at the University of Illinois and the University of Michigan. He joined the SDS and became a close friend of one of its leaders, Tom Hayden. Davis was for several years involved in the group's Economic Research and Action Project, which worked to organize poor urban neighborhoods. By 1967, Davis was increasingly involved in the SDS anti-war activities.

Davis and Hayden joined with the National Mobilization Committee to End the War in Vietnam in planning massive demonstrations to coincide with the Democratic convention in Chicago. Davis met with officials at the Department of Justice to seek their help in obtaining permits from the city of Chicago. He and Hayden also met with attorneys to develop a legal strategy for protection of the demonstrators. In March 1968, Davis and Hayden met with nearly 200 activists and presented the group with an outline of their plans for demonstrations at the convention in Chicago. The document, which Judge Hoffman prohibited the defense from submitting as evidence, stated that the demonstrations "should be nonviolent and legal."

Davis found himself at the center of the police attack on demonstrators in Grant Park on Wednesday of convention week. As he urged the crowd to stay calm, the police moved against the demonstrators and hit Davis on the head. He was both hospitalized and arrested. At the conspiracy trial, Davis was one of only two defendants to testify, and defense attorney Leonard Weinglass asked him to recount the events in Grant Park.

During the months between the defendants' arraignment and the start of the trial, Davis asked Judge Hoffman for permission to travel to North Vietnam and to escort home several American prisoners of war who were released after negotiations by David Dellinger. Judge Hoffman refused the request, but U.S. Court of Appeals Judge Otto Kerner reversed the ruling, allowing Davis to travel.

Davis was convicted on the charge of intent to incite a riot, but the conviction was reversed by the U.S. Court of Appeals for the Seventh Circuit. The government declined to retry Davis on the Anti-Riot Act charge. Near the close of the trial, Judge Hoffman found Davis guilty of 23 counts of contempt and sentenced him to more than two years in jail. The U.S. court of appeals reversed all of the contempt convictions and remanded them for retrial. The government brought only two of the charges for retrial, and Judge Edward Gignoux found Davis not guilty of the two charges. Gignoux found that Davis's remarks to the jury while Bobby Seale was bound and gagged did not cause the breakdown in courtroom decorum, but rather that the disruption of the trial resulted from "the appalling spectacle of a bound and gagged defendant and the marshals' efforts to subdue him." Gignoux also found that the obstruction of the trial following the revocation of David Dellinger's bail was caused by the behavior of spectators, not the comments of Davis and other defendants.

Davis continued his involvement in anti-war activity, including the Washington, D.C., Mayday actions of 1971, when Davis was among the many arrested for attempting to shut down the federal government. In 1972, Davis went to India to meet the Guru Maharaj Ji, and was converted to the guru's Divine Light Mission. In the 1980s, Davis worked as a venture capital consultant, and in 2008 he is the president of the Foundation for a New Humanity.

David Dellinger (1915-2004)

David Dellinger
Courtesy of Bettman/Corbis.

David Dellinger stood apart from the other defendants in his age and in his lengthy experience as a pacifist and activist for social justice. Dellinger was born in Wakefield, Massachusetts, to a well-connected Republican family. He graduated from Yale University and attended Oxford

University. After serving as an ambulance driver for the Loyalists in the Spanish Civil War, he entered Union Theological Seminary to study for the ministry. When Dellinger refused to register for the draft in 1940, he was expelled from the seminary and served one year in a federal prison. When he refused to appear at an draft induction center in 1943, he was again convicted and served two years in a federal prison.

In 1956, Dellinger joined with other Christian pacifists to establish *Liberation* magazine. He organized some of the first protests of American involvement in the Vietnam War. In 1967, as chair of the National Mobilization Committee to End the War in Vietnam, he coordinated a huge anti-war rally in Washington. Dellinger recruited Jerry Rubin to help organize the event that culminated with the march to the Pentagon. Beginning in 1967, Dellinger made several visits to the Paris peace talks, and in the months preceding the conspiracy trial he traveled to Paris to negotiate the release of American prisoners of war and then went to North Vietnam to escort the Americans back to the United States.

Dellinger, as a co-chair of the National Mobilization Committee, was closely involved in planning for the demonstrations in Chicago and hoped to attract huge numbers of people, such as had gathered for the march on the Pentagon in October 1967. At the only rally with a city permit, Dellinger directed the events in Grant Park on Wednesday of convention week, but when police charged on the crowd after a demonstrator lowered the American flag, Dellinger's pleas over the microphone could not stop the violence. Dellinger also clashed with Tom Hayden, who wanted the demonstrators to defend themselves. Later that day, Dellinger attempted to negotiate a permit for a march to the site of the convention, but city officials denied it, and the worst violence of the week followed when police sought to disperse the assembled demonstrators.

Following the indictment of Dellinger and the seven other participants in the demonstrations, he urged the defendants to continue their anti-war activity and to use the trial to publicize their views on the war. Dellinger rejected the advice of potential defense lawyers who suggested their case should focus on narrow legal questions.

The prosecution described Dellinger as "the principal architect especially of the riots which occurred on Wednesday," and the case officially bore his name in the court records. Near the end of the trial, when a police officer serving as a rebuttal witness accused Dellinger of inciting violence in Grant Park, Dellinger responded with what the *New York Times* called a "barnyard epithet," and Judge Hoffman revoked his bail. Dellinger's return to jail prompted the most chaotic scenes in the trial since Bobby Seale had been bound and gagged.

The jury found Dellinger guilty of intent to incite a riot, but the U.S. court of appeals reversed the conviction and remanded the charge for retrial. The government declined to retry him. Near the close of the trial, Judge Hoffman convicted Dellinger of 32 counts of contempt and sentenced him to more than two years and two months in prison. After the court of appeals reversed all of the contempt convictions of the defendants, the government brought eight contempt charges against Dellinger on retrial, and Judge Edward Gignoux found him guilty of seven-the most for any of the defendants or defense attorneys. Dellinger was found guilty on charges related to his courtroom statements, many of them personal insults of the judge. Gignoux found that Dellinger had spoken out when he was adequately represented by his attorneys, and that the outbursts had significantly obstructed the courtroom proceedings. Gignoux did not sentence Dellinger to any additional time in jail.

In 1993, Dellinger published an autobiography, *From Yale to Jail: The Life Story of a Moral Dissenter* .

John Froines

John Froines
Courtesy of Bettman/Corbis.

At the time of the trial, John Froines was an assistant professor of chemistry at the University of Oregon. Froines graduated from the University of California at Berkeley in 1963 and received his Ph.D. in chemistry from Yale University in 1966. Froines had known Tom Hayden since they had trained together as community activists. Like his codefendant Weiner, Froines had served as a marshal for the National Mobilization Committee in Chicago, but Froines and Weiner were the only defendants not related to the leadership of a national organization.

During the defense strategy sessions for the trial, Froines was usually allied with Hayden in support of a clear political focus. Froines traveled with Hayden and Leonard Weinglass to the northern Virginia home of former Attorney General Ramsey Clark to ask him to testify for the defense.

The jury found Froines not guilty of all charges in the indictment, but near the close of the trial Judge Hoffman convicted Froines on ten counts of criminal contempt and sentenced him to six and a half months in jail. The U.S. Court of Appeals reversed the convictions and remanded them for retrial before a different judge in the district court. After the government presented its case in the retrial, the judge acquitted Froines of all remaining contempt charges.

In the spring of 1971, Froines was arrested and again indicted on charges of violating the Anti-Riot Act following his involvement in the Mayday Tribe effort to shut down the federal government in protest of the war in Vietnam. The government dropped the charge. Froines worked for the Occupational Safety and Health Administration during the Carter administration. He later became a professor of environmental health sciences at the University of California at Los Angeles and, as of 2008, he serves as director of the UCLA Center for Occupational and Environmental Health.

Tom Hayden (1939-)

Tom Hayden
Courtesy of Bettman/Corbis.

As a former president of the Students for a Democratic Society and principal author of the key manifesto of student dissent, Tom Hayden was one of the most prominent leaders of the radical political movements that emerged on college campuses in the 1960s. Hayden was born in Detroit, and grew up in Royal Oak, Michigan, where he attended the church of the radio priest and fervent anti-communist, Father Coughlin. Hayden went to the University of Michigan where he served as editor of the *Michigan Daily* and covered the 1960 Democratic convention for his school paper. He joined the Students for a Democratic Society, and as president of the group he drafted the Port Huron Statement that outlined a vision of participatory democracy and personal independence. For several years he worked as a community organizer with an SDS project in Newark, New Jersey. Hayden also became increasingly involved in opposition to American involvement in the Vietnam War. In late 1965, Hayden made his first trip to North Vietnam, and he later returned to that country and Cambodia to secure the release of American prisoners of war.

In the months before the 1968 Democratic National Convention, Hayden and his colleague, Rennie Davis, opened an office in Chicago to plan for a massive demonstration comparable to the anti-war mobilization in Washington, D.C., in October 1967. Although participation in the demonstrations never approached the organizers' goals, Hayden remained as a chief organizer of the week's events, even as the demonstrators seemed to abandon the focused political agenda that Hayden had advocated.

Hayden was one of the six individuals cited by a Daley administration report blaming violence on "outside agitators," and he was one of the eight demonstrators indicted in March 1969. As the defendants planned their strategy, Hayden convinced the defendants to hire Leonard Weinglass, with whom Hayden worked during his community organizing in Newark. Throughout the trial, Hayden was often at odds with other defendants over his determination to maintain a political focus in the trial. Hayden was impatient with what he saw as the unstructured cultural radicalism of Jerry Rubin and Abbie Hoffman.

The jury found Hayden not guilty of the conspiracy charge but guilty of the charge of travel with intent to incite a riot. The conviction was reversed by the U.S. Court of Appeals for the Seventh Circuit and remanded to the district court, but the government declined to retry Hayden. Near the close of the trial, Judge Hoffman convicted Hayden on eleven counts of contempt and sentenced him to more than fourteen months in jail. The U.S. Court of Appeals reversed those criminal contempt convictions and remanded the charges for retrial before another judge. The government brought only one of the contempt charges against Hayden on retrial, and Judge Edward Gignoux found Hayden not guilty. Gignoux found that Hayden's statement in court in response to the physical constraint of Bobby Seale was not responsible for the disruption of the courtroom, but rather that the disruption of the trial resulted from "the appalling spectacle of a bound and gagged defendant and the marshals' efforts to subdue him."

Following the Chicago trial, Hayden continued his work in opposition to the Vietnam War. While working with the Indochina Peace Campaign in 1972, he met Jane Fonda, whom he married. Hayden unsuccessfully challenged incumbent U.S. Senator John Tunney in the 1976 California primary. He won election to the California State assembly in 1982 and the California Senate in 1992 and served until 2000.

Abbie Hoffman (1936-1989)

Abbie Hoffman
Courtesy of Bettman/Corbis.

Abbie Hoffman was one of the most visible and familiar of the Chicago Seven defendants, and his style of cultural politics and confrontation defined much of the defendants' response to Judge

Julius Hoffman and the government prosecutors. The two Hoffmans engaged in verbal sparring throughout the trial, trading one-liners and gaining much of the attention of the press.

Hoffman was born in Worcester, Massachusetts, and attended Brandeis University and graduate school at the University of California at Berkeley. In the early 1960s, he became increasingly involved in social activism and organized northern support for the civil rights movement in the South. In the mid-1960s, Hoffman moved to New York City and organized political theater. His most famous event was in 1967 at the New York Stock Exchange, where, after notifying the press of their intentions, Hoffman and others entered the visitors' gallery and tossed dollar bills to the trading floor. As Hoffman and other cultural radicals in New York planned political theater to coincide with the Democratic convention in Chicago, they devised the idea of Yippie!, a barely organized movement that would simultaneously mimic and mock a political party. Their plans for Chicago focused on a Festival of Life, which they envisioned as part music festival and part public presentation of counter-cultural lifestyle, all with the goal of attracting television coverage.

Hoffman and fellow Yippie Jerry Rubin met with the National Mobilization Committee to coordinate demonstrations at the convention, and the Yippie leaders moved to Chicago to negotiate permits for their events in public parks, but the alliance between the cultural radicals and the political organizers was always uneasy.

Hoffman was highly visible in Chicago during most of the convention week, organizing media events and speaking to crowds in Lincoln Park about expected confrontations with the Chicago police. On the night of the worst violence, however, Hoffman was in jail after his arrest for walking around the city with an obscenity written on his forehead in red lipstick. (He claimed he did it to keep his picture out of the newspaper.) Hoffman was among those cited by Mayor Daley's report blaming the violence on outside agitators, and he was one the eight indicted for conspiracy and intent to incite a riot.

Hoffman was one of the two defendants to take the witness stand, and his extended testimony was a tour de force of his absurdist, subversive verbal style. Hoffman's performance in the courtroom was equally notable, seldom missing an opportunity to undermine the legitimacy of the proceedings.

Judge Hoffman convicted Abbie Hoffman on twenty-three counts of criminal contempt but sentenced him to a comparatively light eight months in jail. The U.S. court of appeals reversed the contempt convictions and remanded them for retrial before another judge. The government prosecuted five of the contempt charges, and Judge Edward Gignoux convicted Hoffman on two of the charges and found him not guilty of the other three. Gignoux convicted Hoffman of the charge related to an extended verbal attack, complete with Yiddish insults, delivered against Judge Hoffman following the revocation of David Dellinger's bail and on the charge related to Abbie Hoffman's appearance in the courtroom in judicial robes, which he flung to the floor. Although Gignoux found that the judicial robe episode did not actually impede the trial, the behavior was "so flagrant, so outrageous, and so subversive" that it rose to the level of "an actual obstruction." Gignoux did not sentence Hoffman to any additional jail time. Hoffman's conviction on the charge of intent to incite a riot was reversed by the court of appeals, and the government made no effort to retry him.

Hoffman published several successful books, including *Revolution for the Hell of It* (1968), *Woodstock Nation* (1969), and *Steal This Book* (1970). He went into hiding after an arrest for cocaine possession and lived under an assumed identity for nearly six years. Hoffman surrendered himself in 1980, after his successful work as an environmental organizer made his exposure likely. He was diagnosed with bipolar disorder in 1980, and he committed suicide in 1989.

Jerry Rubin (1938-1994)

Jerry Rubin
Courtesy of Bettman/Corbis.

Like his fellow Yippie, Abbie Hoffman, Jerry Rubin approached the Chicago conspiracy trial as an opportunity to present a critique of American society and to challenge the legitimacy of the U.S. government.

Rubin was born in Cincinnati and attended Oberlin College before graduating from the University of Cincinnati. He worked for a short time as a sports reporter and then enrolled in graduate school at the University of California at Berkeley. He quickly gave up school for political activism and traveled to Cuba. Back in Berkeley, Rubin participated in the Free Speech Movement in 1964. He organized one of the first teach-ins against the Vietnam War. He also developed a reputation for theatrical behavior when, in 1966, he appeared before the House Un-American Activities Committee dressed as an American Revolutionary soldier.

After an unsuccessful run for mayor of Berkeley, Rubin moved to New York where he merged his political activism with an interest in cultural radicalism. He joined with David Dellinger of the National Mobilization Committee to organize a massive protest against the Vietnam War in October 1967, and it was Rubin who proposed to stage the march in front of the Pentagon. With Abbie Hoffman, Rubin was one of the founders of the Yippie movement, and the two of them moved to Chicago in the spring of 1968 to organize Yippie events and to seek city permits for their gatherings in public parks.

In the week before the Democratic convention, Rubin appeared at a rally at the Chicago Civic Center, where he nominated as president a pig, named "Pigasus." (The organizers were arrested and the pig placed in the custody of the local humane society.) Rubin and other Yippies drew on their media skills to spread wild rumors of non-existent Yippie plans, including a supposed effort to put LSD in the Chicago water supply and a plot to place Yippies disguised as bellhops in the hotels serving convention delegates.

The Daley report on the convention demonstrations cited Rubin as one of the "outside agitators" blamed for the violence. While the grand jury investigated possible indictments related to the convention violence, Rubin continued his political theater. When the House Un-American Activities Committee in October 1968 held hearings on the convention violence, Rubin showed up "bearded, beaded, barefooted, and bare-chested," as the *New York Times* described him. At additional HUAC hearings in December, Rubin arrived at the committee room dressed as Santa Claus.

Rubin was convicted of intent to incite a riot, but the U.S. court of appeals reversed the conviction, and the government declined to retry Rubin on the charge.

At the close of the trial, Judge Hoffman convicted Rubin on fifteen charges of contempt and sentenced him to more than two years in jail. The U.S. Court of Appeals for the Seventh Circuit reversed the convictions and remanded the contempt charges for retrial before another judge in the district court. The government prosecuted only three of the contempt charges, and Judge Edward Gignoux convicted Rubin on two of the charges and found Rubin not guilty on the third. The convictions were on charges related to a vocal attack on Judge Hoffman following the revocation of bail for David Dellinger and to Rubin's appearance, along with Abbie Hoffman, in the courtroom in judicial robes, which they flung to the floor.

Rubin drew media attention again in the 1970s when he withdrew from political activity and started work as an entrepreneur. In the 1980s, he joined Abbie Hoffman on a campus tour dubbed the Yippie versus Yuppie debates. Rubin was killed in a pedestrian accident in Los Angeles in 1994.

Bobby Seale (1936-)

Bobby Seale
Courtesy of Bettman/Corbis.

Bobby Seale was in many ways the unlikeliest of the conspiracy defendants. Seale had met only one other defendant, Jerry Rubin, before their indictment, and some of the defendants did not meet him until they first appeared in the courtroom. Seale had been in Chicago briefly during convention week to give two speeches. Although his case was severed from the others well before the end of the trial, Seale's confrontations with Judge Hoffman and Hoffman's order to have Seale bound and gagged in the courtroom remain the most powerful examples of the breakdown of the judicial process during the conspiracy trial.

At the time of the Democratic National Convention, Seale lived in Oakland, California, and was chairman of the Black Panther Party. The Black Panthers had not participated in the planning for the Chicago demonstrations, but Seale made an overnight trip to deliver two speeches. Seale spoke to a rally in Lincoln Park and talked of the need for black men to arm themselves in protection against the police, whom he repeatedly referred to as the pigs. In the prosecution's opening statement at the trial, Assistant U.S. Attorney Richard Schultz quoted Seale as saying "if they get in our way, we should kill some of those pigs" and talking about "barbecuing that pork."

The inclusion of Seale in the conspiracy indictment perplexed many people, including the other defendants, but it came at a time of numerous prosecutions of Black Panther Party members in different parts of the country and extensive FBI surveillance of the party members. Shortly before the start of the Chicago conspiracy trial, Seale and other members of the party were indicted in Connecticut on charges of conspiracy to murder a suspected police informant. Because of the indictment, Seale was the only defendant held in jail during the length of his time in the Chicago conspiracy trial.

Seale originally retained the Black Panthers' lawyer Charles Garry as his attorney, and Garry appeared at the defendants' arraignment on April 9. When the trial started in September, Garry was recovering from surgery and could not travel, but Judge Hoffman refused to delay the start of the trial. Seale repeatedly refused to allow William Kunstler to represent him, and in a series of increasingly hostile confrontations with the judge, Seale attempted to cross-examine witnesses and otherwise serve as his own counsel. Many of these confrontations ended with Seale's litany of "liar, pig, fascist." On October 29, Judge Hoffman ordered that Seale be bound and gagged by the marshals before any court-room appearance. Newspapers across the country and television networks carried the courtroom drawings of the violently restrained Seale. Within a week, the judge relented, but when Seale again tried to represent himself, Judge Hoffman on November 5 ordered a mistrial in the prosecution of Seale. Judge Hoffman also convicted Seale on sixteen charges of contempt and sentenced him to four years in prison. The day before, a group of lawyers from across the country filed suit in the U.S. district court asking for an order stopping the trial until Seale was allowed to represent himself, but Judge Edwin Robson dismissed the suit on November 5.

The U.S. Court of Appeals for the Seventh Circuit dismissed four of the contempt convictions of Seale and remanded the other twelve for retrial before another judge in the district court. The government declined to prosecute the contempt charges. The court of appeals did not rule on Seale's right to a delay in the trial or the right to represent himself, but it found that the trial judge was obligated to investigate Seale's claims that he was not being represented by an attorney of his choice. If such an inquiry had confirmed Seale's account of meetings with his lawyer and found that Seale was "free from ulterior motivation," Judge Hoffman would have been in error to force Seale to rely on Kunstler as his lawyer.

Seale faced trial on the murder conspiracy charges in New Haven, Connecticut, where thousands of protestors, including Abbie Hoffman, criticized the alleged harassment of the Black Panther Party. The jury deadlocked on the charges against Seale, and he never faced a retrial. In 1973, Seale was a candidate for mayor of Oakland, California, but lost to the incumbent in a runoff. Seale later taught political science and served as an assistant to the dean at Temple University in Philadelphia. In 1988, he published a cookbook, *Barbecue'n With Bobby.*

Lee Weiner

Lee Weiner
Courtesy of Bettman/Corbis.

Lee Weiner was the least familiar of the defendants, with only limited connections to those who had planned the Chicago demonstrations. At the trial he also was the least visible and, according to Tom Hayden, spent much of his time in court reading the *I Ching*. Weiner was a research assistant in the sociology department at Northwestern University and had served at the Chicago demonstrations as a marshal with the National Mobilization Committee to End the War in Vietnam. He was indicted for conspiracy along with the other seven original defendants, and he and John Froines were indicted on a separate charge of teaching the use of incendiary devices.

Weiner was acquitted of both the conspiracy charge and the incendiary device charge. Judge Hoffman convicted Weiner on seven charges of criminal contempt and sentenced him to two months and eighteen days in jail. The U.S. court of appeals reversed the convictions and remanded the charges for retrial before another judge. After the government presented its case in the retrial, Judge Edward Gignoux acquitted Weiner of all remaining contempt charges.

Weiner later worked as a political consultant and with the Anti-Defamation League in New York City.

The attorneys

Thomas A. Foran (1924-2000)

U.S. attorney for the Northern District of Illinois

Thomas A. Foran
Courtesy of Bettman/Corbis.

As U.S. attorney for the Northern District of Illinois, Thomas Foran was the lead prosecutor in the Chicago conspiracy trial. Foran, with the assistance of Richard Schultz, presented a case based largely on the testimony of undercover policemen and paid informants, who told of the defendants' plans to disrupt Chicago during the Democratic convention and to provoke law enforcement officers to resort to violence against the demonstrators. Foran aggressively challenged the defense arguments, and his frequent objections were almost always sustained by Judge Hoffman. Throughout the trial, Foran portrayed the defendants as sophisticated revolutionaries who manipulated the alienation of young people. He also emphasized that most of the defendants were much older than the students they attempted to organize. Within days of the close of the trial, Foran continued to stir controversy when he appeared at a public meeting at a Chicago high school and used anti-gay slurs to describe all of the defendants except Bobby Seale.

In its opinion reversing the criminal convictions of five of the defendants, the U.S. Court of Appeals for the Seventh Circuit criticized Foran for his "considerable number" of derogatory comments about the defense. The appeals court found that Foran's final arguments in the case "went at least up to, and probably beyond, the outermost boundary of permissible inferences from the evidence in his characterizations of defendants." The court cited as particularly offensive Foran's references to "evil men" and "anarchists."

The Chicago-born Foran attended Loyola University and the law school of the University of Detroit before entering into private practice in Chicago. He was well connected in Democratic circles in Chicago and was appointed U.S. attorney by President Johnson in 1968. In his short tenure as U.S. attorney, Foran successfully prosecuted a number of individuals involved in organized crime. Following the election of a Republican President, Foran intended to resign on July 1, 1969, but the Nixon administration's Justice Department requested that Foran stay on as U.S. attorney to prosecute the Chicago conspiracy trial. Following his resignation as U.S. attorney in 1970, Foran returned to private practice in Chicago.

William Künstler (1919-1995)

Attorney for the defendants

William Kunstler
Courtesy of Bettman/Corbis.

William Kunstler served as the lead attorney for the defendants in the Chicago conspiracy trial and cemented his reputation as a lawyer for left-leaning celebrities. Kunstler was born in New

York City and attended Yale University. He then served in the military and graduated from Columbia Law School. As a law student he wrote for various publications and read movie scripts for a major studio. In the early years of his law practice in New York, Kunstler also wrote radio scripts. He gained national attention in 1961 with the publication of a book on the controversial death penalty case of Caryl Chessman. Kunstler represented various civil rights leaders in the 1960s, and he also represented celebrity clients like the comedian Lenny Bruce. He agreed to represent Lee Harvey Oswald after the assassination of President Kennedy, and Kunstler later represented Jack Ruby in an appeal of Ruby's conviction for murdering Oswald.

Although Kunstler often left the more detailed legal work of the Chicago trial to his colleague Leonard Weinglass, it was Kunstler who emphasized what he thought was the political character of the trial. He frequently linked the defendants with American Revolutionaries and historical advocates of social justice and political liberty. The trial, according to Kunstler's opening statement, was "a classic example of the Government against the people." "The real conspiracy in this case is the conspiracy to curtail and prevent the demonstrations against the war in Vietnam." Kunstler was also a highly visible advocate for the defendants outside the courtroom.

At the Chicago trial, Kunstler took the lead in challenging Judge Hoffman and the government prosecutors. His confrontations with the judge resulted in Judge Hoffman issuing contempt convictions on thirty-four charges against Kunstler and imposing a jail sentence of more than four years. The U.S. Court of Appeals for the Seventh Circuit dismissed nine of the charges and remanded the rest for retrial before another judge. The government dropped all but six of the charges, and at the retrial, Judge Edward Gignoux found Kunstler not guilty of four of the charges. The first of Kunstler's contempt convictions resulted from an extended diatribe against Judge Hoffman that constituted "outrageous behavior," according to Gignoux, and that resulted in a substantive delay in the trial. The other conviction was based on Kunstler's refusal to obey the judge's order not to discuss a motion in front of the jury. In both instances, Gignoux found that Kunstler's behavior exceeded any definition of "vigorous advocacy" of the defendants' interests. Gignoux imposed no jail sentence on Kunstler or the other defendants convicted of contempt.

In the years following the Chicago conspiracy trial, Kunstler often represented well-known radicals and notorious criminal defendants. He also appeared in movies and television, occasionally playing himself.

Leonard Weinglass (1933-)

Attorney for the defendants

Leonard Weinglass
Courtesy of Bettman/Corbis.

Leonard Weinglass was the younger and less well-known attorney for the defense. Weinglass graduated from George Washington University and the Yale Law School. After service in the Air Force, he practiced law in Newark, N.J., and taught at the Rutgers Law School. He joined the defense for the Chicago case at the request of Tom Hayden, whom he had defended on several minor offenses arising from Hayden's work with the Students for a Democratic Society. Weinglass took responsibility for the defense of Hayden, Rennie Davis, Abbie Hoffman, and John Froines. Weeks before the trial started, Abbie Hoffman invited Weinglass to accompany him to the Woodstock music festival. The defendants later remembered him as the one who "always did his homework and was there with the necessary cases and precedents when they were needed."

Near the close of the trial, Judge Julius Hoffman convicted Leonard Weinglass of fourteen counts of criminal contempt. The U.S. Court of Appeals for the Seventh Circuit dismissed seven of those counts and remanded the others for retrial before another judge. The government attorneys chose to bring only one of the remaining contempt charges against Weinglass in the retrial, and Judge Edward Gignoux found Weinglass not guilty because the alleged contempt had not obstructed the trial nor had it involved personal insults against Judge Hoffman.

Weinglass later reminisced that he had a "sort of wistful regard" for his experience with Judge Hoffman. "He had a razor-like wit which he would use against you in court. I'd find myself angry and upset but amused at the same time."

Weinglass continued to represent leftist clients, including members of the Weather Underground, and controversial criminal defendants.

Richard J. Daley (1902-1976)

Mayor of Chicago

Mayor Richard J. Daley on the fl oor of the Democratic National Convention
Associated Press, 1968

By 1968, Richard J. Daley had been mayor for more than twenty years, and for much of the nation he was the very image of modern Chicago. After service in the Illinois legislature and state government under Governor Adlai Stevenson, Daley became chair of the Cook County Democratic Central Committee in 1953 and was elected mayor two years later. As mayor and party leader, he commanded an extensive organization that ensured his reelection and helped him efficiently deliver municipal services. Daley also promoted investments in major public works and private construction that helped maintain Chicagos status among American cities. His political influence made him an important player in national Democratic politics. By the time of the Democratic convention, however, Daley's style of urban leadership was an anachronism and subject to charges of cronyism and machine politics.

Daley's reputation suffered a serious blow in the spring of 1968 during the riots that followed the assassination of Martin Luther King. The mayor asked the police superintendent to order police to shoot to kill any arsonist and to shoot to maim looters. A national outcry followed. In 1968, Daley's administration was determined to prevent any kind of civil disturbance during the Democratic convention, and officials refused to issue permits requested by demonstrators. The mayor's administration also mobilized an over-whelming force of police and National Guard troops to maintain order in the city.

National media covering the convention criticized the police response to the demonstrators, and the television networks broadcast Daley's remarkable tantrum on the floor of the convention. Daley responded to the public criticism with a hastily prepared report that blamed the convention violence on "outside agitators" and a "hard core of revolutionaries."

In January 1970, Mayor Daley appeared as a witness for the defense, but his testimony did little to support the defense argument. Daley insisted he had not ordered the denial of permits for demonstrators, but for the most part Daley offered little beyond praise for his staff and U.S. Attorney Foran. Judge Hoffman sustained most of the prosecution's objections to the defense line of questioning of Daley. Defense attorney Kunstler read into the record an "offer of proof," which allows an attorney to present, away from the presence of the jury, information that the judge had not allowed them to present through examination of a witness. Kunstler's order of proof alleged a conspiracy of Daley and President Johnson, with the cooperation of the U.S. attorney, to prevent any demonstrations against the Vietnam War and social injustice.

Despite the damage to his national reputation following the events of 1968, Daley remained popular in much of Chicago and won reelection to a sixth term in 1975.

Media Coverage and Public Debates

During the Democratic National Convention of August 1968, network television coverage of the confrontations between demonstrators and Chicago police shocked the nation and prompted investigations by the city of Chicago, the House Committee on Un-American Activities, and the President's National Commission on the Causes and Prevention of Violence. The media images of the violence disrupting the political process also intensified demands for the criminal prosecution of the police and the demonstrators. The subsequent trial of the demonstrators, closely followed by the media, became the center of a national debate on the fairness of the federal judicial system and on the culture of dissent that arose in the 1960s.

Media coverage had been central to the debate over the demonstrations surrounding the convention, and it would be a subject of controversy leading up to and throughout the Chicago Seven trial. On the first anniversary of the convention riots and weeks before the opening of the trial, Tom Wicker wrote in the *New York Times* "The miracle of television made it visible to all-pierced, at last, the isolation of one America from the other, exposed to each the power it faced."

Chicago police marshal against demonstrators during the Democratic National Convention, 1968
Courtesy of the Chicago History Museum.

The role of the media in the Chicago violence was a polarizing issue. In the days following the convention, Mayor Daley demanded prime time on each of the television networks for a response to what he characterized as distorted coverage of the police violence. Several months later, the Walker Report's review of police violence concluded that "newsmen and photographers were singled out for assault, and their equipment deliberately damaged." Shortly after the report was published, U.S. Attorney Thomas Foran alleged that the television networks had staged shots of the demonstrators' injuries at the hands of the police.

As the trial began in September 1969, the district court for the Northern District of Illinois attempted to manage the expected media crush. Chief Judge William Campbell prohibited cameras and sound equipment from all but one room of the courthouse, and Judge Richard Austin dismissed a suit by the American Civil Liberties Union challenging the ban. Austin announced that "the quickest way to end demonstrations is to have all cameras five blocks from the building." Campbell denied a request from over 100 attorneys to move the trial to a larger courtroom that could accommodate more of the press and hopeful spectators who lined up daily outside the federal courthouse, and the U.S. court of appeals upheld Campbell's decision. Judge Hoffman set aside a section of the courtroom for the press with credentials, but he prohibited them from wearing press credentials in the courtroom, explaining that he didn't want his courtroom to look like "a furniture convention." The limited access did nothing to deter press interest in the trial, and around twenty news outlets, including newspapers like the *New York Times* and the *Washington Post*, assigned reporters to cover the full length of the proceedings.

Everyone in the courtroom took notice of the daily coverage of the trial by national print and broadcast media. The defendants' antics and the long list of celebrity witnesses guaranteed an audience well beyond the judge and jury. The defense held daily press conferences during the lunch break until the judge warned them not to comment on the trial in public. Judge Hoffman proved to be equally adept at attracting press comment, and the chief judge of the court later acknowledged that Judge Hoffman "loved the publicity, bad as it was."

The defendants cultivated media coverage outside of the courtroom in their efforts to convince the public that the court proceedings amounted to a political rather than a criminal trial. At night defendants spoke to community meetings and attended fundraisers held by wealthy supporters. One weekend, the defendants traveled to Washington to join a half-million people at a rally against the Vietnam War. Their public appearances could have a less serious side as well. On a visit to Chicago's Second City comedy club, Abbie Hoffman responded to an audience request with a 45-minute satire of Judge Hoffman. In December 1969, the defendants posed in a group photo for a holiday card that urged recipients to "Make a New Year's Resolution-Join the Conspiracy."

Demonstrators during the Democratic National Convention, 1968
Courtesy of the Chicago History Museum.

Washington Post writer Nicholas Van Hoffman noted within the first weeks of the trial that the proceedings had none of the expected characteristics of a criminal trial. "No one here at the Great Conspiracy Trial thinks of its outcome in terms of guilt or innocence. You are for the government or for the defendants." A *Chicago Sun-Times* reporter found the trial "more sideshow than criminal proceeding."

Outside the courtroom, the cultural and political clashes of convention week played on as background for the trial. A series of protests and demonstrations, most of them small and many barely related to the trial, appeared outside the courthouse. The violence of convention week threatened to reappear in October 1969 during the self-styled "Days of Rage" organized by the Weatherman group and other radical groups emerging from the break up of the Students for a Democratic Society. Protestors clashed with Chicago police and smashed store windows, at one point attempting to reach the hotel where Judge Hoffman and his wife lived.

Very different groups of protestors approached the court to protect defendants' right to representation. When Judge Hoffman threatened to hold the pretrial team of defense lawyers in contempt, nationally prominent lawyers and law professors, including future federal judges, converged on the courthouse to demand a mistrial.

Courtroom drawing of Bobby Seale, seated, bound and gagged during the Chicago conspiracy trial
Howard Brodie, artist. 1969. Library of Congress,
Prints and Photographs Division [LC-USZC4-4870].

The gagging of Bobby Seale, Judge Hoffman's consistently pro-government rulings, and the ill-defined requirements for conviction on the conspiracy charge led many in the press to question the impartiality of the judicial system. Tom Wicker of the *New York Times* asked if the burden of proof "any longer means anything." J. Anthony Lukas noted the many observers "who view what they regard as the excesses on both sides as damaging to the American judicial process and raising questions as to how a court can effectively dispense justice in cases which arouse such strong political passions." The defendants were only too willing to foster these doubts about justice in the federal courts. Rennie Davis said that "Judge Hoffman presides in every court in this country." Alternatively, the letters to the editors of Chicago newspapers indicated popular support for Judge Hoffman.

The guilty verdict for five of the defendants brought familiar popular protests, including a crowd of 5,000 outside the Chicago courthouse and another demonstration in Washington, D.C., where more than 100 people were arrested. The several appeals that brought reversals of the convictions and a rebuke of Judge Hoffman were prominently reported by the national press, but the popular interest in the case never again rose to the levels seen during the trial phase. The proceedings in the court of appeals had none of the dramatic interest of the trial, and, perhaps more important, the protest movement evident at the Democratic convention declined following the killings at Kent State University in the spring of 1970.

Historical Documents

Table of Contents

Testimony of Abbie Hoffman, December 23 & 29, 1969

Abbie Hoffman and Rennie Davis were the only defendants to testify at the trial. Hoffman's appearance was meant to establish the nonviolent intent of the demonstrations and events planned by the Yippies. His opening remarks were more in the nature of a performance than testimony, as was typical of so much of Hoffman's interaction with the court. His answers to the standard opening questions challenged the very forms of a trial and replaced them with something closer to a comedy routine. His claim that he was a resident of Woodstock Nation referred to the book Hoffman published after attending the music festival in August 1969. Hoffman escorted Leonard Weinglass to Woodstock as an introduction to the counterculture. The remarks of December 29 are devoted to the founding and goals of the Yippie party.

[Document Source: *The Conspiracy Trial,*eds., Judy Clavir and John Spitzer (Indianapolis, IN: Bobbs-Merrill Co., 1970), 344-45, 349-50.]

December 23,1969

Mr. Weinglass: Will you please identify yourself for the record?

The Witness: My name is Abbie. I am an orphan of America.

Mr. Schultz: Your Honor, may the record show it is the defendant Hoffman who has taken the stand?

The Court: Oh, yes. It may so indicate.

The Witness: Well, it is not really my last name.

Mr. Weinglass: Abbie, what is your last name?

The Witness: Well, there is some confusion about it because, well, my grandfather, he was a Russian Jew, and he decided to protest the anti-Semitism in the Russian Army and he slew —

Mr. Schultz: Objection. If the defendant has a last name, let him state it, but not —

The Court: All we want to know, sir, is your last name.

The Witness: My slave name is Hoffman. My real name is Shaboysnakoff. I can't spell it.

The Court: There is a lawyer who has filed his appearance in the name of Abbie Hoffman for you. You gave him your name as Abbie Hoffman, did you not?

The Witness: Well, no. It was the Government's idea and the name was Abbott Howard.

Mr. Weinglass: Where do you reside?

The Witness: I live in Woodstock Nation.

Mr. Weinglass: Will you tell the Court and jury where it is?

The Witness: Yes. It is a nation of alienated young people. We carry it around with us as a state of mind in the same way as the Sioux Indians carried the Sioux nation around with them. It is a nation dedicated to cooperation versus competition, to the idea that people should have better means of exchange than property or money, that there should be some other basis for human interaction. It is a nation dedicated to —

The Court: Just where it is, that is all.

The Witness: It is in my mind and in the minds of my brothers and sisters. It does not consist of property or material but, rather, of ideas and certain values. We believe in a society —

The Court: No, we want the place of residence, if he has one, place of doing business, if you have a business. Nothing about philosophy or India, sir. Just where you live, if you have a place to live. Now you said Woodstock. In what state is Woodstock?

The Witness: It is in the state of mind, in the mind of myself and my brothers and sisters. It is a conspiracy. Presently, the nation is held captive, in the penitentiaries of the institutions of a decaying system.

Mr. Weinglass: Can you tell the Court and jury your present age?

The Witness: My age is 33. I am a child of the 60s.

Mr. Weinglass: When were you born?

The Witness: Psychologically, 1960.

Mr. Schultz: Objection, if the Court please. I move to strike the answer.

Mr. Weinglass: What is the actual date of your birth?

The Witness: November 30, 1936.

Mr. Weinglass: Between the date of your birth, November 30, 1936, and May 1, 1960, what if anything occurred in your life?

The Witness: Nothing. I believe it is called an American education.

Mr. Schultz: Objection.

The Court: I sustain the objection.

The Witness: Huh.

Mr. Weinglass: Abbie, could you tell the Court and jury —

Mr. Schultz: His name isn't Abbie. I object to this informality.

Mr. Weinglass: Can you tell the Court and jury what is your present occupation?

The Witness: I am a cultural revolutionary. Well, I am really a defendant-fulltime.

Mr. Weinglass: What do you mean by the phrase "cultural revolutionary"?

The Witness: Well, I suppose it is a person who tries to shape and participate in the values, and the mores, the customs and the style of living of new people who eventually become inhabitants of a new nation and a new society through art and poetry, theater, and music.

Mr. Weinglass: What have you done yourself to participate in that revolution?

The Witness: Well, I have been a rock and roll singer. I am a reporter with the Liberation News Service. I am a poet. I am a film maker. I made a movie called "Yippies Tour Chicago or How I Spent My Summer Vacation." Currently, I am negotiating with United Artists and MGM to do a movie in Hollywood.

I have written an extensive pamphlet on how to live free in the city of New York.

I have written two books, one called *Revolution for The Hell of It* under the pseudonym Free, and one called, *Woodstock Nation*.

Mr. Weinglass: Taking you back to the spring of 1960, approximately May 1, 1960, will you tell the Court and jury where you were?

Mr. Schultz: 1960?

The Witness: That's right.

Mr. Schultz: Objection.

The Court: I sustain the objection.

Mr. Weinglass: Your Honor, that date has great relevance to the trial. May 1, 1960, was this witness' first public demonstration. I am going to bring him down through Chicago.

The Court: Not in my presence, you are not going to bring him down. I sustain the objection to the question.

The Witness: My background has nothing to do with my state of mind?

The Court: Will you remain quiet while I am making a ruling? I know you have no respect for me.

Mr. Kunstler: Your Honor, that is totally unwarranted. I think your remarks call for a motion for a mistrial.

The Court: And your motion calls for a denial of the motion. Mr. Weinglass, continue with your examination.

Mr. Kunstler: You denied my motion? I hadn't even started to argue it.

The Court: I don't need any argument on that one. The witness turned his back on me while he was on the witness stand.

The Witness: I was just looking at the pictures of the longhairs up on the wall....

The Witness: Yes.

We talked about the possibility of having demonstrations at the Democratic Convention in Chicago, Illinois, that was going to be occurring that August. I am not sure that we knew at that point that it was in Chicago. Wherever it was, we were planning on going.

Jerry Rubin, I believe, said that it would be a good idea to call it the Festival of Life in contrast to the Convention of Death, and to have it in some kind of public area, like a park or something, in Chicago.

One thing that I was very particular about was that we didn't have any concept of leadership involved. There was a feeling of young people that they didn't want to listen to leaders. We had to create a kind of situation in which people would be allowed to participate and become in a real sense their own leaders.

I think it was then after this that Paul Krassner said the word "YIPPIE," and we felt that that expressed in a kind of slogan and advertising sense the spirit that we wanted to put forth in Chicago, and we adopted that as our password, really.

December 29, 1969

The Witness: Anita [Hoffman] said that "Yippie" would be understood by our generation, that straight newspapers like the *New York Times* and the U.S. Government and the courts and everything wouldn't take it seriously unless it had a formal name, so she came up with the name: "Youth International Party." She said we could play a lot of jokes on the concept of "party" because everybody would think that we were this huge international conspiracy, but that in actuality we were a party that you had fun at.

Nancy [Kursham] said that fun was an integral ingredient, that people in America, because they were being programmed like IBM cards, weren't having enough fun in life and that if you watched television, the only people that you saw having any fun were people who were buying lousy junk on television commercials, and that this would be a whole new attitude because you would see people, young people, having fun while they were protesting the system, and that young people all around this country and around the world would be turned on for that kind of an attitude.

I said that fun was very important, too, that it was a direct rebuttal of the kind of ethics and morals that were being put forth in the country to keep people working in a rat race which didn't make any sense because in a few years that machines would do all the work anyway, that there was a whole system of values that people were taught to postpone their pleasure, to put all their money in the bank, to buy life insurance, a whole bunch of things that didn't make any sense to our generation at all, and that fun actually was becoming quite subversive.

Jerry said that because of our action at the Stock Exchange in throwing out the money, that within a few weeks the Wall Street brokers there had totally enclosed the whole stock exchange in bulletproof, shatterproof glass, that cost something like $20,000 because they were afraid we'd come back and throw money out again.

He said that for hundreds of years political cartoonists had always pictured corrupt politicians in the guise of a pig, and he said that it would be great theater if we ran a pig for President, and we all took that on as like a great idea and that's more or less-that was the founding.

Mr. Weinglass: The document that is before you, D-222 for identification, what is that document?

The Witness: It was our initial call to people to describe what Yippie was about and why we were coming to Chicago.

Mr. Weinglass: Now, Abbie, could you read the entire document to the jury.

The Witness: It says:

"A STATEMENT FROM YIP!

"Join us in Chicago in August for an international festival of youth, music, and theater. Rise up and abandon the creeping meatball! Come all you rebels, youth spirits, rock minstrels, truth-seekers, peacock-freaks, poets, barricade-jumpers, dancers, lovers and artists!

"It is summer. It is the last week in August, and the NATIONAL DEATH PARTY meets to bless Lyndon Johnson. We are there! There are 50,000 of us dancing in the streets, throbbing with amplifiers and harmony. We are making love in the parks. We are reading, singing, laughing, printing newspapers, groping, and making a mock convention, and celebrating the birth of FREE AMERICA in our own time.

"Everything will be free. Bring blankets, tents, draft-cards, body-paint, Mr. Leary's Cow, food to share, music, eager skin, and happiness. The threats of LBJ, Mayor Daley, and J. Edgar Freako will not stop us. We are coming! We are coming from all over the world!

"The life of the American spirit is being torn asunder by the forces of violence, decay, and the napalm-cancer fiend. We demand the Politics of Ecstasy! We are the delicate spores of the new fierceness that will change America. We will create our own reality, we are Free America! And we will not accept the false theater of the Death Convention.

"We will be in Chicago. Begin preparations now! Chicago is yours! Do it!"

"Do it!" was a slogan like "Yippie." We use that a lot and it meant that each person that came should take on the responsibility for being his own leader-that we should, in fact, have a leaderless society.

We shortly thereafter opened an office and people worked in the office on what we call movement salaries, subsistence, thirty dollars a week. We had what the straight world would call a staff and an office although we called it an energy center and regarded ourselves as a tribe or a family.

Testimony of Rennie Davis, January 24, 1970

Rennie Davis offered the court his account of the events in Grant Park on the afternoon of August 28. The rally was one of the only events for which the city of Chicago granted a permit, but the event ended with some of the worst violence of the week and heightened tensions leading to an even more violent confrontation that evening in front of one of the conventions' delegates' hotels. Davis testified that he attempted to calm the demonstrators and reduce the risk of police violence in the moments before he was beaten.

[Document Source: *The Conspiracy Trial*, eds., Judy Clavir and John Spitzer (Indianapolis, IN: Bobbs-Merrill Co., 1970), 480-81.]

Mr. Weinglass: Now, directing your attention to approximately 2:30 in the afternoon of that same day, do you recall where you were at that time?

The Witness: Yes, I was in Grant Park just south of the refreshment stand. I saw a commotion near the flagpole and shortly after that I heard Dave Dellinger's voice. It was clear that something was happening and Dave indicated that he wanted marshals to move to the flagpole, so I then said to everyone there that we should go toward the flagpole.

Mr. Weinglass: When you went to the flagpole, did you have anything in your hands?

The Witness: I had a speaker system with a microphone.

Mr. Weinglass: As you arrived in the vicinity of the flagpole, what was occurring?

The Witness: The flag had been lowered to halfmast and the police were dragging a young man out of the area. The police seemed to be withdrawing from the area as I arrived, and a lot of people who were gathered around the flagpole began to throw anything they could get their hands on at the police who were withdrawing from the crowd. They threw rocks and boards and lunches and anything that was available right on the ground.

Mr. Weinglass: What were you saying, if anything, at that time on the microphone?

The Witness: I kept directing the marshals to form a line, link arms, and then I constantly urged the people in the crowd to stop throwing things. I said, "You're throwing things at our own people. Move back."

As our marshal line grew, I urged our marshal line to now begin to move back and move the demonstrators away from the police.

Mr. Weinglass: Where did you go?

The Witness: I continued to stand in front of the marshal line that had been formed.

Mr. Weinglass: What did you then observe happen?

The Witness: Well, at that time another squadron of policemen in formation began to advance towards my position.

I was standing in front of our marshal line sort of sandwiched in between our marshal line and the advancing police formation.

Mr. Weinglass: What were you doing as the police were advancing?

The Witness: Well, as the police advanced, I continued to have my back to the police line, basically concerned that the marshal line not break or move. Then the police formation broke and began to run, and at that time I heard several of the men in the line yell, quite distinctly, "Kill Davis! Kill Davis!" and they were screaming that and the police moved on top of me, and I was trapped between my own marshal line and advancing police line.

The first thing that occurred to me was a very powerful blow to the head that drove me face first down into the dirt, and then, as I attempted to crawl on my hands and knees, the policemen continued to yell, "Kill Davis! Kill Davis!" and continued to strike me across the ear and the neck and the back.

I guess I must have been hit thirty or forty times in the back and I crawled for maybe —I don't know how many feet, ten feet maybe, and I came to a chain fence and somehow I managed to crawl either under or through that fence, and a police fell over the fence, trying to get me, and another police hit the fence with his nightstick, but I had about a second or two in which I could stand and I leaped over a bench and over some people and into the park, and then I proceeded to walk toward the center of the park.

Mr. Weinglass: As you walked toward the center of the park, what, if anything, happened?

The Witness: Well, I guess the first thing that I was conscious of, I looked down, and my tie was just solid blood, and I realized that my shirt was just becoming blood, and someone took my arm and took me to the east side of the Bandshell, and I laid down, and there was a white coat who was bent over me. I remember hearing the voice of Carl Oglesby. Carl said, "In order to survive in this country, we have to fight," and then-then I lost consciousness.

Assistant U.S. Attorney Richard Schultz, closing argument for the government, February 11, 1970

According to Richard Schultz, the seven defendants were united in their determination to provoke violence in Chicago during the Democratic convention. Throughout the trial, the prosecution had attempted to explain how the occasional cooperation of seven individuals constituted a conspiracy. Here, Schultz describes the defendants' "tacit understanding" of a shared goal. Schultz also dismisses the long efforts to secure permits and the talk of nonviolence as a ploy to entice unwitting demonstrators into a violent confrontation with police.

[Document Source: *The Conspiracy Trial*, eds., Judy Clavir and John Spitzer (Indianapolis, IN: Bobbs-Merrill Co., 1970), 552-53.]

Let me briefly discuss the conspiracy charge.

We have shown that these defendants, all seven of them, had a mutual understanding to accomplish the objects of the conspiracy, that they had a common purpose of bringing disruption and inciting a violence in this city, and that all seven of them together participated in working together and siding each other to further these plans. Oh, they never explicitly said, "You do that to blow up that," and "I will do that to incite that crowd," that is not how they did it. It was tacit understanding, a working together in all these meetings and all of these conferences that they had, and that is how they conspired.

The only difference between five of the defendants and the remaining two, Rubin and Hoffman, were the ways of getting the people here. Rubin and Hoffman were going to get their people here by a music festival, and the others were going to get their people here by saying they were going to have a counter-convention of the grassroots of America.

All seven defendants worked together jointly for the common purpose and discussed and planned together for the common purpose of creating violent conflict and disruptions in this city. They were going to incite violence in this city by bringing other people here and by coming here themselves. We have proven the defendants guilty on the substantive counts as well as the conspiracy charge, as we charge.

The last area I want to cover are march permits. Most of Davis' direct examination was to impress you on how genuinely he tried to get march permits and an assembly site at the Amphitheatre. Well, he wanted a march permit and he wanted an assembly permit at the Amphitheatre, but it doesn't follow that because he wanted permits he wanted to avoid violence. Don't be fooled by that. Why did Davis want permits for the Amphitheatre? He wanted permits first to make it look like "We are trying to avoid violence. We want permits."

Number two, he wanted permits because they wanted to be where the TV cameras were, at the Amphitheatre.

And, number three, they wanted permits because they wanted the confrontation right at the Amphitheatre, right at the Amphitheatre.

Leonard Weinglass, closing argument for the defendants, February 12, 1970

In his closing arguments, Defense Attorney Leonard Weinglass sought to undermine the prosecutions definition of a conspiracy and to challenge the testimony of government witnesses who claimed the defendants spoke of plans for violence. He then finished by asserting that the trial was a government effort to suppress dissent and that the defendants were in a long tradition of defenders of liberty. When Weinglass sought to link the prosecution to the Salem witch trials and the persecution of Jesus, the U.S. attorney had had enough, and Judge Hoffman upheld the government's objection. Weinglass's remarks were part of a sustained effort to convince the jury of the political character of the trial and to emphasize the historical importance of the outcome.

[Document Source: *The Conspiracy Trial*, eds., Judy Clavir and John Spitzer (Indianapolis, IN: Bobbs-Merrill Co., 1970), 561-62.]

It seems to me that if the lesson of the country teaches anything, it is that the true patriots are the people who take a position on principle and hold to it, and if there are people in this country who feel that the people in Vietnam are not our enemies, but another part of the humanity on this planet against whom this country is transgressing, and they take action, peaceful action, to protest their feeling, like Abe Lincoln did 120 years ago, there is nothing terribly unpatriotic about it, and rather than to derive from hatred for their country, it seems to me to derive from love of country, and these people have always had it difficult.

When Dave Dellinger and Tom Hayden and Rennie Davis, all men in the peace movement, stated shortly after the Convention, "We have won, we have won," Mr. Schultz attempts to indicate to you that what they were talking about is that they have won in their plans to have violence.

I submit to you that the more reasonable interpretation of that is that people in the United States have won and the peace movement has won because people stood up for a principle, they stood up for what they thought was right. They were beaten and struck down in the streets. They were gassed in the park. But far from defeat, they stood, and they stood their ground. What happened here in Chicago during the week of the Convention is an unfortunate incident on the record of this country. But like all other wrongs that have happened, they can be righted only by people who are willing to stand up to the wrong and embrace the truth and the justice that they see and to stand by what they believe to be true.

I submit to you this task is now before you, and whether this wrong, which is the prosecution of those who were the victims of official misconduct and are brought to trial in an attempt to justify that conduct, is ever righted, resides solely and exclusively in your province.

Throughout history it has always been easy to go along. They did it at the Salem witch trials. They went along in Jerusalem —

Mr. Schultz: Oh, objection, if the Court please.

The Court: I see no relationship of the Salem witch trials to this courtroom. I don't think it is comparable. I sustain the objection.

Mr. Weinglass: I merely want to indicate to you in finishing that this case is more than just the defense of seven men. It involves the more basic issue of whether or not those who stand up to dare can do so without grave personal risk and I think it will be judged in that light, and I think while you deliberate this case, that history will hold its breath until you determine whether or not this wrong that we have been living with will be righted by a verdict of acquittal for the seven men who are on trial here.

Thank you.

William Kunstler, closing argument for the defendants, February 13, 1970

Kunstler took one last opportunity to argue that the defendants were being prosecuted for their political beliefs, and he set the case in a broad historical context of political martyrs.

[Document Source: *The Conspiracy Trial*, eds., Judy Clavir and John Spitzer (Indianapolis, IN: Bobbs-Merrill Co., 1970), 567.]

We are living in extremely troubled times, as Mr. Weinglass pointed out. An intolerable war abroad has divided and dismayed us all. Racism at home and poverty at home are both causes of despair and discouragement. In a so-called affluent society, we have people starving and people who can't even begin to approximate the decent life.

These are rough problems, terrible problems, and as has been said by everybody in this country, they are so enormous that they stagger the imagination. But they don't go away by destroying their critics. They don't vanish by sending men to jail. They never did and they never will.

To use these problems by attempting to destroy those who protest against them is probably the most indecent thing that we can do. You can crucify a Jesus, you can poison a Socrates, you can hang John Brown or Nathan Hale, you can kill a Che Guevara, you can jail a Eugene Debs or a Bobby Seale. You can assassinate John Kennedy or a Martin Luther King, but the problems remain. The solutions are essentially made by continuing and perpetuating with every breath you have the right of men to think, the right of men to speak boldly and unafraid, the right to be masters of their souls, the right to live free and to die free. The hangman's rope never solved a single problem except that of one man.

I think if this case does nothing else, perhaps it will bring into focus that again we are in that moment of history when a courtroom becomes the proving ground of whether we do live free and whether we do die free. You are in that position now. Suddenly all importance has shifted to you-shifted to you as I guess in the last analysis it should go, and it is really your responsibility, I think, to see that men remain able to think, to speak boldly and unafraid, to be masters of their souls, and to live and die free. And perhaps if you do what is right, perhaps Allen Ginsberg will never have to write again as he did in "Howl," "I saw the best minds of my generation destroyed by madness," perhaps Judy Collins will never have to stand in any courtroom again and say as she did, "When will they ever learn? When will they ever learn?"

U.S. Attorney Thomas Foran, closing argument for the government, February 13, 1970

For the lead prosecutor, the professed political concerns of the defendants were no more than "bunk." Thomas Foran portrayed the organizers of the demonstrations as fomenters of social chaos. In its decision reversing the criminal convictions of five of the defendants, the U.S. Court of Appeals for the Seventh Circuit would cite Foran's closing remarks as evidence of his unacceptable prejudice against the defendants.

[Document Source: *The Conspiracy Trial*, eds., Judy Clavir and John Spitzer (Indianapolis, IN: Bobbs-Merrill Co., 1970), 572.]

What is their intent? And this is their own words: "To disrupt. To pin delegates in the Convention hall. To clog streets. To force the use of troops. To have actions so militant the Guard will have to be used. To have war in the streets until there is peace in Vietnam. To intimidate the establishment so much it will smash the city. Thousands and thousands of people perform disruptive actions in Chicago. Tear this city apart. Fuck up the Convention. Send them out. We'll start the revolution now. Do they want to fight? The United States is an outlaw nation which had broken all the rules so peace demonstrators can break all the rules. Violate all the laws. Go to jail. Disrupt the United States Government in every way that you can. See you in Chicago."

And these men would have you believe that the issue in this case is whether or not they really wanted permits.

Public authority is supposed to stand handcuffed and mute in the face of people like that and say, "We will let you police yourselves"? How would public authority feel if they let that park be full of young kids through that Convention with no policemen, with no one watching them? What about the rape and the bad trips and worse that public authority would be responsible for if it had?

They tried to give us this bunk that they wanted to talk about racism and the war and they wanted a counter-convention. They didn't do anything but look for a confrontation with the police. What they looked for was a fight, and all that permits had to do with it was where was the fight going to be, and that's all.

And they are sophisticated and they are smart and they are well-educated. And they are as evil as they can be.

Judge Hoffman, charge to the jury, February 14, 1970

Judge Hoffman reminded the jurors of several key points of law that had often been lost in the turmoil of the trial. Recent Supreme Court decisions, such as Brandenburg v. Ohio, had expanded the First Amendment protections of speech that merely advocated illegal action but that was not directly connected to promoting or encouraging that illegal action. Hoffman also informed the jury that the First Amendment protected public assembly without a normally required permit if the individuals organizing the assembly made a reasonable effort to obtain a permit. The jurors were left to decide if the prosecution had established beyond any reasonable doubt that the defendants had intended to incite violence and had taken action to promote that violence.

[Document Source: *The Conspiracy Trial*, eds., Judy Clavir and John Spitzer (Indianapolis, IN: Bobbs-Merrill Co., 1970), 576.]

Ladies and gentlemen of the jury, I shall now instruct you as to what kind of conduct is not prohibited by law, and cannot, therefore, constitute grounds for conviction.

Among the most vital and precious liberties which we Americans enjoy by virtue of our Constitution are freedom of speech and freedom of assembly. The freedoms guaranteed by the First Amendment allow criticism of existing institutions, of political leaders, of domestic and foreign policies and our system of government. That right is unaffected by whether or not it may seem to you to be wrong, intemperate or offensive or designed to undermine public confidence in existing government.

The law distinguishes between mere advocacy of violence or lawlessness without more, and advocacy of the use of force or illegality where such advocacy is directed to inciting, promoting, or encouraging lawless actions. The Constitution does not protect speech which is reasonably and knowingly calculated and directed to inciting actions which violate the law. A conviction can rest only on advocacy which constitutes a call to imminent unlawful action.

You must keep in mind this distinction between constitutionally protected and unprotected speech.

In addition it is a constitutional exercise of the rights of free speech and assembly to march or hold a rally without a permit where applications for permits were made in good faith at a reasonable time prior to the date of march or rally and the permits were denied arbitrarily or discriminatorily.

Where the law refers to an act that is committed knowingly and willfully, it means that the act was done voluntarily and purposely, not because of mistake or accident, with knowledge that it was prohibited by law and with the purpose of violating the law. Thus the defendants cannot be found to have acted willfully and knowingly unless they or any of them did so with a bad purpose of an evil intent. Such knowledge and intent may be proven by the defendants' conduct and by all of the facts and circumstances of the case as shown by the evidence.

If you are not convinced beyond a reasonable doubt that a defendant acted knowingly and willfully, then you must find that the Government has failed to prove the intent necessary and you must, in such an event, acquit that defendant.

U.S. Court of Appeals for the Seventh Circuit, decision on the defendants' appeal of the contempt convictions, May 11, 1972

The court of appeals dismissed some of the contempt convictions against the defense attorneys and reversed all other contempt convictions of the attorneys as well as the defendants. In this excerpt from the opinion written by Judge Walter Cummings, the court of appeals addressed the acceptable behavior of attorneys. While acknowledging that the trial judge must have ultimate authority to regulate behavior in the courtroom, the court of appeals said that a trial judge cannot punish an attorney for reasonable persistence in advocating a client's case. The court also rejected Judge Hoffman's assumption that an attorney should be held responsible for the court-room behavior of a client.

[Document Source: *In re* Dellinger et al., 461 F.2d 389 (1972).]

And where the judge is arbitrary or affords counsel inadequate opportunity to argue his position, counsel must be given substantial leeway in pressing his contention, for it is through such colloquy that the judge may recognize his mistake and prevent error from infecting the record. It is, after all, the full intellectual exchange of ideas and positions that best facilitates the resolution of disputes. However, this is not to say that attorneys may press their positions beyond the court's insistent direction to desist. On the contrary, the necessity for orderly administration of justice compels the view that the judge must have the power to set limits on argument. We simply encourage judges to exercise tolerance in determining those limits and to distinguish carefully between hesitating, begrudging obedience and open defiance.

A reading of the specifications against the attorneys in this case reveals a pattern in the specifications for refusal to obey a court directive to cease argument. That pattern necessitates a brief comment. The record discloses that the trial judge, when ordering counsel to terminate their argument or sit down, frequently added a rejoinder or coupled the order with a statement which called for a response by the attorneys. In such situations, it is our view that an invited, additional response cannot subsequently be viewed as a contemptuous violation of the order.... .

Yet another frequent charge against the attorneys is that they failed to aid the court in maintaining order. While this charge was often coupled with the additional assertion that they actively encouraged their clients in their disruptions, for purposes of remand it is necessary to distinguish between the two situations. An attorney has no affirmative obligation to restrain his client under pain of the contempt sanction, although we do not express an opinion as to the breach of professional ethics that may be involved in this situation. Indeed, compelling an attorney to control the conduct of his client under threat of the contempt sanction might well destroy the confidence in the attorney-client relationship which is necessary to a proper and adequate defense. However, where an attorney encourages disruptive behavior by a client or fans the flames of existing frictions, he cannot find immunity from punishment for such conduct.

U.S. Court of Appeals for the Seventh Circuit, decision on the defendants' appeal of the criminal convictions, November 21, 1972

The U.S. Court of Appeals for the Seventh Circuit reversed the criminal convictions of the five defendants and remanded the cases for retrial at the government's discretion. In the opinion written by Judge Thomas Fairchild, the court of appeals addressed the defendants' arguments in favor of various grounds for reversal, including the constitutionality of the Anti-Riot Act, the composition of the grand jury and the selection of the petit jury, the trial judge's rulings on the admissibility of evidence and testimony of witnesses, the undisclosed communications between the judge and the jury, and the demeanor of the judge and the prosecuting attorneys. The court by a vote of 2-1 upheld the constitutionality of the Anti-Riot Act, but it found other grounds for reversal.

[Document Source: United States v. Dellinger, 472 F.2d 340 (1972).]

Constitutionality of the Anti-Riot Act

The first amendment is premised upon the value of unfettered speech. Constitutional protection is clearly not to be limited, therefore, to mild or innocuous presentation, and it is unrewarding to search for a formula describing punishable advocacy of violence in terms of fervor or vigor. The real question is whether particular speech is intended to and has such capacity to propel action that it is reasonable to treat such speech as action.

The test for the attributes which speech in favor of violent action must achieve before it may be classified as action and thus removed from first amendment protection has been variously phrased-clear and present danger-directed to inciting and likely to incite imminent lawless action-whether the harm sought by expression is immediate and instantaneous and irremediable except by punishing the expression and thereby preventing the conduct-whether the expression is inseparably locked with action.

Our question, in examining the validity of the Anti-riot Act on its face is whether, properly construed, it punishes speech only when a sufficiently close relationship between such speech and violent action is found to exist. Semantically the cases suggest that while a statutory prohibition of advocacy of violence is overbroad, since protected speech is included within advocacy, a prohibition of intentional incitement of violence is not overbroad. The latter depends upon a construction of "incitement" which is sufficiently likely to propel the violent action to be identified with action. . . . It seems to us that the threshold definition of all categories as "urging or instigating" puts a sufficient gloss of propulsion on the expression described that it can be carved away from the comprehensive protection of the first amendment's guarantee of freedom of speech.

Jury Selection

In evaluating this topic, it is important to recall the time when this trial occurred, and to recognize that the division in public attitudes toward the Vietnam war has changed and is changing still. The extent of unpopularity of the war in 1972, when this opinion is written, is not a fair index of the probable opinions on that subject in a cross section selected in September, 1969. Perspective is important. These defendants' plans for activities in Chicago in August, 1968 were first formed when President Johnson was expected to be a candidate to succeed himself. He withdrew March 31, 1968. The 1968 candidacies of Senators Eugene McCarthy and Robert Kennedy, the latter assassinated in June, 1968, were associated with anti-war sentiment. Further crystallization of anti-war sentiment is associated with the Cambodian venture and the Kent State killings, both in the spring of 1970. These episodes had not yet occurred when the jury was selected for this trial in September, 1969. We have no doubt that defendants brought to trial in 1969 upon charges that their anti-war activities were carried beyond constitutional protection were entitled to a testing of their jurors for biased attitudes on this subject.

Perhaps secondary, but significant, were the conflicts of values represented by the so-called youth culture-hippies, yippies and freaks-in contrast with the more traditional values of the vast majority of the community, presumably including most citizens summoned for jury service. Again, we are not unaware that many otherwise qualified members of the community could not be impartial toward, and in fact are often offended by, persons who wear long hair, beards, and bizarre clothing and who seem to avoid the burdens and responsibilities of regular employment. Several defendants would exemplify this conflict.

A similar conflict of values was symbolized in the confrontation between the city police and the demonstrators. A juror's basic sympathies with the actors in these events could easily impair his ability to consider alternative views of the case as presented in court. A venireman's relationship with law enforcement officers would be an important factor to be inquired about in evaluating his ability to be an impartial juror.

In our view, some minimal inquiry into at least these three basic areas was essential to a fair trial of this extraordinary case, at least when defendants requested such inquiry. . . .

These cases demonstrate the danger that widespread publicity about highly dramatic events will render prospective jurors incapable of impartial consideration of the evidence. We think it must follow that where pretrial publicity is of a character and extent to raise a real probability that veniremen have heard and formed opinions about the events relevant to a case, and at least where, as here, the defense has brought the pretrial publicity to the court's attention and requested voir dire inquiry, the court must make inquiry adequate to determine whether anyone has read or heard about the facts, and, if so, what the impact has been on his ability to serve as an impartial juror.

Demeanor of the Judge and Prosecutors

The district judge's deprecatory and often antagonistic attitude toward the defense is evident in the record from the very beginning. It appears in remarks and actions both in the presence and absence of the jury.

The defense presented an extensive case, calling more than 100 witnesses. The judge might, within reason, have alleviated some of the difficulties defense counsel encountered, but he did not do so.

There are a number of areas in the law of evidence in which lawyers and judges differ considerably in interpretation of the rules and where the application of a rule is really governed by the discretion or individual views of the trial judge. When a question is leading; when testimony that another person made a statement is admissible because the making of the statement is relevant, even though the statement also contains assertions of fact; when a question on cross-examination is outside the scope of the direct; when a question is objectionable because repetitive-are all examples of such areas. We shall not attempt the task of reviewing all the rulings on evidence in this case. It does appear, however, that in comparable situations, the judge was more likely to exercise his discretion against the defense than against the government.

Most significant, however, were remarks in the presence of the jury, deprecatory of defense counsel and their case. These comments were often touched with sarcasm, implying rather than saying outright that defense counsel was inept, bumptious, or untrustworthy, or that his case lacked merit. Sometimes the comment was not associated with any ruling in ordinary course; sometimes gratuitously added to an otherwise proper ruling; nearly always unnecessary. Taken individually any one was not very significant and might be disregarded as a harmless attempt at humor. But cumulatively, they must have telegraphed to the jury the judge's contempt for the defense. . . .

In final argument, the United States Attorney went at least up to, and probably beyond, the outermost boundary of permissible inferences from the evidence in his characterizations of defendants. He referred to them as "evil men," "liars and obscene haters,""profligate extremists," and "violent anarchists." He suggested one defendant was doing well as it got dark because "predators always operate better when it gets close to dark."

He yielded to the temptation to exploit the courtroom conduct of various defendants which formed the basis of the contempt citations in *In re Dellinger*. He told the jurors they need not ignore "how those people look and act," "outbursts in the courtroom," "the sudden respect, the sudden decency" occurring "in the last few days as we reach the end of the case," the suggested similarity between the technique the jurors had seen used in the courtroom with the marshals and that allegedly used at the time of the convention with the police.

Dress, personal appearance, and conduct at trial were not probative of guilt. The district judge properly instructed the jurors that they "must not in any way be influenced by any possible antagonism you may have toward the defendants or any of them, their dress, hair styles, speech, reputation, courtroom demeanor or quality, personal philosophy or life style." The United States Attorney should not have urged the jury to consider those things.

We conclude that the demeanor of the judge and prosecutors would require reversal if other errors did not.

Judge Edward Gignoux, decision on the retrial of the contempt convictions-comments on the proper conduct of a trial, December 6, 1973

Judge Gignoux presided over the retrial of the remaining contempt charges against the defendants and their attorneys. After his meticulous review of the contempt specifications and his rejection of all but thirteen of them, Gignoux addressed the impact of Judge Hoffman's management of the case and the general purpose of rules governing courtroom behavior. Gignoux was most concerned with ensuring public confidence in a fair and impartial trial process.

[Document Source: *In re* David T. Dellinger et al., 370 F. Supp. 1304, 1321 —23.]

From the foregoing, it is apparent that the contumacious conduct of the defendants and their lawyers cannot be considered apart from the conduct of the trial judge and prosecutors. Each reacted to provocation by the other, and the tensions generated during four and a half months of so acrimonious a trial cannot be ignored. Indeed, with the exception of the two specifications relating to the "robe" incident . . . , the contumacious conduct of the four remaining defendants can, in each instance, reasonably be said to have been in response, albeit an excessive response, to peremptory action of the judge.

Present government counsel urge that substantial jail sentences for these defendants are necessary to vindicate the judicial process and to deter other defendants and defense counsel from similar misbehavior. After a careful evaluation of the record, however, this Court is convinced that, in the particular circumstances here present, the affirmation of the integrity of trial proceedings and the goal of deterrence have both been achieved by the findings of guilt. The Court is further persuaded that, at this late date, four years after the events which gave rise to these charges, no warrant exists for the imposition of jail sentences additional to the periods of imprisonment which have already been served by the non-lawyer defendants. While Mr. Kunstler was never incarcerated, in the considered judgment of the Court, no purpose, other than the impermissible purpose of vindictiveness, would be served by sentencing him to prison at this time. The condemnation of his conduct and the potentially grave consequences of a criminal contempt conviction to a member of the bar should serve as adequate deterrents to other lawyers who may be disposed to similar misbehavior.

In light of the unique character and long history of this case, and the defendants' attack on the integrity and fairness of the American judicial process, a concluding observation is appropriate. Throughout these proceedings, the defense has asserted that both the 1969 Anti-Riot Act prosecution and the present contempt proceedings have been "political trials" designed to suppress dissent. This position, they claim, gives them license unilaterally to dispense with the standards of civility to which American lawyers and litigants customarily adhere in criminal, as well as civil, trials. It is precisely to preserve the opportunity for the fair and dispassionate resolution of strenuously contested disputes by an impartial tribunal that rules governing the behavior of all the actors in a trial exist....

Trials which proceed in accordance with the law, the rules of evidence and the standards of demeanor not only reaffirm the integrity and viability of the judicial process, but also serve to insure the ability of each one of us to protect the rights and liberties we enjoy as citizens.

Anti-Riot Act

The Chicago conspiracy trial defendants were the first individuals prosecuted under the anti-riot provisions that Congress incorporated in the Civil Rights Act of 1968. The U.S. House of Representatives in 1967 overwhelmingly passed a version of the anti-riot provision in response to the urban riots of that summer and assertions from some members of Congress that African-American political activists had instigated the violence. The Senate included the provision in an open housing bill, and although President Johnson and Attorney General Ramsey Clark did not support the anti-riot provision, the administration accepted it to secure passage of the civil rights measure.

[Document Source: 82 Stat. 75.]

2101. Riots

(a) (1) Whoever travels in interstate or foreign commerce or uses any facility of interstate or foreign commerce or uses any facility of interstate or foreign commerce, including, but not limited to, the mail, telegraph, telephone, radio, or television, with intent -

(A) to incite a riot; or (B) to organize, promote, encourage, participate in, or carry on a riot; or (C) to commit any act of violence in furtherance of a riot; or (D) to aid or abet any person in inciting or participating in or carrying on a riot or committing any act of violence in furtherance of a riot; and who either during the course of any such travel or use or thereafter performs or attempts to perform any other overt act for any purpose specified in subparagraph (A), (B), (C), or (D) of this paragraph shall be fined not more than $10,000, or imprisoned not more than five years, or both. (b) In any prosecution under this section, proof that a defendant engaged or attempted to engage in one or more of the overt acts described in subparagraph (A), (B), (C), or (D) of paragraph (1) of subsection (a) and (1) has traveled in interstate or foreign commerce, or (2) has use of or used any facility of interstate or foreign commerce, including but not limited to, mail, telegraph, telephone, radio, or television, to communicate with or broadcast to any person or group of persons prior to such overt acts, such travel or use shall be admissible proof to establish that such defendant traveled in or used such facility of interstate or foreign commerce.

"The Strategy of Confrontation," report of the Daley administration

Mayor Daley ordered his administration and the city police to prepare a report that would correct what Daley characterized as "unfortunate, inaccurate reporting." The report, quickly drafted under the direction of city counsel Raymond Simon, insisted that the police had been restrained in the face of revolutionary violence, and it offered statistics on the relatively small number of arrests and injuries. The report blamed the violence on the actions of a small group of political activists, and specifically cited Rennie Davis, Tom Hayden, Abbie Hoffman, Jerry Rubin, and David Dellinger, whose brief biographies showed "that they are not strangers to the tactics of confrontation." The American Civil Liberties Union called the report "utterly dishonest" At a press conference displaying confiscated weapons, including a jarred black widow spider, police superintendent James Conlisk announced that in the future the Chicago police would use more tear gas to control mobs.

[Document Source: *"The Strategy of Confrontation: Chicago and the Democratic National Convention - 1968"* Report prepared by Raymond F. Simon, corporation counsel, City of Chicago, Sept. 6, 1968, pp. 49-50.]

Conclusion

The leaders of the dissident movement are nationally known agitators who had arrived fresh from triumphs at Berkeley and Columbia. Their publicly stated purpose in coming to Chicago was twofold. The immediate object was to disrupt the Convention and the City. Their ultimate goal, also publicly proclaimed, was to topple what they consider to be the corrupt institutions of our society, educational, governmental, etc., by impeding and if possible halting their normal functions while exposing the authorities to ridicule and embarrassment. They are anxious to destroy these institutions, but it is unclear as to what replacements they envision, as Senator Daniel Inouye of Hawaii observed in the Convention's Keynote address when he asked "what trees do they plant?"

The dual goals of immediate disruption and ultimate destruction were pursued in Chicago against the government under the guise of a protest against the war in Vietnam. This promised to be a very successful ploy since, as debates at the Convention demonstrated, everyone wants peace and disagreement occurs only over methods.

In spite of such attractive bait, the guerilla or psychological warfare tactics which were employed by these revolutionaries erupted in few serious incidents, the main one being an eighteen minute encounter in front of the Hilton Hotel. As is so often the case, the trusting, the innocent, and the idealist were taken in and taken over. The news media, too, responded with surprising naivete and were incredibly misused. Indeed, any success the revolutionaries achieved in their ultimate objectives of fomenting hatred and ridicule among the citizenry against the authorities was in large part attributable to the almost totally sympathetic coverage extended by reporters to the revolutionary leaders and more understandably, to the attractive idealistic but unwary young people who unwittingly lent them assistance and camouflage....

It seems clear that a nucleus of adult trouble makers avowedly seeking a hostile confrontation with the police will be engaging in the same activities detailed in this report in other cities and towns across the nation. They have announced their intention "to create 200 to 300 Chicagos." All who believe in the essential desirability of our present form of government are challenged to find the best response to what is frequently a violent and revolutionary attack upon our institutions —a response at once effective yet consistent with the dignity and freedom of each and all our citizens.

Walker Report summary

On September 4, 1968, Milton Eisenhower, chair of the National Commission on the Causes and Prevention of Violence, announced that the commission would investigate the violence at the Chicago convention and report its findings to President Lyndon Johnson. A Chicago lawyer, Daniel Walker, headed the team of over 200 members, who interviewed more than 1,400 witnesses to the events and studied FBI reports and film of the confrontations. The report released on December 1, 1968, characterized the convention violence as a "police riot" and recommended prosecution of police who used indiscriminate violence. The report made clear that the vast majority of police had behaved responsibly, but it said that failure to prosecute the police who misbehaved would further damage public confidence in law enforcement.

Chief Judge William Campbell criticized the release of the report before the completion of the grand jury investigation and suggested that the grand jury might need to investigate the motivation for the release. Milton Eisenhower, however, defended the commission's decision to publish the report because of "widespread interest" in the findings. The report was unvarnished in its presentation of the language used by demonstrators and their provocation of the police, but it also blamed the violence on the city government's refusal to allow permits.

[Document Source: *Rights in Conflict. Convention Week in Chicago, August25-29, 1968*. A Report submitted by Daniel Walker, Director of the Chicago Study Team, to the National Commission on the Causes and Prevention of Violence. Introduction by Max Frankel. New York: E.P. Dutton, 1968. pp. 1, 10-11.]

A Summary

During the week of the Democratic National Convention, the Chicago police were the targets of mounting provocation by both word and act. It took the form of obscene epithets, and of rocks, sticks, bathroom tiles and even human feces hurled at police by demonstrators. Some of these acts had been planned; others were spontaneous or were themselves provoked by police action. Furthermore, the police had been put on edge by widely published threats of attempts to disrupt both the city and the Convention.

That was the nature of the provocation. The nature of the response was unrestrained and indiscriminate police violence on many occasions, particularly at night.

That violence was made all the more shocking by the fact that it was often inflicted upon persons who had broken no law, disobeyed no order, made no threat. These included peaceful demonstrators, onlookers, and large numbers of residents who were simply passing through, or happened to live in, the areas where confrontations were occurring.

Newsmen and photographers were singled out for assault, and their equipment deliberately damaged. Fundamental police training was ignored; and officers, when on the scene, were often unable to control their men. As one police officer put it: "What happened didn't have anything to do with police work." . . .

Police violence was a fact of convention week. Were the policemen who committed it a minority? It appears certain that they were-but one which has imposed some of the consequences of its actions on the majority, and certainly on their commanders. There has been no public condemnation of these violators of sound police procedures and common decency by either their commanding officers or city officials. Nor (at the time this Report is being completed-almost three months after the convention) has any disciplinary action been taken against most of them. That some policemen lost control of themselves under exceedingly provocative circumstances can perhaps be understood; but not condoned. If no action is taken against them, the effect can only be to discourage the majority of policemen who acted responsibly, and further weaken the bond between police and community.

Although the crowds were finally dispelled on the nights of violence in Chicago, the problems they represent have not been. Surely this is not the last time that a violent dissenting group will clash head-on with those whose duty it is to enforce the law. And the next time the whole world will still be watching.

The committee to defend the conspiracy

A committee of notable writers, academics, and performers published this call for financial support of the defendants as they approached the start of the trial. The committee warned that the indictment was part of a government effort to silence political dissent and warned that prosecutions under the Anti-Riot Act, which criminalized intent rather than actions, would lead to a "police state" The committee saw the trial as an opportunity to educate the public about the issues that had brought the demonstrators to the Chicago convention. A week before this letter was published, Rennie Davis held a press conference in Chicago to announce fundraising for the legal fees. The defendants now referred to themselves as "The Conspiracy" and they planned meetings across the country to educate the public about the impending trial and "to raise questions of who are the criminals in America today"

[Document Source: *New York Review of Books*, v. 12, n. 12 (June 19, 1969).]

The federal indictment in Chicago of eight political dissenters for conspiracy to promote disorder and riot during the week of the Democratic National Convention is one of the most ominous challenges to political liberty since the passing of Senator Joseph R. McCarthy. It calls for a clear and considered response from all who believe that the preservation of political dissent is now, more than ever, crucial to the survival of democratic process in America.

. . . We are now organizing a large group of sponsors for a national campaign built around the following statement:

"Eight political activists who were prominent in the mass demonstrations of protest during the Democratic National Convention in Chicago are now under federal indictment for criminal conspiracy. They are the first persons to be so charged under Title 18 of the Civil Rights Act of 1968 which makes it a felony to "travel in interstate commerce.... with the intent to incite, promote, encourage, participate in and carry on a riot...."

"The effect of this 'anti-riot' act is to subvert the first Amendment guarantee of free assembly by equating organized political protest with organized violence. Potentially, this law is the foundation for a police state in America.

"In this decade, countless Americans have contributed to the revitalization of politics through freedom rides, peace marches and other demonstrations of protest against impacted political institutions. Yet, from Bull Connor's Birmingham to Richard Daley's Chicago, civil authorities have employed police violence to suppress 'the right of the people peaceably to assemble,' repeatedly invoking the specters of conspiracy, incitement and riot. The Justice Department has now joined the assault on free political action.

"Title 18, the 'anti-riot' provision, was attached to the Civil Rights Act of 1968 by a repressive coalition in the Congress and was aimed at black civil rights activists. Enacted in the wake of the urban riots that followed the murder of Martin Luther King, the rider found support even among members of the Congress who might ordinarily resist the delusion that social disorder is the sinister work of 'outside agitators.'

"The 'anti-riot' clause and the indictment in Chicago are legally and Constitutionally dubious. While *acts* of violence, incitement and disruption are explicitly covered by numerous, long-established state and local laws, conspiracy-which deals not with act but with intent-is a vague concept at best. Prosecution for conspiracy requires no proof of the commission of a crime, nor even of an attempt. Thus the prosecution of conspiracy all too easily becomes political harassment of persons who hold dissenting ideas.

"It is especially surprising that this new law should first be tested in connection with the Chicago disorders. For the events of convention week do reveal, with terrible clarity, that it is local authority and police who decide whether violence attends civil demonstration. In this case, the responsibility of the Chicago authorities is the more striking when it is remembered that several of the eight men under indictment have helped to organize major public demonstrations in other cities, both before and after the week of the Democratic National Convention. None of these demonstrations resulted in riot. . . .

"Confronted by a patently political challenge, the eight defendants have determined on a political response as well as a legal defense. Through their trial they will carry forward the first constitutional challenge to the anti-riot act. They intend, as well, to refocus public attention on the root issues that brought them and thousands of others to Chicago and the Democratic National Convention-the war, racism, the widening power of the military-academic-industrial complex, the enfeeblement of the nation's political process. As a sign of their refusal to be intimidated by the scare label the government would hang upon them, the defendants are calling themselves *The Conspiracy;* and they are inviting other Americans who are similarly committed to radical change in this nation to join *The Conspiracy.* They are also appealing for financial and moral support to Americans who find in this indictment disturbing implications for the safeguard of constitutional liberty and a democratic political life....

Peter Babcox, Noam Chomsky, Judy Collins, Harvey Cox, Edgar Z. Friedenberg, Michael Harrington, Nat Hentoff, Donald Kalish, Christopher Lasch, Sidney Lens, Herbert Magidson, Norman Mailer, Stewart Meacham, Larry David Nachman, Conor Cruise O'Brien, Susan Sontag, Benjamin Spock, I. F. Stone, Harold Taylor

Tom Wicker, " 'Other Thoughts' in Chicago"

Like many journalists covering the Chicago conspiracy trial, Tom Wicker noted that the proceedings often bore little resemblance to other criminal trials. In addition to the colorful witnesses and the theatrical behavior of the judge and defendants, the charge faced by the defendants, according to Wicker, bore little resemblance to other criminal charges and raised fundamental questions about the fairness of the law.

[Document Source: "In the Nation" column, *New York Times*, Jan. 22, 1970.]

An air of unreality hangs over the trial of the so-called "Chicago Seven," and not merely because it keeps turning up such witnesses as Country Joe, the leader of the rock group known as Country Joe and the Fish.

Bearded, wearing an Indian headband and purple boots, he gave his name as Country Joe. And when the prosecution demanded full identification, Judge Julius Hoffman replied in tones of resignation: "Well, I assume his Christian name must be 'Country.' "

But again, it is not just Judge Hoffman's undeniable theatrical gifts nor even the widespread belief-given frequent official voice by the defense counsel-that he favors the prosecution, that makes this landmark trial seem so alien to a conventional assumption of the fitness of things.

Issue Obscured

It is more nearly because there is so little talk or testimony about any of the familiar events that might be thought to be at issue. Surprisingly little is being said about the actual events that surrounded the Democratic convention of 1968, the marches, the police response, the violence in the streets, and although echoes of grim nights in Grant Park keep coming through-their vibrations were certainly bad, as Country Joe put it-the testimony here is focused elsewhere, and rather hazily at that....

And that in the final analysis is why this sometimes ludicrous proceeding seems to have so little relationship, not only just to what happened in Chicago in August of 1968, but to any of our familiar notions of what trials are all about, of what constitutes legal guilt, of what the law's limits are in America.

The Chicago Seven are not being tried for committing acts of violence in August of 1968; nor are they even being tried for having *caused* the violence that did take place.

They are, rather, charged with "conspiring" to disrupt the convention with violence, and it is this "conspiracy" —whether it existed-that is the issue in Judge Hoffman's court. It is at least theoretically possible, therefore, that even had there been no violence at all, the Seven could still be on trial here for taking part in the alleged conspiracy.

Intentions as Cause

Violence did, of course, take place in Chicago in August, 1968. It may be that some, or all of the defendants intended or hoped for violence. But the intention, on the one hand, did not necessarily cause the violence, on the other. If the Seven were on trial here to determine whether acts or intentions of theirs did cause the convention-week violence that actually happened, there would be only a factual question of guilt or innocence to be determined-the usual business of a criminal trial.

But that is not the case. The defendants here are the first to be tried under a provision of the 1968 Civil Rights Act that made it a Federal crime to cross a state line with the intention to cause a riot or a disturbance. The constitutionality of this statute has yet to be determined, but the Chicago trial clearly suggests-as indeed, does the language of the act-that what it seeks to prohibit or penalize is a state of mind, not an overt act.

Burden of Proof

Ironically, it is also pretty clear from this proceeding how difficult it is to prove a state of mind, long afterwards. It is probably more difficult for the prosecution, on whom rests the burden of proof, than for the defendants, which is why Mr. Schultz sound so preposterous in his efforts to show that Rennie Davis was saying one thing to Roger Wilkins while "thinking other thoughts."

Nevertheless, if the issue of a trial actually comes down to "other thoughts," rather than to actual words and deeds, the deeper question may be whether even "the burden of proof" any longer means anything.

The Official Trial Transcript – The Crucial Parts

Table of Contents

Witness Testimonies

Bobby Seale's Testimony (defendant)

MR. KUNSTLER: Would you state your full name?

THE WITNESS: Bobby G. Seale.

MR. KUNSTLER: And, Mr. Seale, what is your occupation?

THE WITNESS: Presently, I am the Chairman of the Black Panther Party.

MR. KUNSTLER: Would you state what is the Black Panther Party for Self-Defense?

THE WITNESS: The Black Panther Party--

MR. SCHULTZ: Objection.

THE COURT: I sustain the objection.

MR. KUNSTLER: Your Honor, every single witness on the stand called by the defense has been entitled to tell what is the organization in which his occupation pertained.

MR. SCHULTZ: We are not litigating the Black Panther Party, your Honor, in this case.

THE COURT: I will let my ruling stand, sir.

MR. KUNSTLER: Mr. Seale, would you state for the Court and jury what your duties are as Chairman of the Black Panther Party?

THE WITNESS: As the Chairman of the Black Panther Party, I am a member of the central committee who have to make speaking engagements, representing the Party's program, the Party's ideology, the social programs that we are setting forth in communities to deal with political, economic, and social evils and injustices that exist in this American society.

I go on a number of speaking engagements. I do quite a bit of coordinating work and direct community organizing in the black community and relate to other organizations whom we have coalitions with. We form alliances and direct these alliances in the same manner that brother Fred Hampton used to do before he was murdered, and we form these alliances with the Young Lords, Puerto Ricans, and also Latino people who are oppressed in America.

MR. KUNSTLER: Mr. Seale, you mentioned the name of Fred Hampton. Who was Fred Hampton?

THE WITNESS: Deputy Chairman--

MR. SCHULTZ: Objection.

THE COURT: I sustain the objection.

MR. SCHULTZ: Your Honor, if you will instruct Mr. Seale that when an objection is pending, he should wait before he answers the question--

THE COURT: Mr. Seale, when an objection is made by the opposing lawyers sitting at that table, wait until the Court decides the objection before you answer, please.

THE WITNESS: Well, should I just give a few seconds to see if there is going to be an objection?

THE COURT: Yes. Wait. It is a good idea.

THE WITNESS: Just to see if there is going to be an objection.

MR. SCHULTZ: I will try to be prompt, your Honor.

MR. KUNSTLER: Mr. Seale, I call your attention to August 27, 1968. Did there come a time when you went to the San Francisco International Airport?

THE WITNESS: Tuesday. That Tuesday in August. It was a Tuesday, I think.

MR. KUNSTLER: Did you then board an airplane?

THE WITNESS: Yes.

MR. KUNSTLER: Do you know the destination of that airplane?

THE WITNESS: Chicago, Illinois.

MR. KUNSTLER: I will ask you now to look at the defense table and I want to ask you this question whether, prior to boarding that airplane, you had ever known Jerry Rubin.

THE WITNESS: No, I had not.

MR. KUNSTLER: David Dellinger?

THE WITNESS: I never seen him before in my life.

MR. KUNSTLER: Abbie Hoffman?

THE WITNESS: I never seen him before in my life before that.

MR. KUNSTLER: Lee Weiner?

THE WITNESS: I never seen him before in my life.

MR. KUNSTLER: Rennie Davis?

THE WITNESS: I never seen him before in my life.

MR. KUNSTLER: Tom Hayden?

THE WITNESS: I had heard of his name but I had never met him or seen him before in my life.

MR. KUNSTLER: John Froines?

THE WITNESS: I never seen him or heard of him before in my life.

MR. KUNSTLER: Can you state to the Court the purpose of your trip to Chicago?

MR. SCHULTZ: Objection, your Honor.

THE COURT: I sustain the objection.

MR. KUNSTLER: Now after you arrived in Chicago on the twenty-seventh of August, did you have occasion at any time later that day to go to Lincoln Park?

THE WITNESS: Yes, it was late in the afternoon.

MR. KUNSTLER: Now when you arrived at Lincoln Park, can you recollect what was going on in the area you went to?

THE WITNESS: The area in the park that I observed was completely occupied by policemen.

The park was generally surrounded by policemen, cops everywhere, and many of those who I looked at and observed to be what I would call or define as pigs. This is what I observed, this is the impression, the facts that existed and what I saw. It was just the cops, and I myself defined it as pigs, were piggyback. This is the general way we talk in the ghetto in expressing a lot of these things.

MR. KUNSTLER: Now did there come a time, Mr. Seale, when you spoke in Lincoln Park that afternoon?

THE WITNESS: Yes, there did come a time when I did speak.

MR. KUNSTLER: I show you D-350 for identification, do you think that you could identify for us what it is?

THE WITNESS: This is a transcript from a tape recording of the speech I made there.

MR. KUNSTLER: I will show you 350-B. Is that the tape from which 350 was made?

THE WITNESS: Yes, I can recognize it.

MR. KUNSTLER: Is that tape a fair and accurate reproduction of your speech as you gave it on
the afternoon of August 27 in Lincoln Park.

THE WITNESS: Yes, it is, except for the fact that the very first line, about half of the sentence on that tape, the very first line of the first sentence that I pronounced in that speech is not on that tape.

MR. KUNSTLER: With the exception of those first three or four words, it is a fair and accurate representation of the speech?

THE WITNESS: Yes.

MR. KUNSTLER: Then I would offer it into evidence.

MR. SCHULTZ: No objection.

MR. KUNSTLER: Your Honor, before this is played we will furnish to the court reporter, to save her hands, a copy of the speech.

MR. SCHULTZ: No objection.

(tape played)

We've come out to speak to some people who're involved, maybe emotionally and maybe in many respects, in a drastic situation of a developing revolution. The revolution in this country at the time is in fact the people coming forth to demand freedom. The revolution at this time is directly connected with organized guns and force.

We must understand that as we go forth to try and move the scurvy, reprobative pigs: the lynching Lyndon Baines Johnsons, the fat pig Humphreys, the jive double-lip-talkin' Nixons, the slick talkin' McCarthys--these murdering and brutalizing and oppressing people all over the world-- when we go forth to deal with them--that they're gonna always send out their racist, scurvy rotten pigs to occupy the people, to occupy the community, just the way they have this park here occupied. You know the Minister of Information, Eldridge Cleaver, who's been nominated as the Presidential candidate, Black Panther candidate, running on the Peace and Freedom ticket. As you know, the brother always says, "All power to the People."

Now just a second here. You must understand what power is. The Minister of Defense, Huey P. Newton, explains and teaches that power is the ability to defend phenomena and make it act in a desired manner.

What phenomena are we talking about? We're talking about the racist, brutal murders that pigs have committed upon black people. We're talking about lynchings that's been going down for four hundred years on black people's heads. We're talking about the occupation troops, right here in Chicago, occupying the black community and even occupying this park where the people have come forth. The phenomenal situation is this: it's that we have too many hogs in every facet of government that exists in this country. We can define that.

But we said the ability to define this social phenomena and also the ability to make it act in a desired manner. How do you make the social phenomena act in a desired manner? I am saying this here, I'm pretty sure you're quite well aware of how you make it act in a desired manner. If a pig comes up to you and you sit down and start talking about slidin' in, rollin' in, jumpin' in, bugalooin' in, dancin' in, swimmin' in, prayin' in and singing "We Shall Overcome," like a lot of these Toms want us to do--we're jivin'. But if a pig comes up to us and starts swinging a billy club. and you check around and you got your piece--you gotta down that pig in defense of yourself. You gonna take that club, whip him over his head, lay him out on the ground and then this pig is acting in a desired manner. All right.

At the same time, many individuals. many groups will run into situations where the pigs are going to attack. Always. Because the pigs have been sent here by the top hog who gave him orders from the power structure to attack the people.

Now listen here. If you gonna get down to nitty-gritty, brothers and people, and you don't intend to miss no nits and no grits, you got to have some functional organization to not only make one individual pig or a number of pigs act in the desired manner but to make this whole racist, decadent power structure act in a desired manner.

The Black Panther Party went forth when brother Huey P. Newton was busted October the 28. He was charged with making a couple of pigs act in a desired manner. And from there, a coalition between the Peace and Freedom Party, a predominately white group, and the Black Panther Party, a black organization, a revolutionary organization, formed this coalition based on the fact that the white people said they were concerned by the fact that their racist power structure in Oakland in California was going to try to railroad Huey P. Newton to the gas chamber and kill him.

Now this coalition developed into a more functional thing: the Peace and Freedom Party in the white community trying to end the decadent racism, the Black Panthers in the black community trying to convince us we've got to defend ourselves, liberate ourselves from the oppressed conditions that are caused by racism. This coalition has gone forth. We think it's a very functional coalition.

So it's very important that we understand the need for organization, cause that's what we deal with. We're not here to be sitting around a jive table vacillating and jiving ourselves. Too many times in the past, the people sit down around tables. When they sit down around these tables they get to arguing about whether or not this white racist wall that black people are chained against is real or not. They want to come talking about some molecular structure of the wall. And the molecular structure of the wall shows that wall is really ninety percent space. So is the white racist wall that we're talking about real or not? We're saying that it's here. You're damned right it's real. Because we're chained against this wall.

And we say this here: don't be out there jiving, wondering whether the wall is real or not. Make sure if you want to coalesce, work, functionally organize, that you pick up a crowbar. Pick up a piece. Pick up a gun. And pull that spike out from the wall. Because if you pull it on out and if you shoot well, all I'm gonna do is pat you on the back and say "Keep shooting." You dig? We won't be jiving.

Now, there are many kinds of guns. Many, many kinds of guns. But the strongest weapon that we have, the strongest weapon that we all each individually have, is all of us. United in opposition. United with revolutionary principles.

So it's very necessary for us to understand the need for functional organization. It's very necessary for us, especially black brothers--listen close--that we have revolutionary principles to guide ourselves by. Because if we just go out in a jive gang, running around in big groups, with rocks and bottles, we're not going to do nothing against 500 pigs with shotguns and .357 Magnums.

What we got to do is functionally put ourselves in organizations. Get every black man in the black community with a shotgun in his home, and a .357 Magnum, and a .45 if he can get it, and an M-1 if he can get it and anything else if he can get it, brothers. Get it and start doing this.

Then, I want to say this here. On the streets, stop running in large groups. That ain't no right tactic. We should run in groups of fours and fives--all around. We cannot continue using these tactics where we lose 3000 arrested or we lose 1 or 200 dead. We gotta stop. So we want to start running in threes, fours, and fives.

Small groups using proper revolutionary tactics. So we can dissemble those pigs who occupy our community, who occupy our community like foreign troops.

Black people, we're saying we're lost. We seem to be lost in a world of white racist, decadent America. I'm saying that we have a right to defend ourselves as human beings. And if some pig comes up to us unjustly treating us injustly, then we have to bring our pieces out and start barbecuing some of that pork.

Brother Huey P. Newton was on the stand yesterday. And they said the brother was so beautiful in cross-examination for a whole day-and-a-half that the jury got mad at the D.A. We hope that brother Huey P. Newton be set free. We go further in our hopes, in our work in in our organization to demand that he be set free.

And we say that if anything happens to Huey P. Newton, the sky is the limit.

Now here are some buckets around and we are here, Huey needs funds, and we hope that you will donate to the Party and other local organizations.

We hope, we sure that you can begin to set up a few things organizationally to deal with the situation in a very revolutionary manner.

So, Power to the People. Power to All the People. Black Power to Black People. Panther Power. Even some Peace and Freedom Power. Power and Free Huey. Thank you.

(end of tape)

MR. KUNSTLER: Now, Mr. Seale, when you used the term "Pig" in that speech, can you define what is meant by the word "pig"?

THE WITNESS: A pig is a person or a policeman who is generally found violating the constitutional rights and the human rights of people, a vile traducer, and he is usually found masquerading as a victim of unprovoked attack.

MR. KUNSTLER: And you also used the term in discussing Huey P. Newton "the sky is the limit." Would you explain what you meant by that?

THE WITNESS: I meant by that that we would exhaust all political and legal means through the courts all the way to the top of the Supreme Court. We would have demonstrations. We will organize the people in together and we will go to the limit to try and get our Minister of Defense free if he is not set free.

MR. KUNSTLER: I have no further question.

THE COURT: Is there any cross-examination?

MR. SCHULTZ: Yes, sir, your Honor, I have some.

Now you said in your speech that was just played before the jury that Huey P. Newton was busted and charged with making a couple of pigs act in a desired manner, did you not, Sir?

THE WITNESS: He was charged with shooting a policeman. He was charged with shooting in defense of himself.

MR. SCHULTZ: So when you said that "individuals should mike pigs act in a desired manner," you were referring to shooting policemen in defense if necessary, isn't that right?

THE WITNESS: Organizationally and functionally, if you look at the whole context of the sentence, what I mean is not what you are inferring.

What I mean is this here--

MR. SCHULTZ: I am asking you what you said, sir. I am asking you, did you not state that?

THE WITNESS: But you also asked me what I mean, Mr. Schultz.

MR. KUNSTLER: I thought he asked him what he meant, too, Your Honor.

MR. SCHULTZ: Let me rephrase the question if I did.

When you stated to the people in Lincoln Park that " they've got to make one individual pig or a number of individual pigs act in the desired manner," you weren't referring to that same desired manner for which Huey Newton was charged, were you?

THE WITNESS: What was that? Rephrase your question again. I am trying to make sure you don't trip me.

MR. SCHULTZ: It was a little complicated, Mr. Seale. It wasn't very well stated.

THE WITNESS: All right.

MR. SCHULTZ: I will ask it to you again.

You said to the people, "They should make one pig or a number of pigs act in the desired manner." You were not then referring to the same desired manner with which Mr. Newton was charged, that is, shooting a policeman? Were you or were you not?

THE WITNESS: No. I can state it in another way in answering the question.

MR. SCHULTZ: No.

THE WITNESS: If you will let me answer the question.

MR. SCHULTZ: You said you were not.

THE WITNESS: Can I answer the question?

THE COURT: You have answered the question. Ask him another question.

MR. SCHULTZ: Were you referring to shooting policemen in the desired manner when you said this: "But if a pig comes up to us and starts swinging a billy club, you're gonna take that club and whip him over the head, and lay him on the ground, and then the pig is acting in a desired manner."

THE WITNESS: I was referring to defending myself.

MR. SCHULTZ: Now you said to the people, did you not, that they should pull the spike from the wall, because "if you pull it out and if you shoot well, all I am going to do is pat you on the back and say 'Keep on shooting'?" Was that for the purpose of making the pig act in the desired manner?

THE WITNESS: That's for the purpose of telling people they have to defend themselves. In that broad sense of that statement, without taking it out of context, that generally means that, and if any individual is unjustly attacked by any policeman, unjustly, at that point he has a human right--

MR. SCHULTZ: To kill the policeman.

THE WITNESS: To defend himself.

MR. SCHULTZ: And that means if necessary to kill that policeman, does it not?

THE WITNESS: If that policeman is attacking me, if he is violating the law, if he is violating the law unjustly, attacking me, –I am not talking about a policeman down the street stopping somebody--

MR. SCHULTZ: That means killing, if necessary, doesn't it?

THE WITNESS: No.

MR. SCHULTZ: You will not kill a policeman, is that right?

THE WITNESS: It is not the desire to kill, and that's what you are trying to put in the tone of it, and it's not that--

MR. SCHULTZ: Will you answer my question?

THE WITNESS: I won't answer that question with a yes or no, your Honor. I have to answer the question my own way.

MR. SCHULTZ: I can rephrase it.

Were you referring to shooting pigs?

THE WITNESS: I was referring to shooting any racist, bigoted pig who unjustly attacks us or brutalizes us in the process of us doing any kind of organizational and functional work to try to change the power structure and remove the oppression.

MR. SCHULTZ: And you said in that context "unjustly attacking you?"

THE WITNESS: In the context of the whole speech, that's what I am talking about.

MR. SCHULTZ: So when you told the people that what we have to do is get every black man in the black community with a shotgun in his home and a .357 Magnum and a .45, if he can get it, and an M-1, if he can get it--you were referring to getting guns for defense, isn't that right'

THE WITNESS: Getting a gun, put a gun in your home, a shotgun.

MR. SCHULTZ: In defense?

THE WITNESS: –or M-1 –you have a right by the Second Amendment of the Constitution to have it.

MR. SCHULTZ: Were you referring to it in self-defense, that is my question, sir?

THE WITNESS: I was referring to it in self-defense against unjust brutal attack by any policeman or pigs or bigots in this society who will attack people.

MR. SCHULTZ: And you said to the people in Lincoln Park "I am referring to unjust brutal attack," didn't you?

THE WITNESS: No. You know what I mean, Mr. Schultz. I am telling you what I am referring to.

MR. SCHULTZ: Now, when you told the people to stop running around in big groups and with rocks and bottles because you can't do anything against 500 pigs with shotguns, and .357 Magnums, was that part of your revolutionary tactics?

THE WITNESS: Definitely. It is a change.

Revolution means change, change away from this old erroneous method of running out in the streets in big numbers and rioting, and throwing rocks and bottles. How are you going to stop a .357 Magnum or shotgun full of some shotgun shells that are being shot at you with rocks and bottles. Stop that. Stop it. Stop the rioting. That is in essence what I am talking about.

Stop those kind of tactics. Use revolutionary tactics. Defend yourself from unjust attacks, et cetera.

MR. SCHULTZ: When you told the people in Lincoln Park, "Pick up a gun, pull the spike from the wall, because if you pull it out and you shoot well, all I'm gonna do is pat you on the back and say, 'Keep on shooting,' " That was part of your revolutionary tactics too, was it not, sir?

THE WITNESS: Yes, sir, and if you look generally--

MR. SCHULTZ: Please, that is all.

THE COURT: You have answered the question.

THE WITNESS: I strike that answer on the grounds that that particular question is wrong because it ain't clear.

THE COURT: I have some news for you, sir.

(there is applause in the courtroom)

THE COURT: I do the striking here, and will the marshals exclude from the courtroom anyone who applauded. This isn't a theater, Anyone who applauded the witness may go out and is directed to leave.

MR. SCHULTZ: Mr. Seale, are you the Bobby G. Seale who was convicted on April 11, 1968, of being in possession of a shotgun in the vicinity of a jail?

THE WITNESS: Yes, I am the same person who was convicted later of being in possession of a shotgun as they charged me of being adjacent to a jail, but as I know by the law, you could have a shotgun as long as it wasn't concealed and as long as you are in a public place, and I was actually in fact on a public sidewalk.

Yes, I was convicted, and the thing was appealed.

MR. SCHULTZ: You had five shotgun shells in that gun, did you not?

THE WITNESS: Yes, in a magazine.

MR. SCHULTZ: Now, Mr. Seale, on Wednesday morning, you gave the second speech, right?

THE WITNESS: I guess that was Wednesday morning, in the middle of the week somewhere.

MR. SCHULTZ: And you said to the people, Mr. Seale, "If the pigs get in the way of our march, then tangle with the blue-helmeted motherfuckers. Kill them and send them to the morgue slab," and you were pointing to policemen at that time, isn't that a fact?

MR. KUNSTLER: This is completely out of the scope of the direct examination, your Honor. It is improper and it is wrong,

THE COURT: No, the witness was brought here to testify about his activities during that period.

I think the Government has the right to inquire. Treating your remarks as objection which you have not made, I overrule the objection.

MR. KUNSTLER: Is your Honor ruling that every witness that takes the stand can be cross-examined on anything?

THE COURT: I said it is my ruling, sir, that that question is a proper one on this record.

MR. SCHULTZ: How many people were you speaking to?

THE WITNESS: Let's see now--

MR. GARRY: Just a minute, Mr. Seale.

I am rising to the part that your Honor has heretofore allowed me to.

Unless we can be given a full transcription of the speech that he gave on that day, I am going to instruct the witness not to answer the question upon the grounds of the Fifth Amendment.

THE COURT: If you so advise him and the witness wants to do it in a proper manner, I will respect his refusal to answer.

MR. GARRY: Mr. Seale, you are entitled and I advise you not to answer this question upon the ground it would tend to incriminate you under the Fifth Amendment of the United States Constitution.

I so advise you to take that advice.

THE COURT: Mr. Seale, you have heard Mr. Garry. If you wish to take advantage of the Fifth Amendment and say to the Court that to answer that question might tend to incriminate you, you may do it, but it must come from you, not from your lawyer.

THE WITNESS: I would like to take the Fifth Amendment on the question, yes, sir.

THE COURT: All right. You needn't answer the question.

MR. SCHULTZ: That is all, your Honor.

THE COURT: Is there any redirect examination?

MR. KUNSTLER: Yes, your Honor.

Mr. Seale, with reference to Mr. Schultz' question regarding the conviction for carrying a shotgun, did you ever go to jail for that?

THE WITNESS: No.

MR. SCHULTZ: Objection, your Honor. That is not proper.

THE COURT: I sustain the objection. The test is the conviction, not the punishment.

MR. KUNSTLER: Mr. Seale, do you recall Mr. Schultz asked you about certain guns?

THE WITNESS: Yes, I do.

MR. KUNSTLER: Now I ask you this question. When you were referring to those guns, did you not use the phrase "in his home"?

THE WITNESS: Yes.

MR. SCHULTZ: Objection to the form of question. Mr. Kunstler is doing the testifying and using the witness as a sounding board.

THE COURT: Yes, the form is bad. I sustain the objection.

MR. KUNSTLER: All right. What did you say in that speech, Mr. Seale, with reference to where those guns were to be?

THE WITNESS: I said "Put the guns in your home, .357 Magnum, M-1, .45s." I referred to these kind of guns or anything else. You have a right to do it, and that , s part of our program in the Party, a constitutional right to arm yourself.

THE COURT: All right. You've answered the question.

MR. KUNSTLER: Now, Mr. Seale, as to the speech that you gave in Lincoln Park on August 27, 1968, what type of person was this speech addressed to?

MR. SCHULTZ: Objection. I asked him nothing about the audience.

THE COURT: I sustain the objection to the question.

MR. KUNSTLER: In the light of that ruling, Your Honor, I have no further questions.

THE COURT: I have sustained the objection.

MR. SCHULTZ: I have no questions.

THE COURT: You may go. Call your next witness, please.

(witness excused)

VOICES: Power to the people! Power to the people!

Abbie Hoffman's Testimony (defendant)

MR. WEINGLASS: Will you please identify yourself for the record?

THE WITNESS: My name is Abbie. I am an orphan of America.

MR. SCHULTZ: Your Honor, may the record show it is the defendant Hoffman who has taken the stand?

THE COURT: Oh, yes. It may so indicate. . . .

MR. WEINGLASS: Where do you reside?

THE WITNESS: I live in Woodstock Nation.

MR. WEINGLASS: Will you tell the Court and jury where it is?

THE WITNESS: Yes. It is a nation of alienated young people. We carry it around with us as a state of mind in the same way as the Sioux Indians carried the Sioux nation around with them. It is a nation dedicated to cooperation versus competition, to the idea that people should have better means of exchange than property or money, that there should be some other basis for human interaction. It is a nation dedicated to--

THE COURT: Just where it is, that is all.

THE WITNESS: It is in my mind and in the minds of my brothers and sisters. It does not consist of property or material but, rather, of ideas and certain values. We believe in a society--

THE COURT: No, we want the place of residence, if he has one, place of doing business, if you have a business. Nothing about philosophy or India, sir. Just where you live, if you have a place to live. Now you said Woodstock. In what state is Woodstock?

THE WITNESS: It is in the state of mind, in the mind of myself and my brothers and sisters. It is a conspiracy. Presently, the nation is held captive, in the penitentiaries of the institutions of a decaying system.

MR. WEINGLASS: Can you tell the Court and jury your present age?

THE WITNESS: My age is 33. 1 am a child of the 60s.

MR. WEINGLASS: When were you born?

THE WITNESS: Psychologically, 1960.

MR. SCHULTZ: Objection, if the Court please. I move to strike the answer.

MR. WEINGLASS: What is the actual date of your birth?

THE WITNESS: November 30,1936.

MR. WEINGLASS: Between the date of your birth, November 30, 1936, and May 1, 1960, what if anything occurred in your life?

THE WITNESS: Nothing. I believe it is called an American education.

MR. SCHULTZ: Objection.

THE COURT: I sustain the objection.

THE WITNESS: Huh.

MR. WEINGLASS: Abbie, could you tell the Court and jury--

MR. SCHULTZ: His name isn't Abbie. I object to this informality.

MR. WEINGLASS: Can you tell the Court and jury what is your present occupation?

THE WITNESS: I am a cultural revolutionary. Well, I am really a defendant--full-time.

MR. WEINGLASS: What do you mean by the phrase "cultural revolutionary?"

THE WITNESS: Well, I suppose it is a person who tries to shape and participate in the values, and the mores, the customs and the style of living of new people who eventually become inhabitants of a new nation and a new society through art and poetry, theater, and music.

MR. WEINGLASS: What have you done yourself to participate in that revolution?

THE WITNESS: Well, I have been a rock and roll singer. I am a reporter with the Liberation News Service. I am a poet. I am a film maker. I made a movie called "Yippies Tour Chicago or How I Spent My Summer Vacation." Currently, I am negotiating with United Artists and MGM to do a movie in Hollywood.

I have written an extensive pamphlet on how to live free in the city of New York.

I have written two books, one called *Revolution for The Hell of It* under the pseudonym Free, and one called, *Woodstock Nation.*

MR. WEINGLASS: Taking you back to the spring of 1960, approximately May 1, 1960, will you tell the Court and jury where you were?

MR. SCHULTZ: 1960?

THE WITNESS: That's right.

MR. SCHULTZ: Objection.

THE COURT: I sustain the objection.

MR. WEINGLASS: Your Honor, that date has great relevance to the trial. May 1, 1960, was this witness' first public demonstration. I am going to bring him down through Chicago.

THE COURT: Not in my presence, you are not going to bring him down. I sustain the objection to the question.

THE WITNESS: My background has nothing to do with my state of mind?

THE COURT: Will you remain quiet while I am making a ruling? I know you have no respect for me.

MR. KUNSTLER: Your Honor, that is totally unwarranted. I think your remarks call for a motion for a mistrial.

THE COURT: And your motion calls for a denial of the motion. Mr. Weinglass, continue with your examination.

MR. KUNSTLER: You denied my motion? I hadn't even started to argue it.

THE COURT: I don't need any argument on that one. The witness turned his back on me while he was on the witness stand.

THE WITNESS: I was just looking at the pictures of the long hairs up on the wall . . .
.

THE COURT: . . . . I will let the witness tell about this asserted conversation with Mr. Rubin on the occasion described.

MR. WEINGLASS: What was the conversation at that time?

THE WITNESS: Jerry Rubin told me that he had come to New York to be project director of a peace march in Washington that was going to march to the Pentagon in October, October 21. He said that the peace movement suffered from a certain kind of attitude, mainly that it was based solely on the issue of the Vietnam war. He said that the war in Vietnam was not just an accident but a direct by-product of the kind of system, a capitalist system in the country, and that we had to begin to put forth new kinds of values, especially to young people in the country, to make a kind of society in which a Vietnam war would not be possible.

And he felt that these attitudes and values were present in the hippie movement and many of the techniques, the guerrilla theater techniques that had been used and many of these methods of communication would allow for people to participate and become involved in a new kind of democracy.

I said that the Pentagon was a five-sided evil symbol in most religions and that it might be possible to approach this from a religious point of view. If we got large numbers of people to surround the Pentagon, we could exorcize it of its evil spirits.

So I had agreed at that point to begin working on the exorcism of the Pentagon demonstration.

MR. WEINGLASS: Prior to the date of the demonstration which is October, did you go to the Pentagon?

THE WITNESS: Yes. I went about a week or two before with one of my close brothers, Martin Carey, a poster maker, and we measured the Pentagon, the two of us, to see how many people would fit around it. We only had to do one side because it is just multiplied by five.

We got arrested. It's illegal to measure the Pentagon. I didn't know it up to that point.

When we were arrested they asked us what we were doing. We said it was to measure the Pentagon and we wanted a permit to raise it 300 feet in the air, and they said "How about 10?" So we said "OK".

And they threw us out of the Pentagon and we went back to New York and had a press conference, told them what it was about.

We also introduced a drug called *lace*, which, when you squirted it at the policemen made them take their clothes off and make love, a very potent drug.

MR. WEINGLASS: Did you mean literally that the building was to rise up 300 feet off the ground?

MR. SCHULTZ: I can't cross-examine about his meaning literally.

THE COURT: I sustain the objection.

MR. SCHULTZ: I would ask Mr. Weinglass please get on with the trial of this case and stop playing around with raising the Pentagon 10 feet or 300 feet off the ground.

MR. WEINGLASS: Your Honor, I am glad to see Mr. Schultz finally concedes that things like levitating the Pentagon building, putting LSD in the water, 10,000 people walking nude on Lake Michigan, and a $200,000 bribe attempt are all playing around. I am willing to concede that fact, that it was all playing around, it was a play idea of this witness, and if he is willing to concede it, we can all go home.

THE COURT: I sustain the objection.

MR. WEINGLASS: Did you intend that the people who surrounded the Pentagon should do anything of a violent nature whatever to cause the building to rise 300 feet in the air and be exercised of evil spirits?

MR. SCHULTZ: Objection.

THE COURT: I sustain the objection.

MR. WEINGLASS: Could you indicate to the Court and jury whether or not the Pentagon was, in fact, exercised of its evil spirits?

THE WITNESS: Yes, I believe it was. . . .

MR. WEINGLASS: Now, drawing your attention to the first week of December 1967, did you have occasion to meet with Jerry Rubin and the others?

THE WITNESS: Yes.

MR. WEINGLASS: Will you relate to the Court and jury what the conversation was?

THE WITNESS: Yes.

We talked about the possibility of having demonstrations at the Democratic Convention in Chicago, Illinois, that was going to be occurring that August. I am not sure that we knew at that point that it was in Chicago. Wherever it was, we were planning on going.

Jerry Rubin, I believe, said that it would be a good idea to call it the Festival of Life in contrast to the Convention of Death, and to have it in some kind of public area, like a park or something, in Chicago.

One thing that I was very particular about was that we didn't have any concept of leadership involved. There was a feeling of young people that they didn't want to listen to leaders. We had to create a kind of situation in which people would be allowed to participate and become in a real sense their own leaders.

I think it was then after this that Paul Krassner said the word "YIPPIE," and we felt that that expressed in a kind of slogan and advertising sense the spirit that we wanted to put forth in Chicago, and we adopted that as our password, really. . . .

Anita [Hoffman] said that "Yippie" would be understood by our generation, that straight newspapers like the New York Times and the U.S. Government and the courts and everything wouldn't take it seriously unless it had a formal name, so she came up with the name: "Youth International Party." She said we could play a lot of jokes on the concept of "party" because everybody would think that we were this huge international conspiracy, but that in actuality we were a party that you had fun at.

Nancy [Kursham] said that fun was an integral ingredient, that people in America, because they were being programmed like IBM cards, weren't having enough fun in life and that if you watched television, the only people that you saw having any fun were people who were buying lousy junk on television commercials, and that this would be a whole new attitude because you would see people, young people, having fun while they were protesting the system, and that young people all around this country and around the world would be turned on for that kind of an attitude.

I said that fun was very important, too, that it was a direct rebuttal of the kind of ethics and morals that were being put forth in the country to keep people working in a rat race which didn't make any sense because in a few years that machines would do all the work anyway, that there was a whole system of values that people were taught to postpone their pleasure, to put all their money in the bank, to buy life insurance, a whole bunch of things that didn't make any sense to our generation at all, and that fun actually was becoming quite subversive.

Jerry said that because of our action at the Stock Exchange in throwing out the money, that within a few weeks the Wall Street brokers there had totally enclosed the whole stock exchange in bulletproof, shatterproof glass, that cost something like $20,000 because they were afraid we'd come back and throw money out again.

He said that for hundreds of years political cartoonists had always pictured corrupt politicians in the guise of a pig, and he said that it would be great theater if we ran a pig for President, and we all took that on as like a great idea and that's more or less—that was the founding.

MR. WEINGLASS: The document that is before you, D-222 for identification, what is that document?

THE WITNESS: It was our initial call to people to describe what Yippie was about and why we were coming to Chicago.

Mk. WEINGLASS: Now, Abbie, could you read the entire document to the jury.

THE WITNESS: It says:

"A STATEMENT FROM YIP!

"Join us in Chicago in August for an international festival of youth, music, and theater. Rise up and abandon the creeping meatball! Come all you rebels, youth spirits, rock minstrels, truth-seekers, peacock-freaks, poets, barricade-jumpers, dancers, lovers and artists!

"It is summer. It is the last week in August, and the NATIONAL DEATH PARTY meets to bless Lyndon Johnson. We are there! There are 50,000 of us dancing in the streets, throbbing with amplifiers and harmony. We are making love in the parks. We are reading, singing, laughing, printing newspapers, groping, and making a mock convention, and celebrating the birth of FREE AMERICA in our own time.

"Everything will be free. Bring blankets, tents, draft-cards, body-paint, Mr. Leary's

Cow, food to share, music, eager skin, and happiness. The threats of LBJ, Mayor Daley, and J. Edgar Freako will not stop us. We are coming! We are coming from all over the world!

"The life of the American spirit is being torn asunder by the forces of violence, decay, and the napalm-cancer fiend. We demand the Politics of Ecstasy! We are the delicate spores of the new fierceness that will change America. We will create our own reality, we are Free America! And we will not accept the false theater of the Death Convention.

"We will be in Chicago. Begin preparations now! Chicago is yours! Do it!"

"Do it!" was a slogan like "Yippie." We use that a lot and it meant that each person that came should take on the responsibility for being his own leader-that we should, in fact, have a leaderless society.

We shortly thereafter opened an office and people worked in the office on what we call movement salaries, subsistence, thirty dollars a week. We had what the straight world would call a staff and an office although we called it an energy center and regarded ourselves as a tribe or a family.

MR. WEINGLASS: Could you explain to the Court and jury, if you know, how this staff functioned in your office?

THE WITNESS: Well, I would describe it as anarchistic. People would pick up the phone and give information and people from all over the country were now becoming interested and they would ask for more information, whether we were going to get a permit, how the people in Chicago were relating, and we would bring flyers and banners and posters. We would have large general meetings that were open to anybody who wanted to come.

MR. WEINGLASS: How many people would attend these weekly meetings?

THE WITNESS: There were about two to three hundred people there that were attending the meetings. Eventually we had to move into Union Square and hold meetings out in the public. There would be maybe three to five hundred people attending meetings. . .
.

MR. WEINGLASS: Where did you go [March 23], if you can recall

THE WITNESS: I flew to Chicago to observe a meeting being sponsored, I believe, by the National Mobilization Committee. It was held at a place called Lake Villa, I believe, about twenty miles outside of Chicago here.

MR. WEINGLASS: Do you recall how you were dressed for that meeting?

THE WITNESS: I was dressed as an Indian. I had gone to Grand Central Station as an Indian and so I just got on a plane and flew as an Indian.

MR. WEINGLASS: Now, when you flew to Chicago, were you alone?

THE WITNESS: No. Present were Jerry, myself, Paul Krassner, and Marshall Bloom, the head of this Liberation News Service.

MR. WEINGLASS: When you arrived at Lake Villa, did you have occasion to meet any of the defendants who are seated here at this table?

THE WITNESS: Yes, I met for the first time Rennie, Tom Hayden—who I had met before, and that's it, you know. . . .

MR. WEINGLASS: Was any decision reached at that meeting about coming to Chicago?

THE WITNESS: I believe that they debated for two days about whether they should come or not to Chicago. They decided to have more meetings. We said we had already made up our minds to come to Chicago and we passed out buttons and posters and said that if they were there, good, it would be a good time.

MR. WEINGLASS: Following the Lake Villa conference, do you recall where you went?

THE WITNESS: Yes. The next day, March 25, 1 went to the Aragon Ballroom. It was a benefit to raise money again for the Yippies but we had a meeting backstage in one of the dressing rooms with the Chicago Yippies.

MR. WEINGLASS: Do you recall what was discussed?

THE WITNESS: Yes. We drafted a permit application for the Festival to take place in Chicago. We agreed that Grant Park would be best.

MR. WEINGLASS: Directing your attention to the following morning, which was Monday morning, March 26, do you recall where you were at that morning?

THE WITNESS: We went to the Parks Department. Jerry was there, Paul, Helen Runningwater, Abe Peck, Reverend John Tuttle--there were a group of about twenty to thirty people, Yippies.

MR. WEINGLASS: Did you meet with anyone at the Park District at that time?

THE WITNESS: Yes. There were officials from the Parks Department to greet us, they took us into this office, and we presented a permit application.

MR. WEINGLASS: Did you ever receive a reply to this application?

THE WITNESS: Not to my knowledge.

MR. WEINGLASS: After your meeting with the Park District, where, if anywhere, did you go?

THE WITNESS: We held a brief press conference on the lawn in front of the Parks Department, and then we went to see Mayor Daley at City Hall. When we arrived, we were told that the mayor was indisposed and that Deputy Mayor David Stahl would see us.

MR. WEINGLASS: When you met with Deputy Mayor Stahl, what, if anything, occurred?

THE WITNESS: Helen Runningwater presented him with a copy of the permit application that we had submitted to the Parks Department. It was rolled up in the Playmate of the Month that said "To Dick with Love, the Yippies," on it. And we presented it to him and gave him a kiss and put a Yippie button on him, and when he opened it up, the Playmate was just there.

And he was very embarrassed by the whole thing, and he said that we had followed the right procedure, the city would give it proper attention and things like that . . . .

December 29, 1969

MR. WEINGLASS: I direct your attention now to August 5, 1968, and I ask you where you were on that day.

THE WITNESS: I was in my apartment, St. Marks Place, on the Lower East Side in New York City.

MR. WEINGLASS: Who was with you?

THE WITNESS: Jerry Rubin was there, Paul Krassner was there, and Nancy. Anita was there; five of us, I believe.

MR. WEINGLASS: Can you describe the conversation which occurred between you and Abe Peck on the telephone?

THE WITNESS: Mr. Peck and other people from Chicago, Yippies--had just returned from a meeting on Monday afternoon with David Stahl and other people from the City administration. He said that he was quite shocked because--they said that they didn't know that we wanted to sleep in the park.

Abe Peck said that it had been known all along that one of the key elements of this Festival was to let us sleep in the park, that it was impossible for people to sleep in hotels since the delegates were staying there and it would only be natural to sleep in the park.

He furthermore told me in his opinion the City was laying down certain threats to them in order to try and get them to withdraw their permit application, and that we should come immediately back to Chicago.

MR. WEINGLASS: After that phone conversation what occurred?

THE WITNESS: We subsequently went to Chicago on August 7 at night.

MR. WEINGLASS: Did a meeting occur on that evening?

THE WITNESS: Yes, in Mayor Daley's press conference room, where he holds his press conferences.

MR. WEINGLASS: Can y ou relate what occurred at this meeting?

THE WITNESS: It was more or less an informal kind of meeting. Mr. Stahl made clear that these were just exploratory talks, that the mayor didn't have it in his power to grant the permits. We said that that was absurd, that we had been negotiating now for a period of four or five months, that the City was acting like an ostrich, sticking its head in the sand, hoping that we would all go away like it was some bad dream.

I pointed out that it was in the best interests of the City to have us in Lincoln Park ten miles away from the Convention hall. I said we had no intention of marching on the Convention hall, that I didn't particularly think that politics in America could be changed by marches and rallies, that what we were presenting was an alternative life style, and we hoped that people of Chicago would come up, and mingle in Lincoln Park and see what we were about.

I said that the City ought to give us a hundred grand, a hundred thousand dollars to run the Festival. It would be so much in their best interests.

And then I said, "Why don't you just give two hundred grand, and I'll split town?"

It was a very informal meeting. We were just sitting around on metal chairs that they had.

All the time David Stahl had been insisting that they did not make decisions in the city, that he and the mayor did not make the decisions. We greeted this with a lot of laughter and said that it was generally understood all around the country that Daley was the boss of Chicago and made all the decisions.

I also said that I considered that our right to assemble in Lincoln Park and to present our society was a right that I was willing to die for, that this was a fundamental human right . . . .

MR. WEINGLASS: On August 14, approximately three days later, in the morning of that day, do you recall where you were?

THE WITNESS: I went to speak to Jay Miller, head of the American Civil Liberties Union. I asked if it was possible for them to work with us on an injunction in the Federal court to sue Mayor Daley and other city officials about the fact that they would not grant us a permit and were denying us our right to freedom of speech and assembly.

MR. WEINGLASS: Now, can you relate to the Court and jury what happened in court when you appeared at 10:00 A.M.?

THE WITNESS: It was heard before Judge Lynch.

There was a fantastic amount of guards all over the place.

We were searched, made to take off our shirts, empty our pockets--

MR. SCHULTZ. That is totally irrelevant. There happened to be threats at that time, your Honor--

THE WITNESS: He is right. There were threats. I had twenty that week.

THE COURT: The language, "There were a fantastic amount of guards," may go out and the jury is directed to disregard them.

MR. WEINGLASS: After the--

THE WITNESS: We came before the judge. It was a room similar to this, similar, kind of wall-to wall bourgeois, rugs and neon lights. Federal courts are all the same, I think.

The judge made a couple of references to us in the room, said that our dress was an affront to the Court.

It was pointed out by a lawyer that came by that Judge Lynch was Mayor Daley's ex-law partner. As as result of this conversation we went back into court about twenty, thirty minutes later.

MR. WEINGLASS: Did you speak to the Court?

THE WITNESS: I spoke to Judge Lynch. I said that we were withdrawing our suit, that we had as little faith in the judicial system in this country as we had in the political system.

He said, "Be careful, young man. I will find a place for you to sleep."

And I thanked him for that, said I had one, and left.

We withdrew our suit. Then we had a press conference downstairs to explain the reasons for that. We explained to the press that we were leaving in our permit application but withdrawing our Federal injunction to sue the city. We said it was a bit futile to end up before a judge, Judge Lynch, who was the ex-law partner of Mayor Daley, that the Federal judges were closely tied in with the Daley and Democratic political machine in Chicago and that we could have little recourse of grievance.

Furthermore, that we suspected that the judge would order us not to go into Lincoln Park at all and that if we did, that we would be in violation of contempt of court, and that it was a setup, and Judge Lynch planned to lynch us in the same way that Stahl was stalling us.

I pointed out that the names in this thing were getting really absurd, similarities. I also read a list of Yippie demands that I had written that morning--sort of Yippie philosophy.

MR. WEINGLASS: Now, will you read for the Court and jury the eighteen demands first, then the postscript.

THE WITNESS: I will read it in the order that I wrote it. "Revolution toward a free society, Yippie, by A. Yippie.

"This is a personal statement. There are no spokesmen for the Yippies. We are all our own leaders. We realize this list of demands is inconsistent. They are not really demands. For people to make demands of the Democratic Party is an exercise in wasted wish fulfillment. If we have a demand, it is simply and emphatically that they, along with their fellow inmates in the Republican Party, cease to exist. We demand a society built along the alternative community in Lincoln Park, a society based on humanitarian cooperation and equality, a society which allows and promotes the creativity present in all people and especially our youth.

"Number one. An immediate end to the war in Vietnam and a restructuring of our foreign policy which totally eliminates aspects of military, economic and cultural imperialism; the withdrawal of all foreign based troops and the abolition of military draft.

"Two. An immediate freedom for Huey Newton of the Black Panthers and all other black people; adoption of the community control concept in our ghetto areas; an end to the cultural and economic domination of minority groups.

"Three. The legalization of marijuana and all other psychedelic drugs; the freeing of all prisoners currently imprisoned on narcotics charges.

"Number four. A prison system based on the concept of rehabilitation rather than punishment.

"Five. A judicial system which works towards the abolition of all laws related to crimes without victims; that is, retention only of laws relating to crimes in which there is an unwilling injured party: i.e. murder, rape, or assault.

"Six. The total disarmament of all the people beginning with the police. This includes not only guns but such brutal vices as tear gas, Mace, electric prods, blackjacks, billy clubs, and the like.

"Seven. The abolition of money, the abolition of pay housing, pay media, pay transportation, pay food, pay education. pay clothing, pay medical health, and pay toilets.

"Eight. A society which works towards and actively promotes the concept of full unemployment, a society in which people are free from the drudgery of work, adoption of the concept 'Let the machines do it.'

"Number ten. A program of ecological development that would provide incentives for the decentralization of crowded cities and encourage rural living.

"Eleven. A program which provides not only free birth control information and devices, but also abortions when desired.

"Twelve. A restructured educational system which provides a student power to determine his course of study, student participation in over-all policy planning; an educational system which breaks down its barriers between school and community; a system which uses the surrounding community as a classroom so that students may learn directly the problems of the people.

"Number thirteen. The open and free use of the media; a program which actively supports and promotes cable television as a method of increasing the selection of channels available to the viewer.

"Fourteen. An end to all censorship. We are sick of a society that has no hesitation about showing people committing violence and refuses to show a couple fucking.

"Fifteen. We believe that people should fuck all the time, any time, wherever they wish. This is not a programmed demand but a simple recognition of the reality around its.

"Sixteen. A political system which is more streamlined and responsive to the needs of all the people regardless of age. sex, or race; perhaps a national referendum system conducted via television or a telephone voting system; perhaps a decentralization of-power and authority with many varied tribal groups, groups in which people exist in a state of basic trust and are free to choose their tribe.

"Seventeen. A program that encourages and promotes the arts. However, we feel that if the free society we envision were to be sought for and achieved, all of us would actualize the creativity within us; in a very real sense we would have a society in which every man would be an artist.'

And eighteen was left blank for anybody to fill in what they wanted. "It was for these reasons that we had come to Chicago, it was for these reasons that many of us may fight and die here. We recognize this as the vision of the founders of this nation. We recognize that we are America; we recognize that we are free men. The present-day politicians and their armies of automatons have selfishly robbed us of our birthright. The evilness they stand for will go unchallenged no longer. Political pigs, your days are numbered. We are the second American Revolution. We shall win.

"YIPPIE."

MR. WEINGLASS: When you used the words "fight and die here," in what context were you using those words?

THE WITNESS: It is a metaphor. That means that we felt strongly about our right to assemble in the park and that people should be willing to take risks for it. It doesn't spell it out because people were capable of fighting in their own way and making their own decisions and We never would tell anyone specifically that they should fight, fistfight.

MR. WEINGLASS: Did you during the week of the Convention and the period of time immediately before the Convention tell any person singly or in groups that they should fight in the park?

MR. SCHULTZ: Objection.

THE COURT: I sustain the objection.

MR. WEINGLASS: Directing your attention to the morning of August 19, 1968, did you attend a meeting on that day?

THE WITNESS: Yes. I went to the office of the Mobilization Committee.

MR. WEINGLASS: Was there a discussion?

THE WITNESS: I never stayed long at these meetings. I just went and made an announcement and maybe stayed ten or fifteen minutes. . . .

MR. WEINGLASS: Was there a course given in snake dancing on that day also?

THE WITNESS: Yes. Yes. People would have a pole and there would be about six people, and then about six people behind them, holding them around the waist, four or five lines of these people with men, women, and kids maybe eight years old in on this whole thing, and people would bounce from one foot to the other and yell "Wash oi, Wash oi," which is kind of Japanese for "Yippie," I guess.

And they would just march up and down the park like this, mostly laughing and giggling, because the newsmen were taking this quite seriously, and then at a certain point everybody would turn in and sort of just collapse and fall on the ground and laugh. I believe we lost about four or five Yippies during that great training.

The exciting part was when the police arrested two army intelligence officers in the trees.

MR. WEINGLASS: During the course of that day when you were in the park, did you notice that the police were hanging any signs in the park?

THE WITNESS: Late in the day, maybe four or five, I became aware that there were police nailing signs on the trees that said "11:00 p.m. curfew," maybe a few other words, but that was the gist of the signs.

MR. WEINGLASS: From Friday, August 23, on to the end of Convention week, did you ever discuss with any people the question of staying in the park after the curfew hours?

THE WITNESS: At a meeting on August 24, that subject came up, and there was lengthy discussion. ..

MR. WEINGLASS: Now, did you hear Jerry Rubin speak at that meeting?

THE WITNESS: Jerry said that the park wasn't worth fighting for; that we should leave at the eleven p.m. curfew. He said that we should put out a statement to that effect.

MR. WEINGLASS: And did you speak at that meeting?

THE WITNESS: I reported on a meeting that morning with Chief Lynskey. I had asked the Chicago cops who were tailing me to take me to Chief Lynskey who was in charge of the area of Lincoln Park. I went up to the chief and said, "Well, are you going to let us have the Festival?"

He said "No festival under any circumstances. If anybody breaks one city ordinance in that park, we clear the whole park."

He said, "You do any one thing wrong and I will arrest you on sight."

He said, "Why don't you try to kick me in the shins right now?"

And I said NBC wasn't there.

And he said, "Well, at least the kid's honest," and stuff like that.

Then I gave a speech to the police that were all assembled and I said, "Have a good time." I said, "The National Guard's coming in, they're probably going to whip you guys up, and I hope your walkie-talkies work better than ours," and stuff like that. And I just walked out.

Then we discussed what we were going to do. I said it was my feeling that Chicago was in a total state of anarchy as far as the police mentality worked. I said that we were going to have to fight for every single thing, we were going to have to fight for the electricity, we were going to have to fight to have the stage come in, we were going to have to fight for every rock musician to play, that the whole week was going to be like that.

I said that we should proceed with the festival as planned, we should try to do everything that we had come to Chicago to do, even though the police and the city officials were standing in our way.

MR. WEINGLASS: During the course of this Saturday and prior to this meeting, did you have occasion to meet Irv Bock in the park?

THE WITNESS: Oh, I met Irv Bock Saturday afternoon during some of the marshal training. Marshal training is a difficult phrase to use for Yippies. We always have a reluctance to marshals because they are telling people what to do and we were more anarchistic than that, more leaderless.

I sort of bumped into Irv Bock. I showed him a--it wasn't a gas mask but it was a thing with two plastic eyes and a little piece of leather that I got, I purchased in an army-navy store for about nineteen cents, and I said that these would be good protection against Mace.

He started running down to me all this complicated military jargon and I looked at him and said, "Irv, you're a cop, ain't you?"

He sort of smiled and said, "No, I'm not."

"Come on," I said, "We don't grow peaceniks that big. We are all quarterbacks. You've got to be a cop."

I said, "Show me your wallet."

So he said, "No, no. Don't you trust me?"

So I said, "Irv," I said, "last night there was a guy running around my house with a pistol trying to kill me," that I had twenty threats that week, and at that point I didn't trust Jerry Rubin. . . .

MR. WEINGLASS: Directing your attention to approximately two o'clock in the morning, which would now be Monday morning, do you recall what you were doing?

THE WITNESS: I made a telephone call to David Stahl, Deputy Mayor of Chicago at his home. I had his home number.

I said, "Hi, Dave. How's it going? Your police got to be the dumbest and the most brutal in the country," I said.

"The decision to drive people out of the park in order to protect the City was about the dumbest military tactic since the Trojans let the Trojan horse inside the gate and there was nothing to be compared with that stupidity."

I again pleaded with him to let people stay in the park the following night. "There will be more people coming Monday, Tuesday, and subsequently Wednesday night," I said, "and they should be allowed to sleep." I said that he ought to intercede with the Police Department. I said to him that the City officials, in particular his boss, Daley, were totally out of their minds.

I said, "I read in the paper the day before that they had 2,000 troops surrounding the reservoirs in order to protect against the Yippie plot to dump LSD in the drinking water. There isn't a kid in the country," I said, "never mind a Yippie, who thinks that such a thing could be done."

I told him to check with all the scientists at the University of Chicago--he owned them all.

He said that he knew it couldn't be done, but they weren't taking any chances anyway . . . .

MR. WEINGLASS: Can you tell the Court and jury where you were in Lincoln Park at approximately 11:30 Monday night?

THE WITNESS: I was walking through the barricade, my wife Anita and I.

MR. WEINGLASS: Did you see Allen Ginsberg at the barricade?

THE WITNESS: Yes. He was kneeling.

There was a crowd of people around. He was playing that instrument that he plays and people were chanting.

There was a police car that would come by and I believe it was making announcements and people would yell at the police car, you know, "Beat it. Get out. The parks belong to the people. Oink Oink. Pig Pig. Pigs are coming. Peace Now."

People were waving flags. People were running around being scared and people were running around sort of joyous. I mean, it was strange, different emotions. It was very dark in that place.

MR. SCHULTZ: The witness is not answering the question any more. He is giving another essay. I object.

MR. WEINGLASS: When the police finally came to the barricade, from what direction did they come?

THE WITNESS: They came in through the zoo.

They proceeded to climb and immediately started to club people.

They were throwing parts of the barricade, trashcans, at people.

MR. WEINGLASS: Now, at the time the police came to the barricade what did you do?

THE WITNESS: Well, I was coughing and spitting because there was tear gas totally flooding the air, cannisters were exploding all around me--I moved with the people out this way, out of the park trying to duck, picking up people that were being clubbed, getting off the ground myself a few times.

The police were just coming through in this wedge, solid wedge, clubbing people right and left, and I tried to get out of the park.

MR. WEINGLASS: Directing your attention to approximately six o'clock the following morning, do you recall where you were?

THE WITNESS: I got in the car of the police that were following me and asked them to take me to the beach--the beach part of Lincoln Park.

MR. WEINGLASS: What was occurring when you got there?

THE WITNESS: Allen Ginsberg and about--oh 150-200 people were kneeling, most of the people in lotus position which is a position with their legs crossed like this--chanting and praying and meditating.

There were five or six police cars on the boardwalk right in back, and there were police surrounding the group. Dawn was breaking. It was very cold, very chilly. People had a number of blankets wrapped around them, sitting in a circle.

I went and sat next to Allen and chanted and prayed for about an hour. Then I talked to the group. People would give talks about their feelings of what was going on in Chicago. I said, "I am very sad about what has happened in Chicago.

"What is going on here is very beautiful, but it won't be in the evening news that night.

"The American mass media is a glutton for violence, and it would be only shots of what was happening in the streets of Chicago."

I said, "America can't be changed by people sitting and praying, and this is an unfortunate reality that we have to face."

I said that we were a community that had to learn how to survive, that we had seen what had happened the last few nights in Lincoln Park. We had seen the destruction of the Festival.

I said, "I will never again tell people to sit quietly and pray for change.". . .

MR. WEINGLASS: Now, directing your attention to approximately 6:00 A.M. the following morning, Wednesday, August 28, do you recall what you were doing?

THE WITNESS: I went to eat. I went with Paul Krassner, Beverly Baskinger, and Anita and four police officers-- Paul also had two Chicago police officers following him, as well as the two that were following me. We walked and the four of them would drive along behind us.

MR. WEINGLASS: Could you describe for the jury and the Court what you were wearing at that time?

THE WITNESS: Well, I had cowboy boots, and brown pants and a shirt, and I had a grey felt ranger cowboy type hat down over my eyes, like this.

MR.WEINGLASS: What, if anything occurred while you were sitting there having breakfast?

THE WITNESS: Well, two policemen came in and said, "We have orders to arrest you. You have something under your hat."

So I asked them if they had a search warrant and I said 'Did you check it out with Commander Braasch? Me and him got an agreement"—and they went to check it out with him, while we were eating breakfast.

MR. WEINGLASS: After a period of time, did they come back?

THE WITNESS: They came back with more police officers—there were about four or five patrol cars surrounding the restaurant. The Red Squad cops who had been following us came in the restaurant, four or five police, and they said, "We checked. Now will you take off your hat?" They were stern, more serious about it.

MR. WEINGLASS: What did you do?

THE WITNESS: Well, I lifted up the hat and I went "Bang! Bang!"

They grabbed me by the jacket and pulled me across the bacon and eggs and Anita over the table, threw me on the floor and out the door and threw me against the car, and they handcuffed me.

I was just eating the bacon and going "Oink Oink!"

MR. WEINGLASS: Did they tell you why you were being arrested?

THE WITNESS: They said they arrested me because I had the word "Fuck" on my forehead. I had put it on with this magic marker before we left the house. They called it an "obscenary."

I put it on for a couple of reasons, One was that I was tired of seeing my picture in the paper and having newsmen come around, and I know if you got that word on your forehead they ain't going to print your picture in the paper. Secondly, it sort of summed up my attitude about the whole thing—what was going on in Chicago.

I like that four letter word—I thought it was kind of holy, actually.

MR. WEINGLASS: Abbie Hoffman, prior to coming to Chicago, from April 1968 on to the week of the Convention, did you enter into an agreement with David Dellinger, John Froines, Tom Hayden, Jerry Rubin, Lee Weiner or Rennie Davis, to come to the city of Chicago for the purpose of encouraging and promoting violence during the Convention week?

THE WITNESS: An agreement?

MR. WEINGLASS: Yes.

THE WITNESS: We couldn't agree on lunch.

MR. WEINGLASS: I have no further questions.

THE COURT: Cross-examine.

MR. SCHULTZ: Thank you, your Honor. . . .

MR. SCHULTZ: Did you see numerous instances of people attacking the Guardsmen at the Pentagon, Mr. Hoffman?

THE WITNESS. I do not believe that I saw any instances of people attacking National Guardsmen. In fact, the attitude was one of comradeship. They would talk to the National Guardsmen continuously and tell them they were not the people that they had come to confront, that they were their brothers and you don't get people to oppose [their ways] by attacking them.

MR. SCHULTZ: Mr. Hoffman, the Guards and the troops were trying to keep the people from entering into the Pentagon for two days, isn't that right?

THE WITNESS: I assume that they were there to guard the Pentagon from rising in the air possibly. I mean, who knows what they are there for? Were you there?

You probably watched it on television and got a different impression of what was happening. That is one aspect of myth-making—you can envisualize hoardes and hoardes of people when in reality that was not what happened.

MR SCHULTZ: Did you see some people urinate on the Pentagon?

THE WITNESS: On the Pentagon itself?

MR. SCHULTZ: Or at the Pentagon?

THE WITNESS: There were over 100,000 people. People have that biological habit, you know.

MR. SCHULTZ: Did you symbolically urinate on the Pentagon, Mr. Hoffman?

THE WITNESS: I symbolically urinate on the Pentagon?

MR. SCHULTZ: Yes.

THE WITNESS: I didn't get that close. Pee on the walls of the Pentagon?

You are getting to be out of sight, actually. You think there is a law against it?

MR. SCHULTZ: Are you done, Mr. Hoffman?

THE WITNESS: I am done when you are.

MR. SCHULTZ: Did you ever state that a sense of integration possesses you and comes from pissing on the Pentagon?

THE WITNESS: I said from combining political attitudes with biological necessity, there is a sense of integration, yes.

MR. SCHULTZ: You had a good time at the Pentagon, didn't you. Mr. Hoffman?

THE WITNESS: Yes I did. I'm having a good time now too. I feel that biological necessity now. Could I be excused for a slight recess?

THE COURT: Ladies and gentlemen of the jury, we will take a brief recess.

(brief recess)

MR. SCHULTZ: On the seventh of August, you told David Stahl that at your liberated area you—

THE WITNESS: What meeting was this, August 7?

MR. SCHULTZ: That's when you just flew in from New York.

THE WITNESS: Crossing state lines—

MR. SCHULTZ: At this meeting on the evening of August 7, you told Mr. Stahl that you were going to have nude-ins in your liberated zone, didn't you?

THE WITNESS: A nude-in? I don't believe I would use that phrase, no. I don't think it's very poetic, frankly.

I might have told him that ten thousand people were going to walk naked on the waters of Lake Michigan, something like that.

MR. SCHULTZ: You told him, did you not, Mr. Hoffman, that in your liberated zone, you would have—

THE WITNESS: I'm not even sure what it is, a nude-in.

MR. SCHULTZ: —public fornication.

THE WITNESS: If it means ten thousand people, naked people, walking on Lake Michigan, yes.

MR.KUNSTLER: I object to this because Mr.Schultz is acting like a dirty old man.

MR. SCHULTZ: We are not going into dirty old men. If they are going to have nude-ins and public fornication, the City officials react to that, and I am establishing through this witness that that's what be did.

THE COURT: Do you object?

MR. KUNSTLER: I am just remarking, your Honor, that a young man can be a dirty old man.

THE WITNESS: I don't mind talking about it.

THE COURT: I could make an observation. I have seen some exhibits here that are not exactly exemplary documents.

MR. KUNSTLER: But they are, your Honor, only from your point of view-making a dirty word of something that can be beautiful and lovely, and--

MR. SCHULTZ: We are not litigating here, your Honor, whether sexual intercourse is beautiful or not. We are litigating whether or not the City could permit tens of thousands of people to come in and do in their parks what this man said they were going to do.

In getting people to Chicago you created your Yippie myth, isn't that right? And part of your myth was "We'll burn Chicago to the ground," isn't that right?

THE WITNESS: It was part of the myth that there were trainloads of dynamite headed for Chicago, it was part of the myth that they were going to form white vigilante groups and round up demonstrators. All these things were part of the myth. A myth is a process of telling stories, most of which ain't true.

MR. SCHULTZ: Mr. Hoffman--

Your Honor, Mr. Davis is having a very fine time here whispering at me. He has been doing it for the last twenty minutes. He moved up here when I started the examination so he could whisper in my ear. I would ask Mr. Davis, if he cannot be quiet, to move to another part of the table so that he will stop distracting me.

THE COURT: Try not to speak too loudly, Mr. Davis.

MR. DAVIS: Yes, sir.

THE COURT: Go ahead.

THE WITNESS: Go ahead, Dick.

MR. SCHULTZ: Didn't you state, Mr. Hoffman, that part of the myth that was being created to get people to come to Chicago was that "We will fuck on the beaches"?

THE WITNESS: Yes, me and Marshall McLuhan. Half of that quote was from Marshall McLuhan.

MR. SCHULTZ: "And there will be acid for all" —that was another one of your Yippie myths, isn't that right?

THE WITNESS: That was well known.

MR. SCHULTZ: By the way, was there any acid in Lincoln Park in Chicago?

THE WITNESS: In the reservoir, in the lake?

MR. SCHULTZ: No, among the people.

THE WITNESS: Well, there might have been, I don't know. It is colorless, odorless, tasteless. One can never tell. . . .

MR. SCHULTZ: The fact is, Mr. Hoffman, that what you were trying to do was to create a situation where the State and the United States Government would have to bring in the Army and bring in the National Guard during the Convention in order to protect the delegates so that it would appear that the Convention had to be held under military conditions, isn't that a fact, Mr. Hoffman?

THE WITNESS: You can do that with a yo-yo in this country. It's quite easy. You can see just from this courtroom. Look at all the troops around--

MR. SCHULTZ: Your Honor, may the answer be stricken?

THE COURT: Yes, it may go out. . . .

MR. SCHULTZ: Mr. Hoffman, in the afternoon on that Thursday you participated ;in a march, and then you laid down in front of an armored personnel carrier at the end of that march, at 16th or 19th on Michigan, laid down on the street?

THE WITNESS: Was that what it was? I thought it was a tank.

It looked like a tank.

Do you want me to show you how I did it? Laid down in front of the tank?

MR. SCHULTZ: All right, Mr. Hoffman. Did you make any gestures of any sort?

THE WITNESS: When I was laying down? See. I went like that, lying down in front of the tank.

I had seen Czechoslovakian students do it to Russian tanks.

MR. SCHULTZ: And then you saw a Chicago police officer who appeared to be in high command because of all the things he had on his shoulders come over to the group and start leading them back toward Grant Park, didn't you?

THE WITNESS: He came and then people left—and went back to the park, yes.

MR. SCHULTZ: Did you say to anybody, "Well, you see that cat?", pointing to Deputy Superintendent Rochford. "When we get to the top of the hill, if the cat doesn't talk right, we're going to hold him there, and then we can do whatever we want and the police won't bother us." Did you say that to anybody out there, Mr. Hoffman?

MR. WEINGLASS: That's the testimony of the intelligence officer, the intelligence police officer of the Chicago Police Department.

THE WITNESS: I asked the Chicago police officers to help me kidnap Deputy Superintendent Rochford? That's pretty weird.

MR. SCHULTZ: Isn't it a fact that you announced publicly a plan to kidnap the head pig—

THE WITNESS: Cheese, wasn't it?

MR. SCHULTZ: —and then snuff him—

THE WITNESS: I thought it was "cheese."

MR. SCHULTZ: —and then snuff him if other policemen touched you? Isn't that a fact, sir?

THE WITNESS: I do not believe that I used the reference of "pig" to any policemen in Chicago including some of the top cheeses. I did not use it during that week. . .

MR. SCHULTZ: You and Albert, Mr. Hoffman, were united in Chicago in your determination to smash the system by using any means at your disposal, isn't that right?

THE WITNESS: Did I write that?

MR. SCHULTZ: No, did you have that thought?

THE WITNESS: That thought? Is a thought like a dream? If I dreamed to smash the system, that's a thought. Yes, I had that thought.

THE COURT: Mr. Witness, you may not interrogate the lawyer who is examining you.

THE WITNESS: Judge, you have always told people to describe what they see or what they hear. I'm the only one that has to describe what I think.

MR. WEINGLASS: I object to any reference to what a person thought or his being tried for what he thought. He may be tried for his intent.

THE COURT: Overrule the objection.

THE WITNESS: Well, I had a lot of dreams at night. One of the dreams might have been that me and Stew were united.

MR. SCHULTZ: Mr. Hoffman, isn't it a fact that one of the reasons why you came to Chicago was simply to wreck American society?

THE WITNESS: My feeling at the time, and still is, that society is going to wreck itself. I said that on a number of occasions, that our role is to survive while the society comes tumbling down around us; our role is to survive.

We have to learn how to defend ourselves, given this type of society, because of the war in Vietnam, because of racism, because of the attack on the cultural revolution—in fact because of this trial.

MR. SCHULTZ: Mr. Hoffman, by Thursday, the twenty-ninth, the last day of the Convention, you knew you had smashed the Democrats' chances for victory, isn't that a fact?

THE WITNESS: No. My attitude was it was a type of psychic jujitsu where the people smash themselves—or the party wrecks themselves. The same way this trial is.

MR. SCHULTZ: By Thursday there was no doubt in your mind when you saw the acceptance speech that you had won, and there would be a pig in the White House in '69?

THE WITNESS: Well, that was our role in coming here, to nominate a pig. That pig did win. He didn't actually—which one did?

MR. SCHULTZ: And you went out for champagne, and you brought it back to Mobilization headquarters and toasted the revolution, you did just that, right?

THE WITNESS: We drank some champagne. It was warm, warm champagne.

MR. SCHULTZ: And toasted to your success, to your victory, isn't that right?

THE WITNESS: We toasted to the fact that we were still alive.

That was the miracle as far as I saw it, is still being alive by that last Thursday.

MR. SCHULTZ: That's all, your Honor.

THE WITNESSS: Right on!

THE COURT: Have you finished your cross-examination?

MR. SCHULTZ: Yes, I have.

THE WITNESS: Right on!

Rennie Davis'Testimony (defendant)

January 23, 1970

MR. WEINGLASS: Will you please identify yourself for the record?

THE WITNESS: Rennie Davis.

MR. WEINGLASS: Do you recall the first time you came to the city of Chicago?

THE WITNESS: The first time I came to the city of Chicago was to visit the international Amphitheatre in a poultry judging contest in 1956. It was the international contest and I had just won the Eastern United States Poultry Judging Contest in 4-H and I came to Chicago to participate at the International Amphitheatre in the contest here.

MR. WEINGLASS: How old were you at that time?

THE WITNESS: I was, I guess, sixteen.

MR. WEINGLASS: Your present age?

THE WITNESS: Twenty-nine.

MR. WEINGLASS: What is your occupation?

THE WITNESS: Since 1967 my primary work and concern has been ending the war in Vietnam. Until the time of this trial I was the national coordinator for the National Mobilization to End the War in Vietnam.

MR. WEINGLASS: Now, directing your attention to the early evening of November 20, 1967, do you recall where you were on that night?

THE WITNESS: I was at the University of Chicago in an auditorium called Judd Hall. It was a meeting of a group called The Resistance. I was a speaker with Bob Ross and David Harris who is the husband of Joan Baez.

MR. WEINGLASS: Could you relate now to the Court and jury the words that you spoke, as best you can recall, on that particular night?

THE WITNESS: I began by holding up a small steel ball that was green, about the size of a tennis ball and I said, "This bomb was dropped on a city of 100,000 people, a city called Nam Ding, which is about sixty-five miles south of Hanoi."

I said, "It was dropped by an American fighter jet, an F-105," and that when this bomb exploded over Nam Ding, about 640 of these round steel balls were spewed into the sky. And I said, "When this ball strikes a building or the ground or slows up in any way, these hammers are released, an explosion occurs which sends out about 300 steel pellets."

"Now one of these balls," I explained, "was roughly three times the power of an old fashioned hand grenade and with 640 of these bombs going off, you can throw steel pellets over an area about a thousand yards long, and about 250 yards wide.

"Every living thing exposed in that 1000-yard area from this single bomb, ninety percent of every living thing in that area will die," I said, "whether it's a water buffalo or a water buffalo boy."

I said that if this bomb were to go off in this room tonight, everyone in the room here would die, but as quickly as we could remove the bodies from the room, we could have another discussion about Vietnam.

I said "This bomb would not destroy this lecture podium, it would not damage the walls, the ceiling, the floor." I said, "if it is dropped on a city, it takes life but leaves the institutions. It is the ideal weapon, you see, for the mentality who reasons that life is less precious than property."

I said that in 1967, the year that we are in, one out of every two bombs dropped on North Vietnam was this weapon. One out of every two. And in 1967 the American Government told the American public that in North Vietnam it was only bombing steel and concrete.

Then I said, "I went to Vietnam not as a representative of the government and not as a member of the military but as an American citizen who was deeply perturbed that we lived in a country where our own government was lying to American people about this war. The American government claimed to be hitting only military targets. Yet what I saw was pagodas that had been gutted, schoolhouses that had been razed, population centers that had been leveled."

Then I said that I am going to the Democratic National Convention because I want the world to know that there are thousands of Young people in this country who do not want to see a rigged convention rubber stamp another four years of Lyndon Johnson's war.

MR. WEINGLASS: I show you an object marked D-325 for identification and can you identify that object?

THE WITNESS: Yes. This was the bomb that I brought back from Vietnam.

MR. WEINGLASS: If the Court please, the defense would like to offer into evidence D-325, the antipersonnel bomb identified by the witness as the object held by him on the night in question.

MR. FORAN: Your honor, the Government objects to this exhibit for the following reasons.

The Vietnamese war, your honor, has nothing whatsoever to do with the charges in this indictment. The Vietnamese war, which is a major difficulty of this country and a major concern of every citizen in this country, has nothing whatever to do with whether or not people in the United States have a right to travel in interstate commerce to incite a riot.

The methods and techniques of warfare have nothing whatever to do with that charge. The methods and techniques of the seeking of the end of the Vietnam war have nothing to do with the charges of this indictment.

The very purpose of the governmental system of the United States is to handle in a purposeful way within the Constitution of the United States the disposition of such complex and difficult and tragic problems that this notion has lived with for about two hundred years. The charges in this indictment your Honor, have nothing to do with this type of testimony or this kind of concept. and for that reason your Honor, the Government objects.

THE COURT: Objection sustained.

MR. KUNSTLER: Your Honor, at this point I would like to move for a mistrial

THE COURT: I deny the motion.

MR. RUBIN: You haven't heard it yet.

THE COURT: Oh, there is no ground for a mistrial.

MR. KUNSTLER: But, your Honor--

THE COURT: I direct the marshal to have this man sit down.

MR. KUNSTLER: Every time I make a motion am I going to be thrown in my seat when I argue it?

MR. DELLINGER: Force and violence. The judge is inciting a riot by asking the marshal to have him sit down.

THE COURT: That man's name is Dellinger?

MARSHAL JONESON: Will you be quiet, Mr. Dellinger?

MR. DELLINGER: After such hypocrisy I don't particularly feel like being quiet. I said before the judge was the chief prosecutor, and he's proved the point.

THE COURT: Will you remain quiet? Will you remain quiet, sir?

MR. DELLINGER: You let Foran give a foreign policy speech, but when he tries to answer it, you interrupt him and won't let him speak.

There's no pretense of fairness in this court. All you're doing is employing a riot--employing force and violence to try to keep me quiet. Just like you gagged Bobby Seale because you couldn't afford to listen to the truth that he was saying to you. You're accusing me. I'm a pacifist.

MARSHAL JONESON: Sit down, please, and be quiet.

MR. DELLINGER: I am employing nonviolence, and you're accusing me of violence, and you have a man right here, backed up by guns, jails, and force and violence. That is the difference between us.

MARSHAL JONESON: Will you sit down?

(applause)

THE COURT: Will you continue, please, with the direct examination of this witness?

MR. DELLINGER: There goes the violence right there.

MR. KUNSTLER: That's the Government in operation, your Honor, as it has been throughout this trial.

THE WITNESS: Your Honor, that's my sister they are taking out of the courtroom.

THE COURT: Even your sister--

MR. RUBIN: Bill, they are taking out my wife.

(cries of "Hey, stop it!")

MR. KUNSTLER: Your Honor, must we always have this, the force and power of the Government?

MR. FORAN: Your Honor--

MR. RUBIN: They are dragging out mv wife--will you please--

THE COURT: We must have order in the courtroom.

MR. FORAN: Your Honor, traditionally in American law, cases are tried in a court-room by the participants in the trial, not the audience, not spectators, not by shouting and screaming. This is the American judicial system, and it's worked very well for two hundred years, and it's not going to change now for these people.

MR. DELLINGER: Yes, kept the black people in slavery for two hundred years and wiped out the Indians, and kept the poor people in problems and started the war in Vietnam which is killing off at least a hundred Americans and a thousand Vietnamese every week, and we are trying to stop it.

MARSHAL JONESON: Sit down.

MR. DELLINGER: And you call that ranting and raving and screaming because we speak the truth.

MARSHAL JONESON: Mr. Dellinger, sit down, please.

MR. FORAN: Your Honor, in the American system there is a proper way to raise such issues and to correct them.

MR. DELLINGER: That was the proper way with Fred Hampton, wasn't it?

MR. FORAN: And to correct them, your Honor, by the proper governmental system, and there is a proper way to do that.

MR. KUNSTLER: This is as to Mr. Rubin's wife. She was thrown out of the court-room, and he is a defendant here. We would like her returned to the courtroom.

THE COURT: No. As long as the marshals are in charge of the behavior of spectators in this courtroom, they will determine who misbehaves.

MR. RUBIN: Am I entitled to a public trial?

THE COURT: No--you have a public trial.

MR. RUBIN: Does a public trial include my wife being in the courtroom? Am I entitled to a public trial?

THE COURT: I don't talk to defendants who have a lawyer.

MR. RUBIN: You didn't listen to my lawyer, so I have to speak. Am I entitled to a public trial?

THE COURT: You may continue with the direct examination of this witness. If you don't, I will just have to ask him to get off the witness stand.

MR. WEINGLASS: Your Honor, the witness has seen from his vantage point his sister forcibly taken from this room. I wonder if we could have a short recess to resolve that?

THE COURT: No recess. No, no. There will be no recess, sir. You will proceed to examine this witness.

MR. WEINGLASS: I direct your attention to February 11, 1968, do you recall where you were?

THE WITNESS: I was in Chicago at what later became the Mobilization office, 407 South Dearborn.

MR. WEINGLASS: What was occurring in the office?

THE WITNESS: I believe it was a planning meeting to talk about the conference that I had requested of the National Mobilization, a bringing together of all groups interested in Chicago.

MR. WEINGLASS: Did you talk about Chicago?

THE WITNESS: Yes. I said that the key questions before us today was what to do in Chicago, what to do at the Convention itself. Then I listed four positions that I proposed as a kind of agenda.

I said position number one would be we should go to the Democratic Convention to disrupt it.

I said there may be people in this room who do believe that the Democratic Convention, which is responsible for the war, should be physically disrupted, torn apart. I said I don't think that is the MOBE's position--but I think that it is essential that we put it on the agenda, It is an issue that has been created in the press and that we vote it up or down so that we can make ourselves clear on this issue.

So issue position number one would be disrupt the Convention.

Position number two, I said, that has been talked about, is that the peace movement should support a candidate. Maybe we should support Eugene McCarthy.

Then I said position number three, that had been talked about by some organizations, was what we called stay-home. This was a position that said that Daley is so concerned about the Convention and having demonstrators come into Chicago that he'd bring in the troops, he'd bring in the police, he'd start cracking heads. And in fact this might play right into Johnson's hands. It might show that the Democratic Party is the party of law and order.

So I said position three, that we should talk about here, is whether or not we should have a demonstration at all.

Then I said position number four is a campaign that begins in the spring, it goes into the fall, it goes into the summer, and then finally brings to Chicago literally every possible constituency of the American people.

MR. WEINGLASS: Now, after you outlined these four alternatives, did you say anything further about them then?

THE WITNESS: Well, there was a very long discussion of these four proposals, and I guess at the end of that discussion I said that it was clear that in this meeting of representatives of major national groups across the country there was not a single person who did not favor position number four.

Then Tom interrupted me, and he said he thought that was wrong.

A group of so-called leaders of organizations shouldn't just get together and decide what position to present to everyone. Tom thought that we should now talk about calling a very large conference of organizations to consider all four alternatives, and then he said that each one of these positions should be written up in a paper and presented to--to this conference.

MR. WEINGLASS: Was such a conference called?

THE WITNESS: Yes, it was. It took place at a place called Lake Villa. It was a YMCA camp, just beside a big lake.

MR. WEINGLASS: Now I show you a document which has been marked D-235 for identification, and I ask you if you can identify that document?

THE WITNESS: Yes, I can. Tom Hayden and I wrote this paper. It's called, "Movement Campaign 1968, an Election Year Offensive."

The paper was mimeographed in our office and then presented to every delegate at this Lake Villa meeting outside of Chicago. This was alternative number four that was agreed upon.

MR. WEINGLASS: I offer into evidence D-235 as Defendant's Exhibit Number D-235.

THE COURT: Show it to counsel.

MR. FORAN: Your Honor, this document was offered once before. This document is some twenty-one pages in length. It contains in it a number of broad summary statements that are not supported by factual data.

Each statement in itself has elements in it that are both irrelevant summary statements of a gross character totally unprovable by evidence, and self-serving in nature, and the law, your Honor, is clear that a self-serving declaration of an act or a party is inadmissible in evidence in his favor.

MR. WEINGLASS: If the Court please, the first time this document was offered, it was through the testimony of the witness Meacham. At that time the Government objected on the ground that the authors of the document were the only persons who could qualify the document for admission. The author is now on the stand, and of course now we are met with the objection that it is self-serving.

If you deny this document then you are proceeding on the assumption, your Honor, that the defendants are guilty and they are contriving documents. That has to be the beginning premise of your thinking if you feel this document is self-serving. If they are innocent, which is what the presumption is supposed to be--then I don't know why the Court would consider that this document would be possibly contrived.

THE COURT: You have here as a witness a very articulate, well-educated, seemingly intelligent witness; why can't he be questioned about his participation in the composition of that document? .

MR. WEINGLASS: The defendants are entitled to the benefit of all of the legal evidence they have indicating their innocence, writings as well as spoken words. If this document contained plans to bomb the Amphitheatre or to create a disturbance or riot in the city streets, we clearly would have had this document in evidence in the Government's case, but it contains the contrary and that is why it is being offered. I think they are entitled to the benefit of anything that indicates their innocence as well as their guilt.

THE COURT: I shall not take it in. I sustain the objection of the Government.

MR. WEINGLASS: Your Honor has read the document?

THE COURT: I have looked it over.

THE WITNESS: You never read it. I was watching you. You read two pages.

THE COURT: Mr. Marshal, will you instruct that witness on the witness stand that he is not to address me.

You may continue sir, with your direct examination.

MR. WEINGLASS: Without referring to the document, what did you say about Chicago, if anything?

MR. FORAN: Your Honor, the form of the question is bad.

THE COURT: I sustain the objection.

MR. WEINGLASS: Did you have occasion to speak at the conference?

THE WITNESS: Yes, I spoke at a workshop Saturday evening. Tom and I were both present because we were presenting our paper.

MR. WEINGLASS: Could you relate to the Court and to the jury what you said at the workshop respecting Chicago?

THE WITNESS: Tom spoke about the paper and what was in it and then someone asked Tom why there was an entire page devoted to the issue about disruption and I answered that question.

MR. WEINGLASS: Do you recall your answer?

THE WITNESS: I said that the reason that this document devotes so much attention to the question of violence and disruption at the Convention is because we think that this is not a demonstration where simply the peace movement comes to Chicago. This is, rather, a demonstration where the peace movement is the instrument to bring literally hundreds of thousands of people to Chicago, and I said that is why it is necessary to make crystal clear our position on disruption.

And I said that is why we feel that we have bent over backwards in this document to make our position on violence and disruption very clear, and we think that we should argue with every organization in the country who is for peace that that must be the strategy in Chicago.

MR. WEINGLASS: Now, directing your attention to the twentieth of July, 1968, do you recall where you were?

THE WITNESS: I was in Cleveland, Ohio, at a meeting in a church in Cleveland.

MR. WEINGLASS: Were any of the other defendants seated here at the table present?

THE WITNESS: Both Dave and Tom were present.

MR. WEINGLASS: Did you speak at that meeting?

THE WITNESS: Yes, I did. I said that I thought what was happening in Chicago was that our original plan to bring a half million American citizens to Chicago was so upsetting to the Mayor of Chicago, who was hosting a Convention of his own party, that there was a real danger that the Mayor had made a decision somewhere along the line to try to scare people away, to try to reduce the numbers of people expected, by stalling on permits and through suggesting that anybody who came to Chicago was going to be clubbed or beaten or Maced.

I said, "On the other hand, I don't want to discourage people into thinking that we are not going to get permits. There are several things in the works that give me a considerable amount of optimism. . . .

MR. WEINGLASS: Directing your attention to the morning of August 2, 1968, do you recall where you were?

THE WITNESS: I was at the Palmer House, at the coffee shop in the basement. I was meeting with David Stahl, the deputy mayor of the City of Chicago, and with me was Mark Simons.

MR. WEINGLASS: Do you recall, did a conversation occur between yourself and David Stahl?

THE WITNESS: Yes, it did. I said that I felt that given the reports that we had seen in the past, that there was some question about our purposes and intentions in coming to Chicago. I said I did not understand any other explanation for the military sort of saber rattling that was going on at that time, the constant talks in the past about disruption of the Convention.

I indicated that the character of the demonstration that was planned by our coalition was not like the Pentagon, where civil disobedience was called for, but was more like the character of the April 15 demonstration in New York, where we hoped to be effective in our protest by numbers and not by militant tactics.

I said that I thought the problem areas that we had to work out were, first of all. the matter of a march and an assembly to the Amphitheatre, and that when we had applied for a permit for the use of Halsted, that that was negotiable and that we have at this point not even applied for how to get to Halsted because we wanted to make this an open meeting between you and me.

I then said that the second area of concern for us was the whole matter of parks, that we thought that integral to our program was having park space set aside by City officials so that people could meet and sleep throughout the week of the Convention.

Then Mr. Stahl indicated to me that he thought it might be difficult for the city to grant a permit for the use of a park; that there was a curfew at I I :00 P.m., and that this would be a violation of a city ordinance to give a permit for park space beyond I 1:00 p.m.

Mr. Stahl was not sure what the feeling of the City would be with respect to an assembly at the Amphitheatre. I said I thought it was very dangerous for us to even consider an area not adjacent to the Amphitheatre, because people on their own would then go down to the area, they would not have marshals, they would not have organization, and the possibility of disruption and violence would be very great.

Then Mr. Stahl said that he agreed, that it probably would create less problems if people did not march as pedestrians but went in an orderly group.

I then asked him, "Well, how do we begin to talk about these matters?"

And he said, that the mayor's office was not responsible for granting of permits, that these matters were the responsibility of the Park District, the Streets and Sanitation Department and the Police Department and the other agencies directly involved, and then I said, "Mr. Stahl, you're not dealing with an out-of-towner. I live in Chicago, and you can say this to the press, but I really wish you wouldn't say it to me." I said, "Everyone knows in this town who makes decisions like this. You can't tell me that the Streets and Sanitation Department head that's appointed by Mayor Daley is going to make a decision independent .of the Mayor," and he sort of smiled at that point and didn't say anything.

Mr. Stahl was very cordial at the end and said, "Thank you very much for what you've said, and I'll relate this back to the appropriate bodies."

MR. WEINGLASS: At approximately six o'clock that night, still on August 21, 1968, do you recall where you were?

THE WITNESS: I was on my way to the Mobilization executive committee meeting, an apartment in Hyde Park.

MR. WEINGLASS: As you were outside, about to enter the apartment, did you have occasion to meet with anyone?

THE WITNESS: Yes. I met with Irv Bock.

MR. WEINGLASS: Now, without going into your conversation with Mr. Bock just now, do you recall what Mr. Bock had in his hand, if anything?

THE WITNESS: He went to his car and he came back and he had--it is hard to describe. It was a very large balloon, and attached to the balloon was a small tube, and stuck in the tube was a cloth fiber, and he took the glass tube and put it into some water, and the air from the balloon would pass through the glass tube in what appeared to be a regular way, so that one bubble would come up and then another and then another and then another, and he explained how this worked.

MR. WEINGLASS: What did he say to you?

THE WITNESS: Well, he said that with this device it's possible to fill the balloon with helium gas and to launch the balloon in the air and allow the helium gas to come out of the balloon in a way that can be computed mathematically so that you know when all of the air will be out of the balloon, and by computing the velocity it's possible to send the balloon up in the air and figure out exactly where it will fall. I said, "Why in the world would anyone be interested in that?"

And he said, "Well, you can attach anything that you want to this balloon, send it up into the air, and then we can drop it on the International Amphitheatre."

And I said, "Well, what would you want to attach to the balloon?" And he said, "Anything you want."

I thanked Irv for his suggestion and went inside.

MR. WEINGLASS: Now, on August 4, do you recall where you were?

THE WITNESS: Yes. I was at a Mobilization steering committee meeting just outside of Chicago. It was in Highland Park at a sort of old fancy hotel that disgusted me. I mean, it was fancy, so I didn't like it.

MR. WEINGLASS: Now, at noon of that day, do you recall where you were?

THE WITNESS: There was a lunch break around noon or 12:30, and the meeting emptied out down towards the lake. I was on a sandy beach on the edge of Lake Michigan, eating my lunch.

MR. WEINGLASS: Were you alone?

THE WITNESS: No, there were a number of people. Irv Bock was present. Well, Tom Hayden, really, and I were together and we talked and ate lunch together.

MR. WEINGLASS: And did you have a conversation with Tom Hayden on the beach?

THE WITNESS: Yes. I told Tom that I had received a letter from Don Duncan who was a close friend of ours and Don had sent us sort of a list of the various kinds of gases that were being used by the Army in South Vietnam. He described in some detail a gas called CS, which he said caused extreme congestion of the chest, a burning sensation in the face, the eyes filled with tears. Actual burns could occur on the face from this. and in heavy dosage, it could cause death.

Don said that he had information that these kinds of new chemicals being used on the people of Vietnam were now going to be used on the peace movement, and he was especially concerned that this might be the case in Chicago.

MR. WEINGLASS: When you and Tom Hayden had that conversation, did you notice the whereabouts of Irv Bock?

THE WITNESS: He was there. I mean, he was close by.

January 24, 1970

MR. WEINGLASS: Directing your attention to August 13, in the evening at approximately six o'clock, did you have occasion to speak with anyone?

THE WITNESS: I spoke with my attorney, Irving Birnbaum, by phone.

MR. WEINGLASS: Do you recall that conversation you had with him on the phone?

THE WITNESS: Yes. I said, "Irv, things are going very badly with permits. This morning the Park District met. I absolutely cannot understand it. Mr. Barry promised us it was going to be on the agenda and it was not even brought up in the meeting."

I said in addition to that, "Yesterday we had a meeting with David Stahl and Richard Elrod where all of the agency heads were supposed to attend, and none of them did." I said that "I feel, very frankly, that the Mayor is now using the permit issue as a kind of political device to scare people away." And I said, "Very frankly, he's being extremely effective."

I then asked Irv whether or not he thought it made sense to file sonic kind of lawsuit against the City and take this whole question of permits into the courts.

Irv then said that he thought that would be a practical proposal, that we should draw up a lawsuit against the City, that the City is using its administrative control over permits to deny fundamental First Amendment and Constitutional rights.

I then said to Irv that Mr. Elrod has been quite emphatic with me about the matter of sleeping in the parks beyond 11:00 p.m. "Do we have any legal basis," I said, "for staying in the parks beyond 11:00?"

Irv Birnbaum said that he thought that very definitely that should be included in the lawsuit because he said that parks were made available for the Boy Scouts and for National Guard troops beyond 11:00 p.m., and that under the Civil Rights Act of equal protection under the law, the same kind of facilities should be made available to American citizens, and he indicated that this should be put in the lawsuit.

MR. WEINGLASS: The following Sunday, which was August 18, do you recall where you were in the morning of that day?

THE WITNESS: Yes. In the morning I was at a union hall on Nobel Street. We were having a meeting of the steering committee of the Mobilization.

MR. WEINGLASS: Were there any other defendants present?

THE WITNESS: Yes. John Froines was present.

MR. WEINGLASS: Do you recall what John Froines said at that particular meeting?

THE WITNESS: I recall that John reported on our work with marshals. He said that we were well under way with training sessions in Lincoln Park.

He then went on to talk about some of the problems that we were having, concerns about police violence, the fact that we were going to have to be very mobile through this week if the police came in to break up demonstrations.

I think at one point he said, "We may have to be as mobile as a guerrilla, moving from place to place in order to avoid arrest and avoid police confrontation."

MR. WEINGLASS: Mr. Davis, directing your attention to Wednesday, August 21, at about 10:30 in the morning, do you recall where you were?

THE WITNESS: I was in this building, in Judge Lynch's chambers.

MR. WEINGLASS: Now, who went with you into the Judge's chambers?

THE WITNESS: An attorney, who was assisting the National Mobilization Committee, Stanley Bass. I believe that Richard Elrod was present, Ray Simon, the Corporation Counsel, was present. Judge Lynch, of course, and others.

MR. WEINGLASS: Could you relate to the Court and jury specific conversations in connection with that lawsuit?

THE WITNESS: Well, Mr. Simon proposed to the Mobilization a number of assembly areas for our consideration. He said he made these proposals rather than the one that we suggested because he thought it unreasonable of the Mobilization to insist on a State Street march, that this Would disrupt traffic too much.

I then told Mr. Simon that I thought these proposals were quite generous, and I was certain that on this matter we could reach an accommodation.

I said, "The problem with your proposal. Mr. Simon, is that it does not address itself to the fundamental issue for us, which is an assembly in the area of the Amphitheatre at the time of the Democratic nomination."

I went on to say that I would make two concrete proposals at this time. I said that it Would be satisfactory to our coalition to consider the area on Halsted Street from 39th on the north to 47th on the south.

I said if that was not acceptable to the City, that there's a large area just west of the parking lot, that would be suitable for our purposes, and I thought would not interfere with the delegates.

Mr. Simons then said that the area on Halsted from 39th on the north to 45th on the south was out of the question for consideration, that it was a security area, he said, and that it was not possible for the City to grant this area to the Mobilization.

He then said that the second area that I had proposed similarly was out of the question because I think he said it was controlled by the Democratic National Convention and the City had no authority to grant that space to the Mobilization.

Then I said, "Assuming both of these areas are just not available, could you, Mr. Simon, suggest an area that would be within eyeshot of the Amphitheatre for an assembly on the evening of the nomination?"

Mr. Simon then said he didn't see why we needed to have an assembly area within eyeshot or close to the Amphitheatre. He said that the City was willing to make other proposals for such an assembly, they would offer us Grant Park, they would offer us Lincoln Park, they would offer us Garfield Park on the west side of Chicago.

MR. WEINGLASS: Now, can you remember where you were in the afternoon of Friday, the twenty-third of August?

THE WITNESS: I think I was in the Mobilization office at that time.

MR. WEINGLASS: Did you receive a phone call at approximately that time in the office?

THE WITNESS: Yes, I did. It was my attorney, Mr. Birnbaum. He said to me that the had just received the opinion of Judge Lynch denying us a permit for an assembly and denying us the right to use parks beyond 11:00 p.m.

I then said, "We should appeal this matter immediately. We are in absolute crisis."

Then Mr. Birnbaum said that, in his professional opinion, no appeal would produce a permit in time for our activities during the week of the Convention, but that he was willing to draw up the papers for appeal for the purpose of preserving the record.

MR. WEINGLASS: I show you D-339 for identification, which is a photograph. Can you identify the persons in that photograph?

THE WITNESS: Myself, Tom Hayden and one of the police tails who followed me through much of the convention week, Ralph Bell.

MR. WEINGLASS: Do you recall when you first saw Mr. Bell, the police tail?

THE WITNESS: Well, on Friday after the phone call from Irv Birnbaum, I then walked out of the building, just to take a long walk alone and to think about what I personally was going to do during this week, and when I came back into the building, there were two men in sort of casual clothes who approached me at the elevator door and flashed badges, said they were policemen, and they were coming up to the office. I went back into the office and they waited outside, and I got Tom, and Tom and I then went back out to talk with them.

MR. WEINGLASS: Could you relate to the Court and jury the conversation that you and Tom Hayden had?

THE WITNESS: Well, one of the gentlemen just flashed his badge for the second time and said, "My name's Officer Bell. This here's Riggio. We're gonna be around you a lot, Davis, so we'll just be around you and going wherever you go from now until the

Convention's over," and I said, "Well, what's the purpose of this?"

And Bell said, "Well, the purpose is to give you protection," and I said, "Well, thank you very much, but I'd just as soon not have your protection."

And then Bell said, "Well, just pretend like you're President and got protection everywhere you go, day and night," and I said, "Well, what if I would request not to have this protection."

And then he said, "Motherfucker, you got the protection, and you try to shake me and you're in big trouble. Now, you cooperate, and we'll get along real fine, hear?"

And I said, "Yes, sir," and walked back into the office.

MR. WEINGLASS: I draw your attention to Monday, August 26, at approximately 2:30 in the afternoon of that day.

Do you recall where you were?

THE WITNESS: Well, that afternoon, Monday, I was in Lincoln Park.

MR. WEINGLASS: When Tom Hayden was arrested, were you at the scene of the arrest?

THE WITNESS: No, sir, I was not. I was in the park at the time, yes.

MR. WEINGLASS: Now, when did you first become aware of the fact that he had been arrested?

THE WITNESS: It was around 2:30. A number of people came to me and said that Tom Hayden and Wolfe Lowenthal had been arrested and I could see the people sort of were spontaneously coming together. Many people were talking about marching on to the police station in response to this arrest.

MR. WEINGLASS: And then after receiving that information, what did you do?

THE WITNESS: Well, I talked to a number of marshals about the urgency of getting on with this march and trying to see that it has direction and that our marshals are involved in this march. I was just sort of concerned that people not run out into the streets and down to the police station, so I got on the bullhorn and started to urge people to gather behind the sound for the march to the police station.

MR. WEINGLASS: Approximately how many people joined the march?

THE WITNESS: Well, my recollection is hazy--over a thousand people, I think, joined the march. I was marching about four or five rows from the front with the sound.

MR. WEINGLASS: Were any defendants in your company at that time?

THE WITNESS: Yes. John Froines was with me, really throughout the march that day.

MR. WEINGLASS: And was this march proceeding on the sidewalk, or was it in the roadway?

THE WITNESS: No, it was on the sidewalk, all the way across the sidewalk until a police officer requested that I urge people to stay on one half of the sidewalk.

MR. WEINGLASS: Now, as you were proceeding south on State Street, were you in the company of any officials of the city of Chicago?

THE WITNESS: Yes. I was in the company of two members of the Corporation Counsel, one of whom was Richard Elrod.

MR. WEINGLASS: As you approached the police station, did you have occasion to speak again to Mr. Elrod?

THE WITNESS: Yes. About a block away from the police station, I spoke with Mr. Elrod. I said, "Mr. Elrod, the police station is completely encircled with uniformed police officers. I'm attempting to move the people out of that area and move past the police station, but you've created a situation where we have to move demonstrators down a solid wall of policemen.

"All that has to happen is for one demonstrator to strike a policeman or for one policeman to be too anxious walking past that line, and we've got a full-scale riot on our hands. I'm just not moving this line until those policemen are taken back into that building." And at that point Mr. Elrod said well, he'd see what he Could do.

MR. WEINGLASS: Did you observe what Mr. Elrod did after that conversation?

THE WITNESS: I didn't see what he did, but minutes later the policemen in formation marched back into the police headquarters at 11th and State.

MR. WEINGLASS: After the police went back into the police headquarters building what did you do?

THE WITNESS: I urged people to march past the police station staying on the sidewalk, staying together, and I think we began to chant "Free Hayden." We continued then east on 11th Street toward Michigan Avenue, and north on the sidewalk on Michigan.

MR. WEINGLASS: As you were proceeding north, what, if anything, did you observe?

THE WITNESS: To the best of my recollection the march had stopped while we were waiting for the other participants to catch up and it was at that moment that some of the people in the demonstration just sort of broke Out of the line of march and ran up a hill. the top of which had the statue of General Jonathan Logan.

MR. WEINGLASS: At that time that the demonstrators broke from the line of march and ran up the hill, were you speaking on the microphone?

THE WITNESS: Not at the time that they broke, no. I had stopped and was waiting for the rest of the people to catch up.

MR. WEINGLASS: Were these people carrying anything in their hands?

THE WITNESS: Yes. They were carrying flags of all kinds, Viet Cong flags, red flags.

MR. WEINGLASS: After you saw them run tip the hill to the statue, what, if anything, did you do?

THE WITNESS: A police formation developed at the base of the hill and began to sweep upward toward the statue and at that point I yelled very loudly that people should leave the statue and go to the Conrad Hilton. I said a number of things very rapidly like, "We have liberated the statue, now we should go to the Conrad Hilton. The Conrad Hilton is the headquarters of the people who are responsible for the arrest. Let's leave the statue, let's liberate the Hilton," basically urging people to get away from the statue.

MR. FORAN: I object to the characterization of the words, your Honor.

THE COURT: The use of the word "urging"?

MR. FORAN: "Basically," from the word "basically," on, I move to strike.

THE COURT: Yes. I don't know precisely what it means.

Read the last answer to him. Try to use words that would satisfy the requirements of an answer to the question, Mr. Witness.

THE WITNESS: I can continue. As the police got right up on the demonstrators and began to club the people who were around the base of the statue, I then said as loudly as I could, "If the police want a riot, let them stay in this area, If the police don't want a riot, let them get out of this area."

MR. WEINGLASS: Did there come a time when you left the area?

THE WITNESS: Yes, I left--after I urged people to leave the area, I then left the area myself. I went back to the Mobilization office.

MR. WEINGLASS: Did you have occasion to meet with Tom Hayden that night?

THE WITNESS: Yes, I did. We went to several places and finally we went to the Conrad Hilton. I guess it was a little before midnight. Tom ran into some friends that he knew, a man named Mr. Alder, and some others. I think Jeff Cowan was present, people that I don't know very well.

And they were involved in various capacities in an official way with the Democratic

Convention, and they invited Tom to come into the Conrad Hilton to watch the Convention on television. So Tom and myself then accompanied them to the entrance on Balbo Street.

MR. WEINGLASS: Were they successful in getting Tom Hayden into the hotel?

THE WITNESS: No. They returned shortly after that, and Tom said we couldn't get in.

MR. WEINGLASS: Then what did you do?

THE WITNESS: I proceeded to walk across the intersection of Balbo, going north on Michigan. Tom Hayden was directly behind, and I guess I was about halfway across the street on Balbo when I heard someone veil very loudly, "Get him, get him " screaming from a distance, and I turned around and saw the policeman who had been following me through the Convention week, Ralph Bell, running very fast, directly at Tom, and he just charged across Michigan Avenue. Tom and I were sort of frozen in our places, and Bell grabbed Tom around the neck and just drove him to the street.

At that point a second police officer in uniform came from behind and grabbed Tom as well, and I believe he actually held the nightstick against Tom's neck. I then took a few steps towards Bell and Tom and this second police officer, and I yelled at Bell, "What do you think you're doing?"

And then this uniformed policeman took his nightclub and chopped me across the neck and then twice across the chest. Then my second police tail whom I hadn't seen at that point, suddenly had me by my shirt, dragged me across the intersection of Balbo and Michigan, and just threw me up against something. I think it was a lightpole. I remember just being smashed against something, and he said--his name was Riggio--he said, "What do you think you're doing, Davis?"

MR. WEINGLASS: Were you placed under arrest at that time?

THE WITNESS: No, I was not.

MR. WEINGLASS: Did you see what happened to Tom Hayden?

THE WITNESS: Tom was put into a paddy wagon, and taken away from the area.

MR. WEINGLASS: What did you do then?

THE WITNESS: Well, I stood still for a moment, just stunned, wandered around alone, then I ran into Paul Potter. Then Paul and I walked back to the office on Dearborn Street.

MR. WEINGLASS: Now, do you recall approximately what time of night you arrived at the office?

THE WITNESS: Well, frankly I don't think that I would recall except that Mr. Riggio when he testified in this trial, indicated the arrest was around midnight, and it's about a five- or ten-minute walk back to the office, so it must have been somewhere between 12:20, 12:30 in that area.

MR. WEINGLASS: When you got back to the office, what, if anything, did you do?

THE WITNESS: Well, I called our legal defense office and explained what had occurred. Then I made a few more phone calls, talked to some people in the office. Paul left the office, and shortly after Paul left, I got in a car and drove towards Lincoln Park.

MR. WEINGLASS: Now, do you recall any of the persons who were in the office at the time you have just indicated?

THE WITNESS: Well, Paul and Carrol Glassman were both in the office, and Jeff Gerth. As a matter of fact, I think it was Jeff Gerth who drove me to Lincoln Park.

MR. WEINGLASS: Now, do you know what time it was that you left the office?

THE WITNESS: Close to one o'clock.

MR. WEINGLASS: Now, when you arrived at Lincoln Park, did you go to the park?

THE WITNESS: No, I did not go into the park. I drove past the park and into the Old Town area, and there I saw Vern Grizzard. I got out of the car and talked to Vernon for a couple of minutes and then Vernon and I got back into the car and we then left the area.

MR. WEINGLASS: Now, approximately twenty-four hours later, very late Tuesday night, do you recall where you were at that time?

THE WITNESS: Well, late Tuesday night I was in Grant Park directly across from the Conrad Hilton Hotel.

MR. WEINGLASS: Now, at 4:00 a.m., were you still in the park?

THE WITNESS: Yes. Yes, I was there certainly up till four o'clock.

MR. WEINGLASS: Did you have occasion at that time to see any of the defendants?

THE WITNESS: Yes, I met with Tom Hayden.

MR. WEINGLASS: Can you describe Tom Hayden's appearance at that time?

THE WITNESS: Well, Tom had a ridiculous hat, and he was sort of dressed in mod clothing. I think he had a fake goatee, as I recall, and for a while he was carrying a handkerchief across his nose and mouth.

I said, "Tom, you look like a fool."

MR. WEINGLASS: Did you and Tom have a conversation after that?

THE WITNESS: Yes. Yes, we did. I said to Tom that I was concerned about the lateness of the hour, I was concerned that television and cameras and photographers and newsmen were now leaving the area; the crowd was thinning out.

I said that this is the kind Of Situation which could lead to problems, and I told Tom that I thought that someone should make an announcement that this has been a great victory. that we're able to survive tinder these incredibly difficult conditions, and that people should now be encouraged to leave the park, and return tomorrow morning. Tom then agreed to make that announcement.

MR. WEINGLASS: The following morning, Wednesday, August 28, do you recall where you were?

THE WITNESS: Wednesday morning before Grant Park I was in the Mobilization office. Fifteen people, something like that, were having a meeting.

MR. WEINGLASS: Do you recall who was present at that meeting?

THE WITNESS: I recall that both Tom and Dave Dellinger were present. Linda Morse I think was there.

MR. WEINGLASS: Will You relate to the Court and jury what the defendants said while they were there, including yourself?

THE WITNESS: Dave said that he thought after the rally in Grant Park the most important thing to do was to continue with our plan to march to the Amphitheatre.

Tom said that there is no possibility of going to the Amphitheatre.

Dave said that the City, even though it has not granted permits, has allowed us to have other marches, and that perhaps they will allow us to go to the Amphitheatre.

Tom insisted that we were not going to the Amphitheatre.

Then David said that he felt that even if the police did not allow us to march, that it was absolutely necessary that we assemble, we line up, and we prepare to go to the Amphitheatre. Dave said that if the police indicate that they are going to prevent this march by force, that we have to at that time say to the world that there are Americans who will not submit to a police state by default; that they are prepared to risk arrest and be taken away to jail rather than to submit to the kind of brutality that we had seen all through the week.

Tom said that he agreed that there were people coming who intended to march, but he said as well there are many people who are not prepared to be arrested and he thought that we needed now to suggest another activity for Wednesday afternoon and evening for those people who were not prepared to he arrested.

Dave said he agreed that those people who were unprepared to be arrested should be encouraged to leave the park and return to the hotels as we had the night before.

I then said that I thought that we needed as well to announce that those people who do not want to participate in either activity should simply stay in the park or go home.

Everyone agreed with that and Dave then said that this should be announced from the platform, these three positions, and that I should inform the marshals of these three positions.

MR. WEINGLASS: Now, directing your attention to approximately 2:30 in the afternoon of that same day, do you recall where you were at that time?

THE WITNESS: Yes, I was in Grant Park just south of the refreshment stand. I saw a commotion near the flagpole and shortly after that I heard Dave Dellinger's voice. It was clear that something was happening and Dave indicated that he wanted marshals to move to the flagpole, so I then said to everyone there that we should go toward the flagpole.

MR. WEINGLASS: When you went to the flagpole, did you have anything in your hands?

THE WITNESS: I had a speaker system with a microphone.

MR. WEINGLASS: As you arrived in the vicinity of the flagpole, what was occurring?

THE WITNESS: The flag had been lowered to halfmast and the police were dragging a young man out of the area. The police seemed to be withdrawing from the area as I arrived, and a lot of people who were gathered around the flagpole began to throw anything they could get their hands on at the police who were withdrawing from the crowd. They threw rocks and boards and lunches and anything that was available right on the ground.

MR. WEINGLASS: What were you saying, if anything, at that time on the microphone?

THE WITNESS: I kept directing the marshals to form a line, link arms, and then I constantly urged the people in the crowd to stop throwing things. I said, "You're throwing things at our own people. Move back."

As our marshal line grew, I urged our marshal line to now begin to move back and move the demonstrators away from the police.

MR. WEINGLASS: Where did you go?

THE WITNESS: I continued to stand in front of the marshal line that had been formed.

MR. WEINGLASS: What did you then observe happen?

THE WITNESS: Well, at that time another squadron of policemen in formation began to advance towards my position.

I was standing in front of our marshal line sort of sandwiched in between our marshal line and the advancing police formation.

MR. WEINGLASS: What were you doing as the police were advancing?

THE WITNESS: Well, as the police advanced, I continued to have my back to the police line, basically concerned that the marshal line not break or move. Then the police formation broke and began to run, and at that time I heard several of the men in the line yell, quite distinctly, "Kill Davis! Kill Davis!" and they were screaming that and the police moved on top of me, and I was trapped between my own marshal line and advancing police line.

The first thing that occurred to me was a very powerful blow to the head that drove me face first down into the dirt, and then, as I attempted to crawl on my hands and knees, the policemen continued to yell, "Kill Davis! Kill Davis!" and continued to strike me across the ear and the neck and the back.

I guess I must have been hit thirty or forty times in the back and I crawled for maybe –I don't know how many feet, ten feet maybe, and I came to a chain fence and somehow I managed to crawl either under or through that fence, and a police fell over the fence, trying to get me, and another police hit the fence with his nightstick, but I had about a second or two in which I could stand and I leaped over a bench and over some people and into the park, and then I proceeded to walk toward the center of the park.

MR. WEINGLASS: As you walked toward the center of the park, what, if anything, happened?

THE WITNESS: Well, I guess the first thing that I was conscious of, I looked down, and my tie was just solid blood, and I realized that my shirt was just becoming blood, and someone took my arm and took me to the east side of the Bandshell, and I laid down, and there was a white coat who was bent over me. I remember hearing the voice of Carl Oglesby. Carl said, "In order to survive in this country, we have to fight," and then--then I lost consciousness.

MR. WEINGLASS: I have completed my direct examination.

THE COURT: Is there any cross-examination of this witness?

MR. FORAN: Mr. Davis, could you tel me what you consider conventional forms of protest?

THE WITNESS: Writing, speaking, marching, assembling, acting on your deepest moral and political convictions, especially when the authority that you--

MR. FORAN: I mean methods. You were going along fine.

THE WITNESS: Well, conventional activity would include those forms and others.

MR. FORAN: All right. And do you support those forms of protest or do you like other forms of protest?

THE WITNESS: It depends on what the issue is.

MR. FORAN: Haven't you stated in the past that you opposed the tendency to conventional forms of protest instead of militant action in connection with Chicago?

THE WITNESS: Well, it really depends at what time that was.

MR. FORAN: Well, in March, say.

MR. WEINGLASS: If he is referring to a prior writing, I would like him to identify it so we may follow it.

MR. FORAN: There is no necessity for me to do that, your Honor.

THE COURT: No, no necessity for that. I order the witness to answer the question if he can. If he can't he may say he cannot and I will excuse him.

Now read the question again to the witness.

THE WITNESS: I understand the question. Maybe if Mr. Foran could define for me what he means by the word "militant," because we may have different views about that word.

THE COURT: There is no necessity for defining words.

THE WITNESS: I would like very much to answer your question, Mr. Foran, but I am afraid that your view of militant and mine are very different, so I cannot answer that question as you phrased it.

THE COURT: He said he cannot answer the question, Mr. Foran. Therefore I excuse him from answering the question.

MR. FORAN: Did you tell that meeting at Lake Villa that the summer of '68 should be capped by a week of demonstrations, disruptions, and marches at the Democratic National Convention clogging the streets of Chicago?

THE WITNESS: Well, I certainly might have said "clogging the streets of Chicago."

MR. FORAN: Did you tell them at that meeting what I just said to you?

THE WITNESS: Well. I may have.

MR. FORAN: Did you ever write a document with Tom Hayden called "Discussions on the Democratic Challenge?"

THE WITNESS: Yes, I recall this. This was written very early.

MR. FORAN: When did you write it?

THE WITNESS: I think we wrote that document around January 15.

MR. FORAN: Have you ever said that "Countless creative activities must be employed that will force the President to use troops to secure his nomination?" Have you ever stated that?

THE WITNESS: That's possible.

MR. FORAN: But in January, in your little document that you and Hayden wrote together, that's what you said you were going to do, wasn't it?

THE WITNESS: Well, you've taken it out of context. I would be happy to explain the whole idea.

MR. FORAN: And it was your intention that you wanted to have trouble start so that the National Guard would have to be called out to protect the delegates, wasn't it?

THE WITNESS: No, it was not.

MR. FORAN: You've stated that, haven't you?

THE WITNESS: No. We thought it might be possible the troops would be brought into the city to protect the Convention from its own citizens, it would be another--

MR. FORAN: From the citizens that were outside waiting to pin the delegates in, is that correct?

THE WITNESS: No. It's not correct.

MR. FORAN: On August 2 you met Stahl for breakfast over at the coffee house and you told him that this was an incendiary situation and that you'd rather die right here in Chicago than in Vietnam, didn't you?

THE WITNESS: No, Mr. Foran. I don't want to die in Chicago or Vietnam.

MR. FORAN: Then you saw Stahl again on August 10, that time at the coffee shop on Monroe Street?

THE WITNESS: Yes, that's right.

MR. FORAN: And you told Stahl that you had housing for 30,000 people, didn't you?

THE WITNESS: That's right.

MR. FORAN: And you told Stahl that you expected at least another 70,000 people to come, and they wouldn't have any place to go, so they had to sleep in the park.

THE WITNESS: I think that I did.

MR. FORAN: And Stahl told you about the park ordinance again, didn't he, reminded you of it, that they couldn't sleep overnight in the park? He also told you about the Secret Service security requirements at the Amphitheater, didn't he, at the August 10 meeting?

THE WITNESS: No, no, absolutely not. On the contrary, there was no indication of a security area until August 21.

MR. FORAN: You told the City that you had to be able to march to the Amphitheatre, didn't you?

THE WITNESS: Well, I told the City that we would assemble in any area that was in proximity to the Amphitheatre.

MR. FORAN: That the terminal point of march had to be the Amphitheatre, didn't you say that?

THE WITNESS: No, I never said that. I talked about eyeshot or being near the Amphitheatre.

MR. FORAN: By the way, you people got permits at the Pentagon, didn't you?

THE WITNESS: Yes, permits were granted for the demonstration at the Pentagon.

January 26, 1970

MR. FORAN: And the Mobilization had planned or some people in it had planned civil disobedience at the Pentagon, isn't that right?

THE WITNESS: What do you mean by civil disobedience?

MR. FORAN: In fact, at the Pentagon, you planned both an active confrontation with the warmakers and the engagement of civil disobedience, didn't you?

THE WITNESS: Well, if 150,000 people gathered in assembly is regarded as an active confrontation, as I regard it, the answer, of course, is yes.

MR. FORAN: Isn't it a fact that on the August 12 meeting with Stahl that you told him that during Convention week the demonstrators were going to participate in civil disobedience? Isn't that a fact?

THE WITNESS: No. May I say what I said?

MR. FORAN: Isn't it a fact that you had found that that was a very successful tactic at the Pentagon?

THE WITNESS: No, I believe that Dave Dellinger said that that was a tactic we did not want to use in Chicago. We had one tactic for the Pentagon and another view for Chicago.

MR. FORAN: Isn't it a fact that that tactic, a permit on the one hand and active confrontation combined with civil disobedience on the other hand, gives the movement an opportunity to get both conventional protest groups and active resistance groups to come together in the demonstration? You have heard Dellinger say that, haven't you?

THE WITNESS: No, he never used those words for Chicago, Mr. Foran. What he always said--

MR. FORAN: Did he say it in connection with the Pentagon?

THE WITNESS: Oh, for the Pentagon? There was no doubt there was a conception for civil disobedience which was wholly different from what we wanted to do in Chicago. Can't you understand? It is so simple. The Pentagon was one thing, Chicago was another thing.

MR. FORAN: I know you would like to explain away what happened in Chicago very much, Mr. Davis, but you also have to take into consideration what happened at the Pentagon was the blueprint for Chicago and you know it.

MR. DELLINGER: You are a liar.

MR. KUNSTLER: Your Honor, every time we try to get one of our witnesses to talk about the Pentagon, who was the quickest on his feet to say "That is outside the scope, you can't go into that--

MR. FORAN:, Not on cross-examination it isn't outside the scope

Isn't it a fact that Mr. Dellinger said that the Mobilization at the Pentagon can have its maximum impact when it combines massive action with the cutting edge of resistance? Didn't he say that?

THE WITNESS: What do you mean "cutting edge of resistance?"

MR. FORAN: Did Mr. Dellinger ever say that?

THE WITNESS: Well, I never heard him use those words.

MR. FORAN: In substance did you hear him say it? In substance?

THE WITNESS: Yes, all right.

MR. FORAN: Isn't it a fact that your plan both at the Pentagon and in Chicago was to combine, in Dellinger's words, the peacefulness of Gandhi and the violence of active resistance? Isn't that a fact?

THE WITNESS:. No, that is not a fact. In fact, that is not even close.

MR. FORAN: May that be stricken, your Honor?

THE COURT: "In fact, that is not even close," those words may go out and the jury is directed to disregard them.

MR. FORAN: You testified on direct examination that on February 11, 1969, you gave a talk at 407 South Dearborn, didn't you?

THE WITNESS: Yes, sir.

MR. FORAN: Very good.

THE WITNESS: Thank you.

MR. FORAN: In the course of that talk you said on direct examination that "there may be people in this room who do believe that the Democratic Convention which is responsible for the war should be physically disrupted."

THE WITNESS: Yes.

MR. FORAN: Isn't it a fact that among the people in that room at 407 South Dearborn who did believe that the Democratic National Convention should be physically disrupted and torn apart were you and Hayden? Isn't that a fact?

THE WITNESS: No, it is not a fact. If you will read my testimony, you will see that--

MR. FORAN: You and Hayden had written--

THE WITNESS: Yes. Now if you will put that document before the jury.

MR. FORAN: –a "Discussion on the Democratic Convention Challenge," hadn't you?

THE WITNESS: We wrote a paper in January that was substantially revised by that very meeting, sir.

THE WITNESS: So you changed your mind between January 15 and February 11, is that your testimony?

THE WITNESS: We did not change our mind. We dropped some of the language that Dave Dellinger criticized as inappropriate, confusing--I think he said the word "disruption" was irresponsible.

MR. FORAN: In addition to you and Hayden, isn't it a fact that another person in that room who wanted to physically disrupt that National Democratic Convention was Dave Dellinger? Isn't that a fact?

THE WITNESS: Your questions embarrass me, they are so terrible. They really do.

MR. FORAN: Well, answer it.

THE WITNESS: The answer is no.

MR. FORAN: Isn't it a fact that Dellinger ran the show at the Pentagon? Isn't that a fact?

THE WITNESS: Sir, our movement doesn't work that way with one man running the show, as you say. It is a movement of thousands of people who participate each year.

MR. FORAN: You said that the Yippies wanted a gigantic festival in the park in Chicago to show the contrast between your culture and the death-producing culture of the Democratic Convention. Did you so testify?

THE WITNESS: I think I said "the death-producing ritual of the Democratic Convention."

MR. FORAN: Isn't it a fact that all the vile and vulgar propaganda the Yippies were passing out was for the purpose of making the City delay on the permit, and to make the authorities look repressive?

THE WITNESS: Sir, no one had to make the City look repressive. The City was repressive.

MR. FORAN: Isn't it a fact that that vile and vulgar advertising along with all of the talk about a rock festival was for the purpose of attracting the guerrilla active resistance types to your protest?

THE WITNESS: No, sir.

MR. FORAN: And the purpose of the permit negotiations was to attract people who believed in more conventional forms of protest, wasn't it?

THE WITNESS: The purpose of the permits was to allow us to have a legal assembly.

MR. FORAN: That is exactly what you had done at the Pentagon, wasn't it, the synthesis of Gandhi and guerrilla, isn't that what you did at the Pentagon?

THE WITNESS: No.

MR. FORAN: Mr. Davis, you testified that you had young Mark Simons request the use of various park facilities for meeting and for sleeping back around the thirty-first of July, isn't that correct?

THE WITNESS: Yes.

MR. FORAN: Now, isn't it a fact that you were always told by every city official that the 11:00 p.m. curfew in the parks would not be waived, isn't that a fact? Stahl told you that again on August 2, didn't he?

THE WITNESS: Not that emphatically.

MR. FORAN: He told you there was an 11:00 p.m. curfew that did not permit sleeping in the parks, did he say that?

THE WITNESS: But in the context at that time it would be waived, as it was waived all the time for the Boy Scouts and the National Guard troops.

MR. FORAN: Well, You didn't consider the Yippies Boy Scouts, did you?

THE WITNESS: Well, I considered that under the Civil Rights Act that American citizens have equal protection of the law.

MR. FORAN: You think that the Yippies with what they were advertising they were going to do in Lincoln Park are the same as the Boy Scouts? Is that what you are saving?

THE WITNESS: Well, as someone who has been very active in the Boy Scouts during all of his young life, I considered--

MR. FORAN: Did you ever see the Boy Scouts advertise public fornication, for heaven's sake?

THE WITNESS: The Yippies talked about a festival of Life and love and--

MR. FORAN: They also talked about public fornication and about drug use and about nude-ins on the beach? They also talked about that, didn't they?

THE WITNESS: They talked about love, yes, sir.

MR. FORAN: You and I have a little different feeling about love, I guess, Mr. Davis.

Now, isn't it a fact that the continuous demands for sleeping in the park were just for the purpose of again making the authorities appear repressive, isn't that a fact?

THE WITNESS: Oh, no. We wanted Soldiers Field as a substitute, or any facility. I indicated to the superintendent that we would take any facilities that could possibly be made available to get around this ordinance problem.

MR. FORAN: Now, in Judge Lynch's chambers, Raymond Simon proposed four different march routes as alternatives to your proposed march routes, didn't he?

THE WITNESS: Surely.

MR. FORAN: And you told him that while they appeared reasonable for daytime demonstrations, they were completely unacceptable to your coalition because there was no consideration of an assembly at the Amphitheater?

THE WITNESS: Yes, sir, I did.

MR. FORAN: Did you accept any of these proposals of the four routes of march?

THE WITNESS: Yes. Well, we accepted the proposal to assemble in Grant Park at 1:00 to 4:00 p.m.

MR. FORAN: And no other proposals were accepted, is that correct?

THE WITNESS: No other proposals were made.

MR. FORAN: Other proposals that Mr. Simon had made to you, you rejected, did you not? You rejected them saying that you wanted to assemble at the Amphitheatre?

THE WITNESS: They were absurd proposals. People everywhere understood why young people were coming to Chicago: to go to the Convention.

MR. FORAN: After all of these meetings, the cause was argued?

THE WITNESS: On August 22, yes, sir.

MR. FORAN: And it was dismissed on the next day, August 23, is that right?

THE WITNESS: That's right, by the former law partner of Mayor Daley.

MR. FORAN: We can strike that statement.

THE COURT: I strike the remark of the witness from the record, and direct the jury to disregard it.

MR. FORAN: Was a motion to disqualify the judge made by your attorneys in this case?

THE WITNESS: No, it was not.

MR. FORAN: Did you instruct them to do so?

THE WITNESS: We discussed it as to whether or not we could get a fair shake from a former law partner of Mayor Daley, and we decided all of the judges were essentially the same, and that most of them are appointed by Daley.

MR. FORAN: So you thought all eleven judges in this district were appointed by Mayor Daley?

THE WITNESS: Not all eleven judges were sitting at that time. We thought that the court might be a face-saving device for the mayor. A mayor who didn't politically want to give permits might allow the courts to give permits. That is why we went into court.

THE COURT: Did you say all of the judges were appointed by Mayor Daley? Does he have the power to appoint judges?

THE WITNESS: No, I think that I indicated that they were all sort of very influenced and directed by the Mayor of the city of Chicago. There is a lot of feeling about it in the city.

There is a lot of feeling of that in this city, Judge Hoffman. You can't really separate the courts from the Daley machine in this town.

THE COURT: Did you know that I was just about the first judge nominated on this bench by President Eisenhower in early 1953?

THE WITNESS: I do know. I understand that. You are a Republican judge.

THE COURT: I am not a Republican judge; I am a judge of all the people. I happen to be appointed by President Eisenhower in the spring of 1953.

THE WITNESS: Yes, sir, I know that.

THE COURT: So do you want to correct your statement about Mayor Daley? If Mayor Daley had his way, he wouldn't have had me. I just want to reassure you if you feel that I am here because of Mayor Daley, I am not really.

THE WITNESS: I see.

THE COURT: Mayor Daley, as far as I am concerned, and so I am told, is a good mayor. I don't think I have ever spoken three sentences to him other than--I don't know whether I spoke to him when he was on the stand here or not. Perhaps I did direct him to answer some questions, I don't know.

MR. FORAN: When you were talking to Judge Lynch, you knew that you were going to have your people stay in the park with or without a permit, didn't you, and you didn't tell the judge that, did you?

THE WITNESS: I told the judge that we wanted to avoid violence and that was the most important thing possible.

MR. FORAN: If you wanted to avoid violence so much, did you tell the people out in the ballfield across the Balbo bridge from the Hilton Hotel that you had 30,000 housing units available and if you don't want trouble in the park, why don't you come take advantage of our housing? Did you say that in Grant Park that day?

THE WITNESS: Mr. Foran, we didn't come to Chicago to sleep.

MR. FORAN: Did you say that? Did you tell those people when you were telling them to go back to Lincoln Park that night for the Yippie Festival, did you tell them, "Don't stay in the park tonight, it might cause trouble. We have got plenty of housing available"? Did you tell them that?

THE WITNESS: We made constant references to the availability of housing through our *Ramparts* wall posters, through announcements at the movement centers. We communicated very well--

MR. FORAN: Your Honor, may I have that stricken'?

THE WITNESS: --that housing was available.

MR. FORAN: Well, as you were leaving that crowd from Lincoln Park, did you ever announce over that bullhorn, "Now look, we don't want any trouble in the park tonight, so any of you people who don't have housing, just let us know. We have thirty thousand housing units available"?

Did you announce that over the bullhorn while you were conducting that march?

THE WITNESS: On that occasion, no. We had other concerns, namely the arrest of Tom Hayden and Wolfe Lowenthal. But we did make constant announcements about--

MR. FORAN: You heard Oklepek testify, did you not, and it is a fact, isn't it, that at the August 9 meeting if the demonstrators were driven from the park, they ought to move out into the Loop and tie it up and bust it up, and you told the people that at that August 9 meeting, didn't you?

THE WITNESS: That is very close, very close. What I said was that they will drive people out of the parks and people will go into the Loop.

MR. FORAN: Your Honor--

THE COURT: The answer is not responsive. Therefore I must strike it.

THE WITNESS: I heard Mr. Oklepek testify to that but it is not a fact. There was something said that he--

MR. FORAN: You did tell people at that time at that meeting that if the police kept the demonstrators in the park and they couldn't get out, that you had an easy solution for it, just riot. That's what you said, didn't you?

THE WITNESS: I have never in all my life said that to riot was an easy solution to anything, ever.

MR. FORAN: And you sat here in this courtroom and you heard Officer Bock and Dwayne Oklepek and Officer Frapolly testify to all of these things, didn't you?

THE WITNESS: I listened to your spies testify about us, yes, sir, and it was a disgrace to me.

MR. FORAN: And isn't it a fact that you structured your testimony sitting at that table--

THE WITNESS: The answer is no.

MR. FORAN: --on direct examination to appear similar to the testimony of the Government's witnesses but to differ in small essentials because you wanted to lend credibility to your testimony? That is a fact, isn't it?

THE WITNESS: It is not a fact and you know it.

MR. FORAN: May we strike that, your Honor. He whispered to the court reporter "and you know it."

THE COURT: Is that what you told the reporter at the end of your answer to the question?

THE WITNESS: No, I made that man to man to Mr. Foran.

MR. FORAN: Your Honor, a lawyer in court is unable to comment on his personal opinions concerning a witness and because of that reason I ask the jury be instructed to disregard Mr. Davis' comment because I cannot properly respond to it.

THE COURT: "And you know it," to Mr. Foran, words to that effect may go out, and the jury is directed to disregard them.

THE WITNESS: I hope after this trial you can properly respond, Mr. Foran. I really do. I hope we have that chance.

MR. FORAN: I don't know what he is--what are you--

THE WITNESS: That you and I can sit down and talk about what happened in Chicago and why it happened.

THE COURT: Mr. Witness--

THE WITNESS: I would like to do that very much.

THE COURT: Mr. Witness--

MR. FORAN: Your Honor--

THE COURT: Do you hear me, sir?

THE WITNESS: Yes, I do.

THE COURT: You didn't--

THE WITNESS: I am sorry.

THE COURT: You paid no attention to me.

I direct you not to make any volunteered observations. I have made this order several times during your testimony.

THE WITNESS: I apologize.

THE COURT: I do not accept your apology, sir.

January 27, 1970

MR. FORAN: You and your people wanted to have violence in Lincoln Park, didn't you?

THE WITNESS: No, sir. We wanted to avoid violence.

MR. FORAN: You wanted it for one purpose. You wanted it for the purpose of discrediting the Government of the United States, isn't that correct?

THE WITNESS: I wanted to discredit the Government's policies by bringing a half million Americans to Chicago at the time of the Convention.

MR. FORAN: Have you ever said that you came to Chicago to display a growing militant defiance of the authority of the government?

THE WITNESS: I don't recall saying that.

MR. FORAN: Could you have said it?

THE WITNESS: Well, that would be out of context. I would talk about the war. I would talk about racism.

MR. FORAN: Have you ever said it in context or out of context?

THE WITNESS: But the context is all-important, don't you see? It is most important.

MR. FORAN: Not in a statement like that. Have you ever said that?

THE WITNESS: Show me the document.

MR. FORAN: I am asking you a question. I want you to tell me.

THE WITNESS: I don't recall ever saying that.

MR. FORAN: And you wanted violence at the International Amphitheatre also, didn't you?

THE WITNESS: Just the opposite.

MR. FORAN: Isn't it a fact that you wanted violence in order to impose an international humiliation on the people who ruled this country? Isn't that a fact?

THE WITNESS: It is my belief that it was you wanted the violence, Mr. Foran, not me.

MR. FORAN: Your Honor, may that be stricken, and may I have the question answered?

THE COURT: Certainly, the statement may go out. The witness is directed to be careful about his answers. Please read the question for the witness.

(question read)

THE WITNESS: I did not want violence, Mr. Foran.

MR. FORAN: You did want to impose an international humiliation on the people who ruled this country, isn't that correct?

THE WITNESS: I am afraid that our government has already humiliated itself in the world community, sir.

MR. FORAN: Now, you had another alternative to the march to the Amphitheatre, didn't you?

THE WITNESS: Yes, sir.

MR. FORAN: And that was for people who didn't want to march to drift away in small groups from the Bandshell and return to the hotel areas in the Loop.

THE WITNESS: That is right.

MR. FORAN: And it was planned, wasn't it, that they were to come back to the Hilton Hotel in force and cause a violent confrontation with the police, wasn't it?

THE WITNESS: No, of course not.

MR. FORAN: Was the objective of the second alternative to paralyze the "magnificent mile" of Michigan Avenue?

THE WITNESS: No, that is a Government theory, a Government theory to try to figure out and explain away what happened in Chicago.

MR. FORAN: You have actually stated, haven't you, that all of those things I have been asking you about were the things that you accomplished in Chicago, haven't you?

THE WITNESS: You mean violent confrontations and tearing up the city and--

MR. FORAN: That the purpose of your meeting in Chicago was to impose an international humiliation on the people who rule this country, to display a growing militant defiance of the authority of the Government, to paralyze the "magnificent mile" of Michigan Avenue. You have said all of those things, haven't you, that that was your purpose in coming to Chicago and that you achieved it?

THE WITNESS: No, I never indicated that that was our purpose in coming to Chicago.

MR. FORAN: Did you ever write a document, coauthor one with Tom Hayden, called "Politics After Chicago?"

THE WITNESS: I may have.

MR. FORAN: I show you Government's Exhibit No. 104 for identification and ask you if that is a copy of it.

THE WITNESS: Yes. You have butchered the context, just as I suspected.

MR. FORAN: Now, have you and Mr. Hayden stated in this "Politics After Chicago" that since the institutions of this country cannot be changed from within, the people will take to the streets? Have you stated that?

THE WITNESS: Yes. I wish you would read the whole context.

MR. FORAN: You have stated that, have you not?

THE WITNESS: Yes.

MR. FORAN: You have stated "We learned in Chicago what it means to declare that the streets belong to the people."

THE WITNESS: Yes.

MR. FORAN: Did you state that the battle line is no longer drawn in the obscure paddies of Vietnam or the dim ghetto streets, but is coming closer to suburban sanctuaries and corporate board rooms? The gas that fell on us in Chicago also fell on Hubert? The street that was paralyzed was the "magnificent mile" of Michigan Avenue?

THE WITNESS: Yes. That is quite different from what you said before.

MR. FORAN: Did you state this:

"Our strategic purpose is two-fold: To display a growing militant defiance of the authority of the Government."

Did you state that?

THE WITNESS: It is possible. Read the whole document.

MR. FORAN: You stated that, didn't you?

THE WITNESS: Why don't you read the whole document or give it to the jury?

MR. FORAN: You have stated that your program is to discredit the authority of the Government which is deaf to its own system and railroad an election through America as if Vietnam were the caboose?

THE WITNESS: Boy, that's right on.

MR. FORAN: You stated that, did you not, that you wanted to discredit the authority of a Government which is deaf to its own citizens?

THE WITNESS: Well, I embrace those words. I don't know if I said them, but those words are just right.

MR. FORAN: And you believe that you won what you called the Battle of Chicago, don't you?

THE WITNESS: What do you mean by the Battle of Chicago?

MR. FORAN: Have you ever called what occurred in Chicago during the Convention the Battle of Chicago?

THE WITNESS: Yes, and I have defined it and I wonder if you would let me define it here. I will be happy to answer the question.

MR. FORAN: Have you ever stated in the words that I have asked you, "We won the Battle of Chicago"? Have you ever said that in any context?

THE WITNESS: You are not interested in the context, I suppose.

MR. FORAN: In any context, Mr. Davis.

THE WITNESS: Yes, I believe we won the battle in Chicago.

MR. FORAN: That you--it was your--your program would include press conferences, disruptions and pickets dramatizing whatever demands you wanted?

THE WITNESS: May I see the context so we can clarify it?

MR. FORAN: I show you Government's Exhibit No. 99. It starts at the top.

THE WITNESS: Yes. I was right.

MR. FORAN: Now, you feel that the Battle of Chicago continues, don't you?

THE WITNESS: Yes, I believe that contest that will shape the political character in the next decade was really shaped in Chicago in the context between the Daleys and the Nixons, and the Hayakawas, and the Reagans and the young people who expressed their hopes in the streets in Chicago. And I think, frankly, in that context, it is going to be clear it is not the Daleys, or the Humphreys, or the Johnsons who are the future of this country. We are the future of this country.

MR. FORAN: Isn't it a fact that you have said, Mr. Davis, that the Battle of Chicago continues today. The war is on. The reason we are here tonight is to try to figure out how we are going to get the kind of mutiny that Company A started in South Vietnam and spread it to every army base, every high school, every community in this country. That is what you said about the Battle of Chicago continuing today, isn't it?

THE WITNESS: Young people in South Vietnam--

MR. FORAN: Haven't you said just exactly what I read to you, sir?

MR. WEINGLASS: Your Honor, could we have the date of that statement?

THE COURT: Certainly, if you have the date, give it to him.

THE WITNESS: August 28, 1969.

MR. FORAN: On the one year anniversary of what happened on Wednesday, August 28, 1968?

THE WITNESS: A year after the Convention.

MR. FORAN: Isn't it a fact that you have said, "If we go about our own work, and if we make it clear that there can be no peace in the United States until every soldier is brought out of Vietnam and this imperialistic system is destroyed." Have you said that?

THE WITNESS: I don't recall those exact words, but those certainly are my sentiments, that we should not rest until this war is over and until the system--

MR. FORAN: And until this imperialistic system is destroyed?

THE WITNESS: Until the system that made that war is changed, the foreign policy

MR. FORAN: The way you decided to continue the Battle of Chicago, the way you decided to fight the Battle of Chicago, was by incitement to riot, wasn't it?

THE WITNESS: No, sir, by organizing, by organizing within the army, within high schools, within factories and communities across this country.

MR. FORAN: By inciting to riot within high schools, and within colleges, and within factories, and within the army, isn't that right, sir?

THE WITNESS: No. No, sir. No, I am trying to find a way that this generation can make this country something better than what it has been.

MR. FORAN: Your Honor, he is no longer responding to the question.

THE COURT: I strike the answer of the witness and direct the jury to disregard it.

MR. FORAN: And what you want to urge young people to do is to revolt, isn't that right?

THE WITNESS: Yes, revolt.

MR. FORAN: And you have stated, have you not, "That there can be no question by the time that I am through that I have every intention of urging that you revolt, that you join the Movement, that you become a part of a growing force for insurrection in the United States'") You have said that, haven't you?

THE WITNESS: I was standing right next to Fred Hampton when I said that, who was murdered in this city by policemen.

MR. FORAN: Your Honor, I move to strike that.

THE COURT: Yes, the answer may certainly go out. The question is wholly unrelated to one Fred Hampton.

MR. FORAN: Wouldn't it be wonderful, your Honor, if the United States accused people of murder as these people do without proof, without trial, and without any kind of evidence having been presented in any kind of a decent situation

MR. KUNSTLER: A man is murdered in his bed, while he is sleeping, by the police.

MR. FORAN: With nineteen guns there.

THE COURT: I am trying this case. I will ask you, Mr. Kunstler, to make no reference to that case because it is not in issue here.

MR. FORAN: In Downers Grove on August 30, you told all of the people out there, "We have won America." Didn't you tell them that? Didn't you tell them that?

THE WITNESS: I believe that I said--

MR. FORAN: Didn't you say that to them out at Downers Grove, sir?

THE WITNESS: Yes, sir, I did.

MR. FORAN: I have no further cross-examination.

THE COURT: Redirect examination.

MR. WEINGLASS: Redirect is unnecessary, your Honor.

Jesse Jackson's Testimony (minister)

MR. KUNSTLER: Would you state your full name?

THE WITNESS: Jesse Louis Jackson.

MR. KUNSTLER: Mr. Jackson, what is your position?

THE WITNESS: I am a Christian minister employed by the Southern Christian Leadership Conference.

MR. KUNSTLER: Reverend Jackson, in what capacity are you employed by the Southern Christian Leadership Conference?

THE WITNESS: As director of its economic arm, Operation Breadbasket.

MR. KUNSTLER: Could you state for the jury what Operation Breadbasket is?

THE WITNESS: Operation Breadbasket is an economic movement that is designed to be the antidote to the racist domination of our black community by engaging in boycotts and consumer withdrawals from the companies that have an imperialistic relationship with our community. That is, the companies control the capital and blacks are merely reduced to consumers. So far, we've been able to get about five thousand jobs directly, perhaps ten thousand indirectly, but more importantly, we've been able to develop black institutions as a result of this movement.

MR. KUNSTLER: By the way, who is president of the Southern Christian Leadership movement?

THE WITNESS: Dr. Ralph Abernathy. . .

MR. KUNSTLER: Reverend Jackson, I call your attention to the third weed in August, 1968. Did you have an occasion to see Rennie Davis?

THE WITNESS: Yes. At my house here in Chicago.

MR. KUNSTLER: Did you have a conversation at that time with Mr. Davis?

THE WITNESS: Yes, we had three or four issues to discuss. One was the relationship between the assassination of Dr. King and some things that we wanted to happen during the Convention. Rennie really wanted to know what was on my mind about the Convention and I told him that the reason we had not pursued relentlessly through any legal process who killed Dr. King was, that we thought that what killed him was an atmosphere that had been created because the nation was so split over the war question, and somehow if the Democratic Convention really became consistent with democracy, perhaps something could come in that Convention that would indicate a real sorrow for his assassination as opposed to just a holiday.

Then Rennie told me he would like to try to go to Hanoi. He felt that if I went to Hanoi that I could talk with the prisoners that were to be released and that through this process we could make the negotiations in Paris more meaningful . . . .

I related to Rennie that the shoot to kill order had come out, and therefore we had heard rumblings that if blacks participated in a big demonstration, that we would be shot down. We had talked with some of the policemen, and we saw some shotgun shells that had overkill pellets in them, so some of us who were afraid that some of the younger blacks might get involved in riots had begun to hold some workshops on he South and West sides.

So Rennie told me that he saw the danger, but what kind of decision was I going to make? I told him we felt that if blacks marched downtown there would be a massacre, and it wasn't that we were afraid to go, but we still were hung up because we had some dissenting delegations among us from Mississippi and Georgia. We wanted to support them.

So Rennie said that perhaps the only thing that could do, rather than my being caught in so much ambiguity, was that he was trying to get a legal permit through the city, and asked me what was my advice in case he didn't get the legal permit. I told him that I hoped he got the legal permit, but even if he didn't that it would be consistent with Dr. King's teaching that we then got a moral permit. Rather than getting permission from the city, we'd have to get a commission from our consciences and just have an extralegal demonstration, that probably blacks should participate, that if blacks got whipped nobody would pay attention, it would just be history. But if whites got whipped, it would make good news: that is, it would make the newspapers.

Rennie told me he didn't understand what I was saying. I told him that I thought long haired whites was the new style nigger, and if he didn't think they would get whipped, to try it.

We finally decided that we would explain to our people what the demonstration was about, that we would hope the permits would come through, that Dr. Abernathy was going to come back to the black community with the buggy and the mules. But we were afraid of the tremendous police build up in our community, so we felt too helpless to just put our heads in a meat grinder, and therefore I would spend my time working in the black community telling blacks not to get involved, and I would hope that those who were involved would appreciate that we were with them, but we just couldn't be there physically because chaos was anticipated as opposed to peace.

This was the substance of that conversation as I recall it.

MR. KUNSTLER: I have no further questions.

THE COURT: Is there any cross-examination of this witness?

MR. FORAN: Reverend Jackson, did you call Mr. Davis or did Mr. Davis call you?

THE WITNESS: He called me, then I called him back.

MR. FORAN: That is all.

THE COURT: You may go, thank you.

(applause)

The marshals will exclude everyone that they have seen applaud.

MR. KUNSTLER: Your Honor, with the testimony of Reverend Jackson, the defense has concluded its presentation of live witnesses. We do have a film that we hope to qualify. We think we will be able to procure the cameraman. We also have a few documents that we are still working on which we may present to the Court.

THE COURT: I would give consideration to recessing until Monday, provided counsel for the defense will rest or will go forward with the remainder of whatever evidence it has.

MR. SCHULTZ: Your Honor, if that evidence is going to be in addition to what Mr. Kunstler stated-- that is, that they not over the weekend decide on another dozen or thirty witnesses to start up again.

THE COURT: Mr. Kunstler represented that was the last witness, as he put it.

It that is the way you want to leave it, with the condition that you must rest Monday, if you don't have anything further, I am perfectly willing to put this case over to Monday morning.

MR. KUNSTLER: That is agreeable, you Honor.

THE COURT: The jury may now be excused until Monday morning at ten o'clock and I will ask counsel and the parties to remain . . . .

MR. KUNSTLER: I am going to go back on my representation anyway with one more witness, your Honor. We had originally contacted Dr. Ralph Abernathy to be a witness for the defense in this case. Dr. Abernathy was then out of the country and has just returned and is willing to appear as a witness for the defense. He is arriving at this moment at O'Hare Airport.

We think his testimony is crucial inasmuch as the Government has raised the issue of the mule train and I think your Honor may recall the testimony of Superintendent Rockford where the Superintendent tried to give the that the mule train was afraid of the demonstrators and therefore the police obligingly led it through the line.

Also Mr. Abernathy made a speech at Grant Park directly related to the events of the night of Wednesday, August 28. I did not know that he would be back in the country when I spoke to your Honor on Friday Afternoon. His testimony is not long and it would be the last witness we would offer subject only to those records

THE COURT: I certainly am not going to wait for him.

Who will speak for the Government?

MR. SCHULTZ: I will, your Honor.

The Government is ready to start its case this morning.

We are ready to go and would like to proceed with the trial. We would like to put on our first witness this morning.

THE COURT: There have been several witnesses called here during this trial whose testimony the Court ruled could not even be presented to the jury— singers, performers, and former office holders, I think in the light of the representations made by you unequivocally, sir, with no reference to Dr. Abernathy, I will deny your motion that we hold--

MR. KUNSTLER: Your Honor, I think what you have just said is about the most outrageous statement I have ever heard from a bench, and I am going to say my piece right now if you wish to.

You violated every principle of fair play when you excluded Ramsey Clark from that

witness stand. The *New York Times,* among others, has called it the ultimate outrage in American justice.

VOICES: Right on.

MR. KUNSTLER: I am outraged to be in this court before you. Now because I made a statement on Friday that I had only a cameraman, and I discovered on on Saturday that Ralph Abernathy, who is the chairman of the Mobilization is in town, and he can be here, I am trembling because I am so outraged. I haven't been able to get this out before, and I am saying it now, and then you can put me in jail if you want to. You can do anything you want with me, because I feed disgraced to be here.

To say to us on a technicality of my representation that we can't put Ralph Abernathy on the stand. He is the cochairman of the Mobe. He has relevant testimony. I know that doesn't mean much in this court when the Attorney General of the United States walked out of here with his lips so tight he could hardly breath, and if you could see the expression on his face, you would know, and his wife informed me that he never felt such anger at the United States Government as at not being able to testify on that stand.

I have sat here for four and a half months and watched the objections denied and sustained by your Honor, and I know that this is not a fair trial. I know it in my heart. If I have to lose my license to practice law and if I have to go to jail, I can't think of a better cause to go to jail for and to lose my license for--

A VOICE: Right on.

MR. KUNSTLER: —than to tell your Honor that you are doing a disservice to the law in saying that we can't have Ralph Abernathy on the stand. You are saying truth will not out because of the technicality of a lawyer's representation. If that is what their liberty depends upon, your Honor, saying I represented to you that I had a cameraman that was our only witness, then I think there is nothing really more for me to say.

THE COURT: There is not much more that you could say, Mr. Kunstler.

MR. KUNSTLER: I am going to turn back to my seat with the realization that everything I have learned throughout my life has come to naught, that there is no meaning in this court, and there is no law in this court—

VOICES: Right on.

MR. KUNSTLER: —and these men are going to jail by virtue of a legal lynching—

VOICES: Right on.

MR. KUNSTLER: And that your Honor is wholly responsible for that, and if this is what your career is going to end on, if this is what your pride is going to be built on, I can only say to your Honor, "Good luck to you."

VOICES: Right on. Right on.

THE COURT: Out with those applauders.

MR. DAVIS: I applauded to, your Honor. Throw me out.

THE COURT: Unfortunately, you have to remain, Mr. Davis, but we note that you applauded. You say you applauded.

MR. SCHULTZ: Your Honor, may we proceed with this trial?

THE COURT: Yes. But they must—we must have the defendants rest here when they have no more evidence.

MR. KUNSTLER: Your honor, we are not resting. We are never going to rest, your honor is going to do the resting for us because we have a witness who is available and ready to testify.

THE COURT: I will do the resting for you.

MR. KUNSTLER: You will have to do it for us, your Honor. We are not resting.

THE COURT: Mr. Clerk, let the record show that the defendants have in effect rested.

MR. SCHULTZ: Your Honor, may the defendants and their counsel then not make any reference in front of this jury that they wanted Dr. Abernathy to testify?

MR. KUNSTLER: No, no.

THE COURT: I order you not to make such a statement.

MR. KUNSTLER: We are not going to abide by any such comment as that. Dr. Ralph Abernathy is going to come into the courtroom, and I am going to repeat my motion before the jury.

THE COURT: I order you not to.

MR. KUNSTLER: Then you will have to send me to jail, I am sorry. We have a right to state our objection to resting before the jury.

THE COURT: Don't do it.

MR. KUNSTLER: Your Honor, what is an honest man to do when your Honor has done what he has done? What am I to do? Am I to stand here and say, "Yes, yes, yes."

THE COURT: I will ask you to sit down. I have heard enough from you along that line this morning, sir. I have never as a lawyer or a judge heard such remarks in a courtroom made by a lawyer.

MR. KUNSTLER: Your Honor, no one has heard of such conduct as is going on in this courtroom from the bench. This is the ultimate outrage. And I didn't say that, the editorial writers of the *New York Times* said that.

MR. SCHULTZ: May we proceed, your Honor?

THE COURT: Yes. I have ordered the jury brought in.

Norman Mailer's Testimony (author)

MR. KUNSTLER: Would you state your full name, please?

THE WITNESS: Norman Mailer is my full name. I was born Norman Kingsley Mailer, but I don't use the middle name.

MR. KUNSTLER: Would you state, Mr. Mailer, what your occupation is?

THE WITNESS: I am a writer.

MR. KUNSTLER: I show you D-344 for identification and ask you if you can identify this book.

THE WITNESS: This is a book written by me about the march on the Pentagon and its title is *The Armies of the Night*.

MR. KUNSTLER: Can you state whether or not this book won the Pulitzer Prize)

THE WITNESS: It did.

MR. SCHULTZ: Objection.

THE COURT: I sustain the objection. I strike the witness' answer and I direct the jury to disregard it.

MR. KUNSTLER: Can you state what awards this book has won?

THE WITNESS: The book was awarded the National Book Award and the Pulitzer Prize in 1969.

MR. KUNSTLER: I call your attention, Mr. Mailer, to--let me withdraw that.

Did you have a conversation with Jerry Rubin after the Pentagon?

THE WITNESS: Yes, I did in December in my home. I had called Mr. Rubin and asked him to see me because I was writing an account of the march on the
Pentagon. I was getting in touch with those principals whom I could locate. Mr. Rubin was, if you will, my best witness. We talked about the details of the march on the Pentagon for hours. We went into great detail about many aspects of it. And in this period I formed a very good opinion of Mr. Rubin because he had extraordinary powers of objectivity which an author is greatly in need of when he is talking to witnesses.

MR. SCHULTZ: Your Honor--Mr.Mailer--

THE COURT: I will have to strike the witness' answer and direct the jury to disregard every word of it.

MR. SCHULTZ: Your Honor, would you instruct Mr. Mailer even though he can't use all of the adjectives which he uses in his work, he should say "he said" and "I
said," or if he wants to embellish that, then "I stated" and "he stated." But that's the way it is related before a jury.

THE COURT: We are simple folk here. All you have to do is say "he said", if anything, "I said," if anything, and if your wife said something, you may say what she said.

I strike the witness' answer, as I say, and I direct the jury to disregard it.

MR. KUNSTLER: Now, was anything said in the conversation about what happened at the Pentagon?

THE WITNESS: Mr. Rubin went in to considerable detail about his view of the American military effort in Vietnam and the structure of the military and industrial establishment in America, and it was in Mr. Rubin's view--

MR. SCHULTZ: Your Honor, could he state what Mr. Rubin said relating to what he observed at the Pentagon?

THE WITNESS: This is Mr. Rubin s view. Mr. Rubin said it was his view, Counselor, he said that military-industrial establishment was so full of guilt and so horrified secretly at what they were doing in Vietnam that they were ready to crack at the smallest sort of provocation, and that the main idea in the move on the Pentagon was to exacerbate their sense of authority and control.

MR. KUNSTLER: Mr. Mailer, was anything said about Chicago in this conversation?

THE WITNESS: Yes. Mr. Rubin said that he was at present working full time on plans to have a youth festival in Chicago in August of 1968 when the Democratic Convention would take place and it was his idea that the presence of a hundred thousand young people in Chicago at a festival with rock bands would so intimidate and terrify the establishment that Lyndon Johnson would have to be nominated under armed guard.

And I said, "Wow."

I was overtaken with the audacity of the idea and I said, "It's a beautiful and frightening idea."

And Rubin said, "I think that the beauty of it is that the establishment is going to do it all themselves. We won't do a thing. We are just going to be there and they won't be able to take it. They will smash the city themselves. They will provoke all the violence."

And I said, "I think you're right, but I have to admit to you that I'm scared at the thought of it. It is really something."

And he said, "It is. I am going to devote full time to it."

I said, "You're a brave man."

MR. KUNSTLER: Now did you go to Chicago?

THE WITNESS: Yes.

MR. KUNSTLER: I call your attention to approximately 5:00 P.m. on August 27, 1968. Do you know where you were then?

THE WITNESS: Yes. I was in my hotel room with Robert Lowell and David Dellinger and Rennie Davis.

MR. KUNSTLER: Would you state what was said during that conversation?

THE WITNESS: The conversation was about the possibility of violence on a march that was being proposed to the Amphitheatre.

Mr. Lowell and I were a little worried about it because we were McCarthy supporters and we felt that if there was a lot of violence it was going to wash out McCarthy's last remote chance of being nominated.

And Mr. Dellinger said to me, "Look, you know my record, you know I've never had anything to do with violence." He said, "And you know that we have not been the violent ones. For every policeman that has been called a pig, those police have broken five and ten heads. You know that I never move toward anything that will result in violence," he said, "but at the same time I am not going to avoid all activity which could possible result in violence because if we do that, we'll be able to protest nothing at all. We are trying at this very moment to get a permit, We are hoping we get the permit, but if they don't give it to us, we'll probably march anyway because we have to: it's why we're here. We're here to oppose the war in Vietnam and we don't protest it if we stay in our rooms and don't go out to protest it."

He then asked me to speak at Grant Park the next day.

MR. KUNSTLER: Did You accept that invitation?

THE WITNESS: No, I didn't. I said I was there to cover the Convention for Harper's Magazine, and I felt that I did not want to get involved because if I did and got arrested, I would not be able to write my piece in time for the deadline, and I was really very concerned about not getting arrested, and losing three, or four, or five days because I had eighteen days in which to write the piece, and I knew it was going to be a long piece.

MR. KUNSTLER: I call your attention to the next day, Wednesday, the twenty-eighth of August, between 3:30 and 4:00 P.m. approximately. Do you know where you were then?

THE WITNESS: Yes, I was in Grant Park. I felt ashamed of myself for not speaking, and I, therefore, went up to the platform and I asked Mr. Dellinger if I could speak, and he then very happily said, "Yes, of course."

MR. KUNSTLER: Can you state what you did say on Wednesday in Grant Park?

THE WITNESS: I merely said to the people who were there that I thought they were possessed of beauty, and that I was not going to march with them because I had to write this piece. And they all said, "Write, Baby." That is what they said from the crowd.

MR. KUNSTLER: Now, Mr. Mailer, I call your attention to Thursday, August 29, did you give another speech that day?

THE WITNESS: Yes, that was in Grant Park on Thursday morning, two or three in the morning.

MR. KUNSTLER: Do you recall what you said?

THE WITNESS: Yes. That was--

MR. SCHULTZ: Objection. What he said is not relevant. What he said at the Bandshell where the Bandshell performance was sponsored by the defendants, that is one thing, but where he makes an independent statement-

THE COURT: There hasn't been a proper foundation for the question.

MR. KUNSTLER: I will ask one question.

THE COURT: I sustain the objection.

MR. KUNSTLER: Mr. Mailer, at the time you spoke, did you see any of the defendants at this table in the vicinity?

THE WITNESS: No, I don't think so.

MR. KUNSTLER: Then I have no further questions.

THE COURT: Is there any cross-examination?

MR. SCHULTZ: A few questions, your Honor.

Mr. Mailer, when you had your conversation with Rubin at your home, did Rubin tell you that the presence of a hundred thousand young people would so intimidate the establishment that Johnson would have to call out the troops and National Guard?

THE WITNESS: He did not use the word intimidate, as I recollect.

MR. SCHULTZ: Did he say that the presence of these people will provoke the establishment and the establishment will smash the city themselves?

THE WITNESS: That was the substance of what he said, yes.

MR. SCHULTZ: All right. Now at your speech in Grant Park, didn't you say that we are at the beginning of a war which would continue for twenty years and the march today would be one battle in that war?

THE WITNESS: Yes, I said that.

MR. SCHULTZ: But you couldn't go on the march because you had a deadline?

THE WITNESS: Yes. I was in a moral quandary. I didn't know if I was being scared or being professional and I was naturally quite upset because a man never likes to know that his motive might be simple fear.

THE COURT: I thought you said you had to do that piece.

THE WITNESS: I did have to do the piece, your Honor, but I just wasn't sure in my own mind whether I was hiding behind the piece or whether I was being professional to avoid temptation.

MR. SCHULTZ: Did you tell the crowd, Mr. Mailer, at the Bandshell, "You have to be beautiful. You are much better than you were at the Pentagon?" Did you tell them that?

THE WITNESS: Yes. I remember saying that.

MR. SCHULTZ: You were talking about their physical appearance rather than their actions?

THE WITNESS: That is right. To my amazement these militant activities seemed to improve their physique and their features.

MR. SCHULTZ: I have no further questions.

THE COURT: Is there any redirect examination?

MR. KUNSTLER: Could you state if Rubin didn't use the word "intimidate" as you have answered Mr. Schultz, what word he did use? What was his language?

THE WITNESS: It would be impossible for me to begin to remember whether Mr.Rubin used the word "intimidate" or not. I suspect that he probably did not use it because it is not his habitual style of speech. He would speak more of diverting, demoralizing the establishment, freaking them out, bending their mind, driving them out of their bird.

I use the word "intimidate" because possibly since I am a bully by nature, I tend to think in terms of intimidation, but I don't think Mr. Rubin does. He thinks in terms of cataclysm, of having people reveal their own guilt, their own evil.

His whole notion was that the innocent presence of one hundred thousand people in Chicago would be intolerable for a man as guilt-ridden as Lyndon Johnson. When this conversation took place, Lyndon Johnson was still President and the war in Vietnam gave no sign of ever being diminished in its force and its waste.

MR. KUNSTLER: I have no further questions.

Richard Daley's Testimony (mayor of Chicago)

MR. KUNSTLER: What is your name?

THE WITNESS: Richard Joseph Daley.

MR. KUNSTLER: What is your occupation?

THE WITNESS: I am the mayor of the City of Chicago.

MR. KUNSTLER: Is that the chief executive officer of the City of Chicago?

THE WITNESS: It is referred to occasionally as that.

MR. KUNSTLER: Now, Mayor Daley, how many executive departments do you have in the City of Chicago?

THE WITNESS: Approximately thirty-five.

MR. KUNSTLER: By whom are they headed?

THE WITNESS: Cabinet officers appointed by the mayor and confirmed by the City Council.

MR. KUNSTLER: How are they removed?

THE WITNESS: They are only removed bv cause and also by trial before the Police Board.

MR. KUNSTLER: Have you ever had occasion to remove the head of any executive department yourself?

MR. FORAN: Objection, your Honor.

THE COURT: I sustain the objection.

MR. KUNSTLER: Have you ever had occasion to remove a superintendent of police?

MR. FORAN: Objection, your Honor,

THE COURT: I sustain the objection.

MR. KUNSTLER: Mayor Daley, who appoints the Police Board?

THE WITNESS: The mayor of the City of Chicago.

MR. KUNSTLER: Now with specific reference to the superintendent of police, what is his name?

THE WITNESS: James Conlisk.

MR. KUNSTLER: Was Superintendent Conlisk recommended by the Police Board?

MR. FORAN: I object to this. Now it is immaterial.

THE COURT: I sustain the objection.

MR. FORAN: Let's get on to the Democratic Convention if we are going to get there.

MR. KUNSTLER: Now, who was the chairman of the Park Commission in 1968, specifically during the period from the first of the year going through August?

THE WITNESS: The proper designation is president, not chairman. The president was William McFetridge.

MR. KUNSTLER: Is this the same William McFetridge who announced your first candidacy for mayor in 1954?

MR. FORAN: Objection, your Honor.

THE COURT: I sustain the objection.

MR. KUNSTLER: He was for many years a very close personal friend of yours. is that correct?

MR. FORAN: I object to that. It is clearly immaterial. It is a leading form of question.

THE COURT: I sustain the objection.

MR. KUNSTLER: Your Honor, this is a key portion of our interrogation, the relationship of the witness to--

THE COURT: It may be a key portion but--

MR. FORAN: Then let him ask the proper questions, your Honor.

THE COURT: I am ruling on it only as a matter of the law of evidence, sir. Whether it is key or not isn't important to me.

MR. KUNSTLER: Is it not true, Mayor Daley, that Mr. McFetridge once said the parks were not for dissenters?

MR. FORAN: Objection.

THE COURT: I sustain the objection.

MR. KUNSTLER: Mayor Daley, do you know a Federal judge by the name of Judge Lynch?

THE WITNESS: Yes.

MR. KUNSTLER: William Lynch.

At one time did you practice law with him?

MR. FORAN: Your Honor, I object to the form of the question.

THE COURT: I sustain the objection.

MR. KUNSTLER: Mayor Daley, what is your relationship with Thomas Foran, the U.S. Attorney who is in this courtroom today?

THE WITNESS: I think he is one of the greatest attorneys in this country and the finest man I have met in private and public life.

MR. KUNSTLER: Your Honor, I would ask that that answer be stricken as not responsive as to what is his relationship.

THE COURT: I would like to have that said about me, but I agree with you that it is not responsive.

MR. KUNSTLER: Your Honor, something is happening in the rear row. I don't know what it is.

THE COURT: Will you let the marshals take care of the rear row?

(jury excused)

A SPECTATOR: The marshals are interrupting the trial.

MR. KUNSTLER: Your Honor, something is happening in the back row. A marshal is going down--a woman marshal is going down--

VOICE: Ouch!

Ow, don't step on me, please!

VOICES: He isn't doing anything.

She didn't do anything.

MR. KUNSTLER: Your Honor, that is one of our staff people. I don't understand--I would like the Court to inquire--

THE COURT: Regardless of who the person is, if the person has been disorderly, the marshal must ask the person to leave.

VOICES: What's going on?

Leave him alone.

Hey, leave him alone.

Leave him alone.

Ouch!

Leave her alone.

(shouts and screams)

VOICES: Stop it. Hey, stop that. Leave them alone.

(shouts and screams)

VOICES: You're hitting Frank in the face.
　　Leave him alone, Leave him alone.

(shouts and screams)

VOICES: Just leave him alone.
　　You're still hitting him.
　　Leave him alone.

MR. KUNSTLER: The defendants request to know what happened.

THE COURT: The marshals will explain at an appropriate time.

MR. KUNSTLER: We have information, your Honor, that some of the people doing the removing are not marshals, but employees of the City of Chicago, and we have a man standing there with his coat on who obviously is not a marshal. We would like to know who he is.

MR. WEINGLASS: He is the one who was hitting Frank.

THE COURT: If everybody will be quiet and listen to the testimony of the witness, the questions of the lawyers, there will be no disorder.

MR. KUNSTLER: We have asked your Honor to conduct an inquiry. Nothing could be fairer than that. I am not asking you to believe--

VOICES: Hey! Hey!
　　For crying out loud!
　　Come on, will you!
　　For Christ's sake!

MR. FORAN: Your Honor, that is the defendant Davis going back there, running to the spectator section of the courtroom.

(shouts and screams)

VOICES: Leave him alone!

THE COURT: The place for Mr. Davis is at the defendants table and in his chair.
　　Bring in the jury, Mr. Marshal.
　　The Court directs the spectators to be orderly. If any spectator is not orderly, he will be appropriately dealt with by the Court.

MR. KUNSTLER: Your Honor, I just want to request if the person in the brown suit is a marshal. Since some of our people have been beaten up, I would like to know who that man is.

MR. FORAN: Oh, your Honor.

MR. DELLINGER: It's true.

MR. FORAN: --I object to the comment of Mr. Kunstler, your Honor. That's outrageous. I ask the jury be directed to disregard his comments.

THE COURT: Yes, I do direct the jury--

MR. KUNSTLER: Your Honor, if he will show his badge, we will be happy.

THE COURT: He doesn't have to be a marshal--

MR. KUNSTLER: To stand there in the position of authority?

THE COURT: I don't know who he is. I don't know most of the marshals.

MR. KUNSTLER: Your Honor is not going to ask him for the production of the badge?

THE COURT: No, no. No, no.

MR. KUNSTLER: Your Honor, it's our information this is a personal bodyguard of the witness.

THE COURT: Will you please proceed, sir, with the direct examination of this witness? Otherwise I will direct the witness to leave the witness stand.

MR. KUNSTLER: Mayor Daley, do you hold a position in the Cook County Democratic Committee?

THE WITNESS: I surely do, and I am very proud of it.

I am the leader of my party. I am the leader of the Democratic Party in Cook County. .
.

MR. KUNSTLER: I call your attention, Mayor Daley, to the week of August 28, 1968. Did you attend any sessions of the Democratic National Convention?

THE WITNESS: I did.

MR. KUNSTLER: And were you there during the nominating speeches for the various candidates?

THE WITNESS: I was.

MR. KUNSTLER: Mayor Daley, on the twenty-eighth of August, 1968, did you say to Senator Ribicoff--

MR. FORAN: Oh, your Honor, I object.

MR. KUNSTLER [continuing]: –"Fuck you, you Jew son of a bitch, you lousy motherfucker, go home"?

MR. FORAN: Listen to that. I object to that kind of conduct in a courtroom. Of all the improper, foolish questions, typical, your Honor, of making up questions that have nothing to do with the lawsuit.

THE COURT: May I suggest to you, sir, that this witness is your witness and you may not ask him any leading questions even of the sort that you proposed--especially, rather, of the sort that I heard a part of a moment ago.

MR. KUNSTLER: I have the source, your Honor. I will be glad to read it into the record.

THE COURT: I order you now, Mr. Kunstler, not to ask leading questions. Under the law you may not ask him such questions.

MR. KUNSTLER: Well, your Honor, then I would renew my motion out of the presence of the jury to have a hearing on the question of whether he is or is not a hostile witness.

THE COURT: I will be glad to do that. I'll excuse you, ladies and gentlemen of the jury, for a few moments.

(jury excused)

MR. KUNSTLER: Your Honor, Rule 43(b), Federal Rule of Civil Procedure, states that a party may interrogate any unwilling hostile witness by leading questions and contradict and impeach him in all respects as if he had been called by the adverse party.*

Witnesses procured by the U.S. Attorney, particularly Mr. Simon, indicated that the City of Chicago had in every way cooperated with these defendants in the procuring of permits and that the City of Chicago had refused permits.

In fact, if your Honor recalls, Mr. Baugher testified that he couldn't understand why the permits were not issued.

Your Honor, the only way we are ever going to get to the truth of this matter is by being able to ask cross-examination questions of the Mayor. He is the chief executive officer, as he testified, of the City of Chicago.*

THE COURT: The motion of the defense will be denied. The Court finds that there is nothing in the testimony of the witness that has indicated hostility. His manner has been that of a gentleman. He's answered questions straightforwardly, pursuant to the oath administered by the clerk of the court.

Bring in the jury.

(jury enters)

MR. KUNSTLER: Mayor Daley, who is David Stahl? Do you know him?

THE WITNESS: He is a very fine young man, the Deputy Mayor, who is interested in public life. He is a former vice-president of one of the outstanding corporations in Chicago and he is doing an outstanding job for the people of our city.

MR. KUNSTLER: I will assume with all of the people I ask you about they are very fine young men and so on.

It will save time.

THE WITNESS: I would say that anyone that served in government today is a fine young man because of what they are trying to do.

MR. KUNSTLER: I direct your attention, Mayor Daley, to March 28, 1968: do you recall any conversation or meeting with Mr. Stahl with reference to the Youth International Party?

THE WITNESS: I gave Mr. Stahl the same instructions I gave any other department, certainly, to meet with them, to try to cooperate with them, and do everything they could to make sure that they would be given every courtesy and hospitality while they were in the city of Chicago.

MR. KUNSTLER: Did you consider that the use of nightsticks on the heads of demonstrators was hospitable?

MR. FORAN: Objection, your Honor.

THE COURT: I sustain the objection.

MR. FORAN: It's a leading question.

MR. KUNSTLER: Prior to the Democratic National Committee choosing Chicago for its 1968 convention, did you have any discussions with Mr. Bailey or any other official of the Democratic National Committee?

THE WITNESS: Yes.

MR. KUNSTLER: Did those instructions relate to the coming of the Convention to Chicago?

MR. FORAN: Your Honor, I object to that as a leading question.

THE COURT: I sustain the objection.

MR. KUNSTLER: Did you discuss in any of these discussions the war in Vietnam?

MR. FORAN: Your Honor, I object to the question.

THE COURT: I sustain the objection.

MR. KUNSTLER: In any of those discussions with Mr. Bailey, did you have any conversation about the black community in Chicago?

MR. FORAN: Same objection exactly, your Honor. Object to it.

THE COURT: I sustain the objection.

MR. KUNSTLER: Mayor Daley, in your experience as the mayor of this city which goes back, I understand, to 1955, have you ever had knowledge of people sleeping in Lincoln Park overnight?

MR. FORAN: Your Honor, I object to the form of the question. It is leading,

THE COURT: That is right. I sustain the objection.

MR. KUNSTLER: Your Honor, we have tried to get a declaration of a hostile witness here without success. You have the discretion, your Honor, to declare a hostile witness which would make things-

THE COURT: If that is true I do not choose to exercise my discretion to suspend the law. MR. KUNSTLER: Did any of these defendants to your knowledge attempt to meet with you with reference to the Democratic National Convention prior to August 25?

MR. FORAN: Object to the leading character of the question, your Honor, and I ask that counsel be admonished.

THE COURT: I sustain the objection, and I remind you of my order, Mr. Kunstler.

MR. KUNSTLER: Mayor Daley, do you believe that people have the right to demonstrate against the war in Vietnam?

MR. FORAN: Your Honor, I object to the form of the question. It's an improper question.

THE COURT: I sustain the objection to the question.

MR. KUNSTLER: Now, Mayor Daley, you've testified that you were at the Democratic National Convention on Wednesday, August 28, and I questioned you about a statement with reference to Senator Ribicoff.

Can you indicate what you did say to Senator Ribicoff on that day?

MR. FORAN: Your Honor, I object to the form of the question, and again I ask that counsel be admonished.

THE COURT: I sustain the objection, and I remind you again and admonish you, Mr. Kunstler, of my order.

MR. KUNSTLER: Your Honor, I have tried to reiterate ten times that in view of the nature of this witness, it is impossible to examine him and get to the truth of anything with these restrictions--

THE COURT: This witness is no different from any other witness.

MR. KUNSTLER: But, your Honor, that isn't so. He is different from any other witness. He is the Mayor of the city-

THE COURT: The fact that he happens to occupy a high public place--other than that, he is a witness. In this court he is just a witness.

MR. KUNSTLER: We are trying, your Honor, to get to the truth of what happened during Convention week.

THE COURT: You must get at the truth through proper questions, sir.

MR. FORAN: Through the law of evidence, your Honor, that it has taken five hundred years to achieve.

MR. KUNSTLER: Your Honor, it is obvious to me that in view of the Court's rulings and in view of the restrictions under which I am working, that it is impossible to question this witness adequately as we have desired to do.

I would now, in view of the responses to my last twenty questions here, like to read into the record an offer of proof of what we had hoped to prove through this witness if we had been able to ask him either impeaching or questions as a hostile witness.

I have prepared that offer of proof and would be prepared to read it into the record at this point.

THE COURT: I will excuse you for a few minutes, ladies and gentlemen of the jury.

(jury excused)

MR. KUNSTLER: Your Honor, the defendants make the following offer of proof. Had the Mayor been designated a hostile witness, the defendants would have offered proof through his testimony to show the following:

1. That there was a conspiracy, overt or tacit, between Mayor Daley and the Democratic administration of Lyndon B. Johnson to prevent or crush any significant demonstrations against war, poverty, imperialism, and racism. and in support of alternative cultures at the 1968 Democratic National Convention.

2. That the members of this conspiracy planned and executed the use of every means at their disposal, including the open and blatant encouragement of violence toward demonstrators by police and other military forces, in order to prevent or crush such public exhibition of dissatisfaction with American domestic and foreign policies.

3. That in so doing the conspirators were determined to continue the fraudulent myth that the people of the United States had a real voice in their government and that they would have a significant choice in the national election of 1968 between candidates supporting virtually identical policies of war, imperialism, racism, and the continued degradation and exploitation and oppression of youth, ethnic, socioeconomic, racial and other minorities.

4. That Mayor Daley obtained and maintains in power in Chicago bv the creation and maintenance of a corrupt political machine which is supported by those individuals and corporations standing to gain the most bv a continuation of present American domestic and foreign policies.

5. That this political machine is determined, whatever the cost, to prevent meaningful solutions to the problems presently facing the people of the United States and those of the rest of the world.

6. That the conspirators have embarked on a program of intense and brutal repression against all those who are seeking such solution, including but not limited to individuals and organizations committed to the end of the war in South Vietnam and the immediate and unconditional withdrawal of American troops therefrom, the right of black people and other racial, ethnic, or socioeconomic minorities to control their own communities, the right of rebellion against oppression, and the bedrock right of all people to adopt a new way or style of life.

7. That in furtherance of this conspiracy, Mayor Daley, among other things:

(a) On April 1 5, 1 968, ordered his police to respond to the assassination of Dr. Martin Luther King, Jr., with orders to shoot to kill arsonists and shoot to maim or cripple looters in the black community.

(b) Attempted first to obstruct the peace parade of the Chicago Peace Council on April 27, 1968, and then brutalized the marchers therein as a warning to peace demonstrators to stay away from the Democratic National Convention.

(c) Attempted first to obstruct the demonstrations at the Democratic National Convention in August of 1968 and then harassed, victimized, and brutalized the participants therein.

(d) Attempted to mislead the people of Chicago and the United States as to the nature and cause of such obstructive and brutal tactics.

8. That in furtherance of this conspiracy, Mayor Daley utilized the services of members of his political machine, including those of Thomas Foran, the United States Attorney for the Eastern District of Illinois and a former assistant Corporation Counsel of the City of Chicago.

9. That the indictment in this case was procured as a result of the said conspiracy in order to:

(a) shift the deserved blame for the disorders Surrounding the Democratic Convention from the real conspirators to deliberately selected individuals symbolizing various categories and degrees of dissent from American foreign and domestic policies.

(b) punish those individuals for their role in leading and articulating such dissent and

(c) deter others from supporting or expressing such dissent in the future.

10. That the indictments of eight Chicago policemen, simultaneously with the instant one" were deliberately planned and procured to match the charges against the defendants and thus give the fraudulent illusion that an even-handed standard of Justice was being applied.

11. That Mayor Daley and his administrators have for years victimized the black community in the City of Chicago by means which include chronic police violence, economic oppression, and the abuse of Federal and state programs.

12. That Mayor Daley and his administration have for years harassed, intimidated, and terrorized young people in the City of Chicago who have adopted and maintained life styles of which he disapproves including the wearing of long hair and unconventional clothing.

13. That Mayor Daley maintains power in Chicago by a combination of:
   (a) political patronage;
   (b) furthering the interests of the city's financial and mercantile communities;
   (c) oppression of racial, ethnic, socioeconomic and other minorities.

14. That behind the mayor are powerful corporate interests who determine broad public policy in Chicago but are responsible to no one elected or public body. These interests govern Chicago for self-serving private gains instead of social needs: urban renewal works to enrich these private interests and against poor and working people who are robbed of their homes-, no public programs effectively halt the polluting of our air and water by these powerful interests. The city practices genocide against the black community and in particular the Black Panther Party, which no group of citizens can effectively check or reverse without dislodging these private interests from their control over public officials and institutions.

VOICE: Right on.

MR. KUNSTLER: This is our offer of proof. This is what we would have hoped to have proved had we been able to have the mayor declared. as we think he ought to be, a hostile witness.

THE COURT: Your offer is made a part of the record, sir.

MR. KUNSTLER: With that, your Honor, we have no further questions because of the reasons I have indicated.

THE COURT: Is there any cross-examination? Oh, just a minute. We must have the jury in.

(jury enters)

MR. FORAN: Mr. Daley, in your conversations with anyone did you ever suggest that a permit be denied to any applicant or applicants for a march permit relating to the Democratic Convention?

THE WITNESS: No, I never did.

MR. FORAN: In your conversations with anyone did you ever suggest that a permit be denied to any applicant or applicants for a permit to use any of the parks in this city?

THE WITNESS: No.

MR. FORAN: That is all.

James Riordan's Testimony (deputy chief of police)

February 4, 1970

MR. SCHULTZ: Please state your name.

THE WITNESS: James D. Riordan.

MR. SCHULTZ: And what is your occupation?

THE WITNESS: Deputy Chief of Police in the Chicago Police Department.

MR. SCHULTZ: Now, calling your attention specifically to approximately 5:45 in the evening on Wednesday, August 28, do you recall where you were?

THE WITNESS: I was about fifty feet south of Balbo on Columbus Drive in Grant Park on the east sidewalk.

There were approximately, about 1500 people on the sidewalk from the location where I was standing back to about 9th Street. This was a group of people that wanted to march.

MR. SCHULTZ: And where were you in relation to this group of people that wanted to march?

THE WITNESS: I was in front of them. I stopped the march.

MR. SCHULTZ: Now, at 5:45 that evening on Columbus Drive, did you have occasion to see David Dellinger?

THE WITNESS: I did. He was confronting me at the head of the march.

MR. SCHULTZ: Now, at approximately 5:45, what if any announcements were made?

THE WITNESS: There was announcement made approximately thirty or forty yards back to the south of the front of the march by an unknown man with a loudspeaker.

MR. SCHULTZ: What if anything did you hear on the bullhorn?

THE WITNESS: I heard this unidentified speaker announce to the group that inasmuch as the march had been stopped, to break up in small groups of fives and tens, and to go over into the Loop, to penetrate into the hotels, the theaters, and stores, and business establishments where the police could not get at them, and disrupt their normal activity, and. if possible, to tie up the traffic in the Loop.

MR. SCHULTZ: After that announcement was made, what if anything did you observe the people in your area do?

THE WITNESS: The march disintegrated, and approximately 500 people crossed Columbus Drive and walked west through the ballfield toward the Illinois Central bridge on Balbo.

MR. SCHULTZ: Did Dellinger say anything when this announcement was made?

THE WITNESS: I did not hear him say anything.

MR. SCHULTZ: Did you see where he went?

THE WITNESS: He left with the head of the group that were carrying the flags.

MR. DELLINGER: Oh, bullshit. That is an absolute lie.

THE COURT: Did you get that, Miss Reporter?

MR. DELLINGER: Let's argue about what you stand for and what I stand for, but let's not make up things like that.

THE COURT: All of those remarks were made in the presence of the Court and jury by Mr. Dellinger.

MR. KUNSTLER: Sometimes the human spirit can stand so much, and I think Mr. Dellinger reached the end of his.

THE COURT: I have never heard in more than a half a century of the bar a man using profanity in this court or in a courtroom.

MR. HOFFMAN: I've never been in an obscene Court, either.

THE COURT: I never have as a spectator or as a judge. I never did.

MR. KUNSTLER: You never sat here as a defendant and heard liars on the stand, your Honor.

MR. SCHULTZ: Now, your Honor, I move that that statement--how dare Mr Kunstler--

MR. KUNSTLER: I say it openly and fully, your Honor.

MR. SCHULTZ: Your Honor, we had to sit with our lips tight, listening to those defendants, to those two defendants, Mr. Hayden and Mr. Hoffman, perjure themselves. I mean Davis and Hoffman.

MR. KUNSTLER: A little Freudian slip, your Honor.

MR. SCHULTZ: Your Honor, I have no further direct examination.

MR. DELLINGER: You're a snake. We have to try to put you in jail for ten years for telling lies about us, Dick Schultz.

MARSHAL JONESON: Be quiet, Mr. Dellinger.

MR. DELLINGER: When it's all over, the judge will go to Florida, but if he has his way, we'll go to jail. That is what we're fighting for, not just for us, but for all the rest of the people in the country who are being oppressed.

VOICES: Right on.

THE COURT: Take that man into custody, Mr. Marshal. Take that man into custody.

VOICES: Right on, right on.

MR. SCHULTZ: Into custody?

THE COURT: Into custody.

VOICES: Right on.

MR. DAVIS: Go ahead, Dick Schultz, put everybody in jail.

MR. DELLINGER: Dick Schultz is a Nazi if I ever knew one.

MR. SCHULTZ: Your Honor, will you please tell Mr. Davis to walk away from me?

MR. DELLINGER: Put everybody in jail.

THE COURT: Mr. Davis, will you take your chair.

MR. HOFFMAN: Nazi jailer.

THE COURT: You may proceed with your cross-examination.

MR. KUNSTLER: Chief Riordan, what time did the march disintegrate?

THE WITNESS: Oh, I would say about six o'clock.

MR. KUNSTLER: Now, would it surprise you, Chief, to know that some forty minutes later, Superintendent Rochford stated that the march was still present, and that he had a conversation with Dave Dellinger at 6:40 that night on that very spot?

MR. SCHULTZ: Objection, your Honor.

THE COURT: I don't deal in surprises. That is always an improper question.

THE WITNESS: It could have happened.

THE COURT: I sustain the objection.

MR. KUNSTLER: At approximately six o'clock, that time was when you say Dave Dellinger left that scene, isn't that correct?

THE WITNESS: That is true. He left my presence.

MR. KUNSTLER: Have you had any conversation with Superintendent Rochford about this?

THE WITNESS: No, sir.

MR. KUNSTLER: Do you know yourself that Superintendent Rochford was there forty minutes later talking to Dave Dellinger and the march had not disintegrated?

MR. SCHULTZ: Objection, your Honor.

THE COURT: I sustain the objection.

MR. KUNSTLER: Chief Riordan, at any time after you heard this speaker make those remarks, did you get on the radio and alert the police in the city of Chicago that a mob was invading the Loop?

THE WITNESS: No, sir.

MR. KUNSTLER: You heard the words, and did nothing?

THE WITNESS: That's right. I reported in to the Yard, the communications center.

MR. KUNSTLER: When did you do that?

THE WITNESS: When I arrived there.

MR. KUNSTLER: At what time did you arrive there?

THE WITNESS: 6:45.

MR. KUNSTLER: And what you had heard over a loudspeaker forty-five minutes earlier about invading the Loop and penetrating the stores and tying up traffic, you didn't think that was important enough to alert a Chicago policeman, is that correct?

THE WITNESS: That is not correct.

MR. KUNSTLER: I have no further questions.

(jury excused)

THE COURT: I have some observations to make here, gentlemen.

Time and again, as the record reveals, the defendant Dave Dellinger has disrupted sessions of this court with the use of vile and insulting language. Today again he used vile and obscene language which, of course, is revealed by the record.

I propose to try to end the use of such language if possible, and such conduct, by terminating the bail of this defendant.

I do not, if I can help it, intend to permit such tactics to make a mockery out of this trial.

I hereby, Mr. Clerk, terminate the bail of the defendant David Dellinger and remand him to the custody of the United States Marshal for the Northern District of Illinois for the remainder of this trial.

MR. KUNSTLER: Your Honor, is there not going to be any argument on this?

THE COURT: No argument.

MR. KUNSTLER: I would like to say my piece. He is my client, and I think this is an utterly--

(There is disorder in the courtroom.)

MR. KUNSTLER: You brought this on, your Honor. This is your fault. This is what happened in Chicago. You exerted the power, and I would like to argue the point.

THE COURT: You won't argue the point.

MR. KUNSTLER: I will argue, your Honor, that your Honor's action is completely and utterly vindictive, that there is no authority that says because a defendant blurts out a word in court--

THE COURT: This isn't the first word, and I won't argue this.

MR. DAVIS: This court is bullshit.

THE COURT: There he is saying the same words again.

MR. DAVIS: No, I say it.

MR. KUNSTLER: That was not even David Dellinger who made the last remark.

MR. SCHULTZ: It was Davis, the defendant Davis who just uttered the last--

MR. RUBIN: Everything in this court is bullshit.

MR. DAVIS: I associate myself with Dave Dellinger completely, 100 percent. This is the most obscene court I have ever seen.

MR. RUBIN: You are going to separate us. Take us, too.
Take us all. Show us what a big man you are. Take us all.

MR. DAVIS: Mr. Rubin's wife they are now taking--

MR. RUBIN: Keep your hands off her. You see them taking away my wife?

MR. DAVIS: Why don't you gag the press, too, and the attorneys, gag them?

MR. KUNSTLER: Your Honor, there was no need for your action.

THE COURT: The court will be in recess. Mr. Marshal--

THE MARSHAL: Sit down, Mr.–

MR. KUNSTLER: Your Honor, is there no decency left here? Can't we just argue the point?

THE COURT: You will have to go away from that lectern. You can't stand there and insult the United States District Court.

MR. KUNSTLER: Everything in this case is an insult.

THE COURT: You just insulted me again and you have done if often.

MR. KUNSTLER: Every argument is not an insult.

THE COURT: This case is recessed.

THE MARSHAL: Everyone please rise.

THE COURT: Clear the courtroom.

MR. DAVIS: You can jail a revolutionary, but you can't jail the revolution.

MR. HOFFMAN: You are a disgrace to the Jews. You would have served Hitler better. Dig it.

THE MARSHAL: That was Mr. Hoffman, your Honor.

THE COURT: I saw him and I heard him.

MR. RUBIN: You are a fascist, Hoffman--

THE MARSHAL: Clear the court.

THE COURT: Clear the courtroom, Mr. Marshal.

MR. DAVIS: Get as many people as you can. Just like the Convention all over again.

THE MARSHAL: Clear the court.

THE COURT: Clear the court.

A FEMALE VOICE: You little prick.

MR. RUBIN: You are fascist.

THE MARSHAL: Get out of the courtroom.

Let's go.

MR. HOFFMAN: Oh, yes, I forgot, it's a public trial.

Robert Murray's Testimony (police sergeant)

MR. SCHULTZ: Will you please state your name?

THE WITNESS: Robert Murray.

MR. SCHULTZ: What is your occupation, please, Mr. Murray?

THE WITNESS: I am a Police Sergeant with the Chicago Police Department.

MR. SCHULTZ: Mr. Murray, during the week of the Democratic National Convention in August of 1968, where were you assigned, please?

THE WITNESS: I was dressed in casual clothes, wash pants and jacket.

MR. SCHULTZ: On Sunday evening, August 25, 1968, in Lincoln Park, between nine and ten o'clock at night, did you have occasion to observe a person named Jerry Rubin?

THE WITNESS: Yes, sir, I did.

MR. SCHULTZ: At the time you saw Rubin what, if anything, did he have on his head?

THE WITNESS: He was wearing a football helmet.

MR. SCHULTZ: When you observed Rubin, what, if anything, was he doing?

THE WITNESS: The first time I observed him he was standing there and he was talking with a newsman from ABC.

MR. SCHULTZ: Would you relate, please, what you heard?

THE WITNESS: The conversation was on a first-name basis and the newsman said, "Well, Jerry, how di you feel your program will be accepted on the college campuses this fall?" and I heard Mr. Rubin say, "Well, I feel that it will be accepted very well by the kids because they are fed up with the power structure."

The newsman said, "Well, we are going to get some coffee. We haven't had our coffee yet." and Mr. Rubin said, "Well, wait, don't go right now. We're going out in the ball field," and he pointed in the direction of the ball field, and he says, "we want to see what these pigs are going to do about it," pointing to the police officers that were standing in front of this park house.

MR. SCHULTZ: How many police officers were standing there?

THE WITNESS: There were ten policemen and one sergeant.

MR. SCHULTZ: Were they dressed in police uniform?

THE WITNESS: Yes, they were.

MR. SCHULTZ: Would you continue?

THE WITNESS: He said, "We're going out to the ball field. We want to see what these pigs are going to do when we go out there." And the newsman said, "Well, when are you going?" And he said, "Right now." He said, "O.K., we'll wait." And Mr. Rubin and the other man he was with walked out onto the ball field and I just stood there behind the newsman.

MR. SCHULTZ: What occurred then?

THE WITNESS: Then I heard this man that was with him say to Mr. Rubin, "Now's the time for the flares or the fires." I don't know which word it was.

MR. SCHULTZ: Then what did you hear, please?

THE WITNESS: I heard Mr. Rubin say, "No, not now," and the other man said, "Nothing's happening. Now's the time for the flares or the fires."

Then I heard Mr. Rubin say, "OK, go get them." and at this this man turned and went out of the park going west.

MR. SCHULTZ: Then what occurred, please?

THE WITNESS: Then Mr. Rubin turned and he began to shout in a loud voice, and he used some profanity.

MR. SCHULTZ: Your Honor, I want to ask that the witness be permitted to state what was said, even though some of those words are profane words, your Honor. They are four-letter words.

THE COURT: It occurs to me that it isn't necessary to obtain the permission of the Court. A witness may testify to what he heard. I don't mean to say that people will necessarily enjoy hearing profane words, but if profane words were spoken, part of a conversation, part of something an individual had said, I think it is appropriate in law that the witness so testify.

MR. SCHULTZ: Would you relate what Rubin said when he was waving with his arm?

THE WITNESS: He looked over his shoulder, and he says, "look at these motherfucking pigs standing over here."

He says, "They have to be standing in the park protecting the park, and the park belongs to the people. Let's get these fuckers out of here."

MR. SCHULTZ: Then what occurred, please?

THE WITNESS: Well, the people began getting up, picking up their belongings and blankets and started walking over by him, and they also shouted the same things.

MR. SCHULTZ: As the people started to get up, did you observe Rubin at that time?

THE WITNESS: Yes sit.

MR. SCHULTZ: Did he say anything else ?

THE WITNESS: Yes, sir. He says, "The pigs are in our park. They're —-" the same word I just used —- "m-f-ers, they're shitheads," and he began to walk toward them.

MR. SCHULTZ: What, if anything, did the people who got up--what did they start to do, please Mr. Murray?

THE WITNESS: The people with Mr. Rubin were yelling, "They're m-f-ers and they're s.o.b.'s"

MR. SCHULTZ: Where was Rubin in relation to the other people as he was walking to where the policemen were?

THE WITNESS: He was right in front of them.

MR. SCHULTZ: What did the police do as the crowd approached them.

THE WITNESS: They backed up against the wall.

MR. SCHULTZ: Would you relate, please, what, if anything, you observed Rubin do?

THE WITNESS: Well, as the crowd approached and stopped they were yelling things, and Mr. Rubin yelled, "You're children are pigs, you're pigs, why don't you get out of the park? Let's get them out of the park!" and the crowd was yelling "White honky m-f-ers, get out of our park! And then I heard Mr. Rubin say, "Look at them. They look so tough with their arms folded. Take off your guns, and we'll fight you hand to hand." And the crowd began to yell the same things.

MR. SCHULTZ: Then what occurred, please?

THE WITNESS: Then I observed Mr. Rubin take a cigarette butt and flick it.

MR. SCHULTZ: And then what occurred, please?

THE WITNESS: Well, then people in the crowd started throwing cans, bottles, stones, small rocks, paper--newspapers that had been crumpled--paper bags, food wrappings.

MR. SCHULTZ: What, if anything, were the ten policemen and the sergeant doing at this time, please?

THE WITNESS: Well, some of the police officers were ducking, and some of them were just standing there in a position like this. (demonstrating)

MR. SCHULTZ: Did you observe where Rubin went-- if he went anywhere--near the end of this ten minute period that you have just described?

THE WITNESS: Almost everyone in this crowd of approximately 200 was screaming something, and I observed Mr. Rubin, who was to my right, start walking backwards out of the crows.

MR. SCHULTZ: Now, calling you attention to the twenty-sixth of August, did you have occasion to see the defendant Jerry Rubin in Lincoln Park on that night?

THE WITNESS: Yes sir, I did.

MR. SCHULTZ: Would you relate what you heard, please?

THE WITNESS: I heard Mr. Rubin saying that the pigs started the violence, and he says, "Tonight, we're not going yo give up the park. We have to fight them. We have to meet violence with violence." He says, "The pigs are armed with guns and clubs and Mace, so we have to arm ourselves," with any kind of weapon they could get.

MR. SCHULTZ: Do you recall any further statements by him at this time?

THE WITNESS: I don't recall what else he said, but he ended it with saying, "And don't forget our gigantic love-in on the beaches tomorrow."

MR. SCHULTZ: Did you have occasion to see Rubin again that night?

THE WITNESS: I saw him walking through the park, walking up to small groups, having a conversation with them and leaving, going from group to group.

MR. SCHULTZ: What did you hear said, please?

THE WITNESS: I heard him say that "We have to fight the pigs in the park tonight," that "we're not going to let them take the park."

MR. SCHULTZ: Now, just before eleven o'clock that evening—this is on Monday night, August 26, 1968—what, if anything, did you observe the crowd do?

THE WITNESS: Well, I observed the crowd—people in the park running through the park, gathering up—carrying park benches and tables. All the tables in the park, they were carrying them to the northeast corner of the park. They were breaking branches off the trees, big limbs. There was lumber, carrying it like over their shoulders, and they were taking all the wastebaskets that were in the park, and some of them the regular type basket and others box-shape, and they were carrying it back to this northeast corner of the park. At this time many people were entering the park, and this crowd became larger and larger by the minute, and they kept piling different items on top, and jamming baskets in between tables and benches, and they were shouting, "Hell, no, we won't go! The park belongs to the people! Fuck Lynsky! Kill the cops!" Things like that.

MR. SCHULTZ: And while the crowd was shouting these things, what, if anything, did the police do?

THE WITNESS: Well, a car approached with microphones on the roof, and it ws making an announcement that the park was closed and anybody found in there would be placed under arrest, and of course, when this car would start the announcement, the shouts and screams were louder, and then rocks— some of the people behind the barricade ran to the left of the barricade and came closer to this police car and threw rocks at it.

MR. WEINGLASS: If your honor please, I object to this line of questioning. There has been no foundation. There have been no preliminary questions as to what defendant, if any, was nearby relating to this incident.

THE COURT: You may justify the asking of the question.

MR. SCHULTZ: Yes, your Honor. Two hours prior to this incident, this witness testified the defendant Rubin encouraged this action. This is the product or part of the product—

MR. WEINGLASS: That is precisely what I was talking about. I think this is most unfair to permit a summation in front of the jury.

THE COURT: I overrule the objection.

MR. SCHULTZ: And then after the police car was hit by the objects, what occurred, please?

THE WITNESS: Shortly after, eight to ten policemen approached.

MR. SCHULTZ: And what occurred, please?

THE WITNESS: Objects came from the crowd, from behind the barricade again, bricks and stones, mostly, bottles and cans, and one policeman turned, started running back, fell down, and they cheered, and the policemen retreated.

Then they came up again but behind them came a skirmish line, one line of policemen shoulder-to-shoulder behind them, and the police shot gas-- I should say threw gas--at the barricade.

MR. SCHULTZ: Then what occurred?

THE WITNESS: Well, everything, objects just pulled out from behind the barricade, people behind the barricade rolled these wastebaskets that were filled with paper, they lit them and they rolled them down the incline toward the policemen.

Finally, just as the police got close to the barricade, everybody started running out of the park.

MR. SCHULTZ: Did you run out of the park?

THE WITNESS: Yes.

MR. SCHULTZ: Your Honor, I have no further questions on direct examination.

* * * * * * *

MR. KUNSTLER: Now, you have testified on direct, as I understand it, that on Sunday, August 25, you had been in Lincoln Park, is that correct, at some time, about between 9:00 and 10:00 p.m.?

THE WITNESS: That's correct.

MR. KUNSTLER: Were you told to watch any particular people?

THE WITNESS: No, sir, I was not.

MR. KUNSTLER: Did you know Jerry Rubin before you entered the park?

THE WITNESS: No, sir, I did not.

MR. KUNSTLER: Had you ever seen him before?

THE WITNESS: Personally, no, sir.

MR. KUNSTLER: Had you seen pictures of him?

THE WITNESS: Yes, sir, on TV and newspapers and magazines.

MR. KUNSTLER: When you saw him in the park that day, you recognized him because you had seen him on TV and in magazines, is that correct?

THE WITNESS: Well, I thought it was him, and then there was a boy standing next to me, a teenager, and he said, "There's Jerry Rubin with the helmet. Now things will start happening."

MR. KUNSTLER: And there is no doubt in your mind, is there, Sergeant, that this was Sunday, August 25?

THE WITNESS: No, sir, there's no doubt.

MR. KUNSTLER: Is it not true, Sergeant Murray, that you told the FBI that this incident occurred on Monday August 26, 1968, instead of Sunday, August 25, 1968?

THE WITNESS: That's correct.

MR. KUNSTLER: When did you come to the conclusion that you had reported as to the incident some two weeks afterwards happened on a different day than you told the FBI?

THE WITNESS: I found out my mistake the first time that I was interviewed by a U.S. Attorney, who was U.S. Attorney Cubbage.

MR. KUNSTLER: Now, you also told the FBI, did you not, that the second incident which you have described as happening on August 26, on Monday evening, you told the FBI, did you not that that occurred on Tuesday night, August 27?

THE WITNESS: That is correct.

MR. KUNSTLER: And is it your testimony now that that, too, was a mistake

THE WITNESS: Yes, sir, it is.

MR. KUNSTLER: Now, when you first saw Mr. Rubin between nine o'clock and ten o'clock on the 25th, as you now testify, what was he wearing in addition to the football helmet.

THE WITNESS: Well, the football helmet was white, it had a blue stripe down the middle, it had a number "88" on the back. He had a sweater or sweatshirt, as I recall, tied around his waist with the sleeves like tied in front, and I believe he was wearing blue jeans or work clothes, as I would describe them.

MR. KUNSTLER: You said Rubin made some remarks to the police such as "you're pigs," and "Get out of the park" and "take off the guns and we'll fight you," and so on.

THE WITNESS: Yes, sir.

MR. KUNSTLER: Now, at that moment I think you said that Jerry Rubin flicked a cigarette butt, is that correct?

THE WITNESS: That's right.

MR. KUNSTLER: Had you seen Jerry Rubin smoking up to this time?

THE WITNESS: No, sir, I didn't.

MR. KUNSTLER: Never saw him smoke, did you?

THE WITNESS: No, sir.

MR. KUNSTLER: When did you see him light his cigarette?

THE WITNESS: I didn't see him light the cigarette.

MR. KUNSTLER: How did the cigarette suddenly appear in his hand, if you know?

THE WITNESS: I don't know.

MR. KUNSTLER: It suddenly is there, is that what you are saying?

THE WITNESS: Yes. He was right to my right, and he took his arm like this, and that's when I saw him flip the cigarette like this.

MR. KUNSTLER: When he flicked the cigarette, what else happened?

THE WITNESS: Well, other people started throwing things.

MR. KUNSTLER: Was that the signal in your mind for other people to throw cigarettes? Is that what you regarded it as?

MR. SCHULTZ: If the Court please, I object to that.

THE COURT: I sustain the objection.

(the court is adjourned for the day)

October 3, 1969

MR. KUNSTLER: Your Honor, in the hope of possibly nipping this in the bud, I would like to ask your honor to at least caution the prosecution to adhere to Canon 7 of the American Bar Association's annually adopted standards and I am referring to the one called "Ethical Consideration" which states:

"A lawyer should not make unfair or derogatory personal reference to opposing counsel. Harangue and offensive tactics by lawyers interfere with the ordinary administration of justice and have no proper place in our legal system."

The remarks that were made by Mr. Foran and Mr. Schultz over the course of this trial on the personal level, the references to television actors and Channel Seven and the like, as well as others which are in the record—

THE COURT: I made a reference to your appearance on television.

MR. KUNSTLER: But not in a derogatory way, you Honor.

THE COURT: I would say a lawyer should always be a gentleman in court. Ours is first of all, Mr. Kunstler, a profession of good manners. I insist on a lawyer having good manners before I even determine whether he is a good lawyer.

MR. KUNSTLER: Your Honor, we were called unethical. I can't think of a grosser insult to an attorney in a courtroom than to be called unethical by opposing counsel. If that is not derogatory—

THE COURT: I wish you would read a document you filed here which I have ordered impounded, and I don't know how you describe that—

MR. KUNSTLER: Your Honor, that is a legitimate attack in a disqualification motion and your Honor knows that as well as I do. That is a legitimate attack.

THE COURT: Don't tell me what I know. I know what that document is because I am a student, I hope, of English. And you should follow the same rules, Mr. Kunstler, and I will ask the Government lawyers to do as I suggest.

Mr. Schultz, if you think some very forceful criticism of counsel on the personal level is indicated, in such an event please ask me to exclude the jury.

MR. SCHULTZ: We will do that, your Honor.

THE COURT: Mr. Marshal, please bring in the jury

(jury enters)

You may continue with the cross examination of this witness, Mr. Kunstler.

MR. KUNSTLER: Sergeant, you testified on direct that on Monday evening you saw a barricade being built, is that correct?

THE WITNESS: Yes, sir.

MR. KUNSTLER: Did you see any physical contact between the police and the people in the vicinity of the barricade.

THE WITNESS: No, sir. I saw bricks and bottles and I saw some of them hitting the policemen.

MR. KUNSTLER: Did you see any of the policemen hit by any of this material.

THE WITNESS: Well, there was one of them that went down as if he was hit, but I couldn't see him get hit. But I saw others being hit as they turned running, I saw things hitting them.

MR. KUNSTLER: Now, Sergeant, just a few more questions, and I am now going back to the preceding night.

Sergeant, I want you to detail for me exactly what Mr. Rubin was wearing on the night of Sunday, August 25, when you first saw him.

THE WITNESS: He was wearing a football helmet. It had a blue stripe down the middle, I would estimate a half-inch stripe, down the middle of this helmet, from the forehead to the neck.

MR. KUNSTLER: Now, you mentioned something about the numbers "88," as I recall, Where were they?

THE WITNESS: On the back, on "8" on the left of the stripe and one "8" on the right of the stripe.

MR. KUNSTLER: Now, Mr. Rubin had this helmet on his head, I understand, during all of the time you saw him on Sunday night.

THE WITNESS: Yes, sir.

MR. KUNSTLER: Can you describe for us the length of Mr. Rubin's beard that night?

THE WITNESS: Well, it--it was not long.

MR. KUNSTLER: But would you say in a matter of inches?

THE WITNESS: Half inch, quarter inch, half inch, something like that.

MR. KUNSTLER: What about Mr. Rubin's height? How tall would you say he was?

THE WITNESS: Five-seven.

MR. KUNSTLER: And how much did he weigh, if you can estimate?

THE WITNESS: About 145 pounds.

MR. KUNSTLER: Now, are you absolutely certain that the man you saw that night with the football helmet with "88" on it was the same defendant, Jerry Rubin, who is sitting here in court today?

THE WITNESS: Yes, sir.

MR. KUNSTLER: There is no question in your mind whatsoever?

THE WITNESS: No, sir.

MR. KUNSTLER: All right. May I have the witness, please

MR. SCHULTZ: Objection.

THE COURT: May you have what?

MR. KUNSTLER: I want him to look at a man, your Honor, and ask him if that was not the man he saw in the park that night.

THE COURT: I sustain the objection.

MR. KUNSTLER: Your Honor, it is like a document. It is perfectly proper to ask if this was the man he saw.

MR. SCHULTZ: Your Honor, it might be out of order, but it will save time. I won't object to that.

THE COURT: You won't object to it?

MR. SCHULTZ: No.

THE COURT: I thought you did. Your objection is valid.
    If the Government doesn't object, let him walk in.

(Robert Levin enters the courtroom)

MR. KUNSTLER: Would you put on the helmet on, please?
    Are you absolutely sure that this is not the man you saw that night in Lincoln Park?

THE WITNESS: Absolutely.

MR. KUNSTLER: You are absolutely certain?

THE WITNESS: Yes, I am. He's too big.

MR. KUNSTLER: Would you turn around also and show him the back of the helmet.

THE WITNESS: That's a motorcycle helmet.

MR. KUNSTLER: That is not the helmet you saw that night?

THE WITNESS: No, it was a football helmet.

MR. KUNSTLER: Your Honor, I have no further questions.

MR. SCHULTZ: Your Honor, may we have for the record an identification of this individual who walked into the courtroom?

THE COURT: Yes. Tell us who your exhibit is.

MR. KUNSTLER: Your Honor, the exhibit is a man named Robert Levin, L-E-V-I-N. Your Honor, I would just like to mark this helmet for identification as Defendants' D-15.

MR. WEINGLASS: This was your first assignment as an undercover agent, is that correct?

THE WITNESS: That's not correct. I at no time was told that I was an undercover agent.

MR. WEINGLASS: Do you recall your interview with the Federal Bureau of Investigation characterizing yourself as an undercover person?

THE WITNESS: They may have said I was undercover, but I said I worked plainclothes and milled in the crowd and tried to get information.

MR. WEINGLASS: Now, when you were told to gather information, were you told to gather information about any particular person?

THE WITNESS: No, sir, I was not.

MR. WEINGLASS: You were just to wander through the park?

THE WITNESS: Yes, sir, I was.

MR. WEINGLASS: You were just to wander through the park?

THE WITNESS: Yes, sir, I was.

MR. WEINGLASS: And report back to your superiors?

THE WITNESS: Yes, sir.

MR. WEINGLASS: Could you tell the jury how it is that you are able to recall approximately thirteen months later the precise words used by Jerry Rubin on Sunday night, August 25, without the benefit of a single note, a single recorded word, or any other note to refresh your recollection?

MR. SCHULTZ: Objection, if the Court please.

MR. WEINGLASS: Could you tell us how you could recall the precise words used, Sergeant?

THE WITNESS: Well, when I set down and really thought about it, and I thought about this incident, it came back very clearly because I was shocked at what was happening, and I remembered it.

MR. WEINGLASS: So, approximately two months later you sat down and you tried to remember and you remembered verbatim what Jerry Rubin said on Monday night, August 26, in the thirty-second speech, is that correct?

THE WITNESS: Yes; I remembered what others said too there.

MR. WEINGLASS: Now you did not testify that you heard Jerry Rubin say anything about erecting a barricade?

THE WITNESS: No, I didn't hear Mr. Rubin say at any time, "We're going to build a barricade," no.

MR. WEINGLASS: As a matter of fact, Jerry Rubin wasn't in the park at the time the barricade was up, isn't that true?

MR. SCHULTZ: Objection, if the Court please.

THE COURT: I will sustain the objection.

MR. WEINGLASS: Sergeant Murray, as I understand your testimony, you never saw Jerry Rubin with a weapon in his hand?

THE WITNESS: That is correct. I never saw him with a weapon.

MR. WEINGLASS: I have concluded my cross-examination.

THE COURT: All right. Mr. Marshal, the court will be in recess until two o'clock.

Frank Riggio's Testimony (police detective)

October 13, 1969

MR. FORAN: Will you state your name, please?

THE WITNESS: Frank Riggio.

MR. FORAN: What is your occupation, Mr. Riggio?

THE WITNESS: I am a detective with the Police Department, City of Chicago.

MR. FORAN: Calling your attention to August of 1968 during the Convention, were you given any specific assignment?

THE WITNESS: I was to keep Rennie Davis under surveillance.

MR. WEINGLASS: At this point, this witness having identified himself now as a surveillance agent, -on behalf of the defendant Rennie Davis I make the objection that a twenty-four-hour surveillance constitutes a constitutional invasion of a citizen's privacy contrary to the Fourth Amendment and I object to this witness being permitted to give any testimony in a Court of law on the ground that his conduct constituted a violation of the United States Constitution.

THE COURT: I will overrule the objection.

MR. FORAN: Calling your attention to August 25, 1968, did you see either Davis or Hayden?

THE WITNESS: Yes, we were in Lincoln Park. My partner and I began to follow Mr. Davis and Mr. Hayden, who were walking together by themselves. They would come to a group of people and stop and talk and then proceed through the group, and then as my partner and I would try to follow, the group would close up and block our way and make it difficult for us to keep Mr. Davis and Mr. Hayden in sight.

MR. FORAN: How long did you follow them around the park that day?

THE WITNESS: Oh, approximately two hours.

MR. FORAN: As you were following them from group to group, at about that time, at ten o'clock, what occurred?

THE WITNESS: Mr. Davis and Mr. Hayden came to a group of people where they stopped and talked to Wolfe Lowenthal. As they stopped and talked to him, Mr. Davis began to proceed toward Stockton Drive. Mr. Hayden and Mr. Lowenthal began to walk off in a different direction. My partner and I began to return to our own vehicle.

MR. FORAN: As you approached the front of your vehicle, what happened?

THE WITNESS: As we approached the front of the vehicle, we could hear a hissing noise coming from the vehicle. We then proceeded around the side of the vehicle and we observed two figures crouched at the right rear tire. At this time, my partner and I shouted to the two figures, and identified ourselves as police officers. As we approached the two figures stood up, one ran off--as I approached I noted it was Tom Hayden stood at the rear tire of the vehicle, I could see that the tire of the vehicle was, for all intents and purposes, flat.

I pursued the figure who had run off toward the group of people who were in the park at the time. He ran a short distance, stopped and turned around and faced me, at which time I grabbed him and began to bring him back to the vehicle. All this time my partner had stayed with Mr. Hayden at the rear of our vehicle.

MR. FORAN: Who was it, by the way, that you had?

THE WITNESS: It was Mr. Wolfe Lowenthal.

MR. FORAN: What happened when you got back to the vehicle?

THE WITNESS: When we got back to the vehicle we informed Mr. Hayden and Mr. Lowenthal that they were under arrest for the damage they had done to the squad car and told them to get into the vehicle.

MR. FORAN: What happened at this time?

THE WITNESS: Mr. Hayden and Mr. Lowenthal at this time refused to get back into the vehicle, and they began to struggle with both my partner and myself. They began to pull away from us, shove us. They braced themselves against the opening of the rear door and would not get into the vehicle.

During this time they began to shout, "Help! Get these policemen! Don't let these policemen arrest us! Help us! Don't let them get us!"

MR. FORAN: What happened then?

THE WITNESS: At this time the crowd began to run over to the vehicle and began to force my partner and myself along with Mr. Hayden and Mr. Lowenthal into the corner formed by our open door and the vehicle itself. The crowd began to scream, "We're not going to let you arrest them!" Somebody yelled, "Get their guns!" Another one yelled, "Get the police! Get these policemen and turn them over to us! We're not going to let you take them!"

MR. FORAN: What occurred then?

THE WITNESS: At this time we informed Mr. Hayden and Mr. Lowenthal that we couldn't possibly effect their arrest at this time but that on the next occasion that we saw them, we would place them under arrest, and at this time they ran off with the crowd of people.

MR. FORAN: What was the crowd doing as they ran off?

THE WITNESS: Screaming and clapping, jumping up and down.

MR. FORAN: Now, did you have occasion to see Hayden and Lowenthal again?

THE WITNESS: The next day I saw them, I believe it was the twenty-sixth of August, in Lincoln Park.

MR. FORAN: Did you see Hayden?

THE WITNESS: Yes. When we first saw them we stopped and informed a uniformed sergeant and a squad of uniformed policemen that our intention was to arrest these two men and to have them pull up a wagon as we approached the group.

MR. FORAN: What happened as you approached the group?

THE WITNESS: As we approached the group, Mr. Hayden and Mr. Lowenthal stood up and informed the group, "Here come the two coppers from last night. They are going to arrest us."

At this time, my partner and I walked into the group and informed Mr. Hayden and Mr. Lowenthal that they were under arrest, and at this time the squadrol had pulled up into the crowd.

MR. FORAN: Now, what did you do then?

THE WITNESS: As we began to walk Mr. Hayden and Mr. Lowenthal into the squadrol, the crowd began to scream, "You can't arrest them!" and "Why are you taking them?" and "We won't let you arrest them!"

MR. FORAN: Do you remember any particular persons in the crowd?

THE WITNESS: I remember one young lady and one young man in particular.

MR. FORAN: Do you know that man's name, Mr. Riggio?

THE WITNESS: Not offhand, no.

MR. FORAN: Will you look over there and see if you can find him at that table?

THE WITNESS: It is the fellow in the blue shirt sitting right over there [indicating].

MR. FORAN: May the record show, your Honor, that the witness has identified Mr. John Froines?

MR. FORAN: Mr. Riggio, at that time did you have a conversation with Mr. Froines?

THE WITNESS: I did. The defendant said, "I demand to know why you are arresting these two." I informed him they were being arrested for a violation that had occurred the previous night. He then stated that, "We are not going to let you take them. If you try to take them all hell is going to break loose in this city."

MR. FORAN: What happened then?

THE WITNESS: At this time, with the help of the uniformed patrolmen, I got into the squadrol along with the defendants Hayden and Lowenthal, and proceeded to 21 South State Street.

MR. FORAN: What did you do when you got there?

THE WITNESS: We began our normal booking procedures of the two defendants.

MR. FORAN: Calling your attention to later on that same evening, close to midnight, where were you?

THE WITNESS: We were at the intersection of Michigan and Balbo Avenue.

MR. FORAN: Who did you see there at the corner of Balbo and Michigan?

THE WITNESS: I saw the two defendants, Rennie Davis, Tom Hayden, and also Wolfe Lowenthal, crossing the intersection of Balbo.

MR. FORAN: What did you and your partner do at that time?

THE WITNESS: I fell into step behind Mr. Davis. My partner fell into step behind Mr. Hayden.

MR. FORAN: What, if anything, happened as you crossed the street?

THE WITNESS: I heard Mr. Hayden, who was a step or two in back of me, say, "Here he comes again," or "Here he is again." And then he said, "You," and he used a profanity.

MR. FORAN: What words did he call you?

THE WITNESS: He said, "Here he is again, you motherfucker." At that time I turned around and observed the defendant Hayden spit at my partner, at which time my partner grabbed Mr. Hayden and Mr. Hayden then fell to the street. The crowd was beginning to rush to the incident which was now occurring.

Mr. Davis turned and began to shout, "They've got Tom again. Let's go help Tom," and they began to rush back toward my partner and Tom Hayden. At this time, with the help of uniformed officers, we pushed the crowd back across Balbo Drive.

MR. FORAN: What did you do then?

THE WITNESS: At this time after the crowd had gotten back, I went back to my partner and Mr. Hayden, and we took Mr. Hayden to a squadrol and placed him in a squadrol.

THE COURT: I think we have reached the time when we normally recess. . .

Mr. Riggio, my name is William Kunstler. I am one of the attorneys for the defendants. On Sunday, August 25, in Lincoln Park, you were arresting Hayden and Lowenthal —for what?

THE WITNESS: For obstructing us.

MR. KUNSTLER: As far as you know, how were they obstructing you?

THE WITNESS: If we had received an emergency call or any sort of communication from the squad operator we wouldn't be able to fulfill it with a flat tire.

MR. KUNSTLER: And then you indicated Mr. Hayden screamed for help.

THE WITNESS: Correct. Mr. Lowenthal also screamed.

MR. KUNSTLER: And then what happened?

THE WITNESS: A large group of people began to form around our vehicle.

MR. KUNSTLER: And you reached a decision that it would be the better part of discretion not to effectuate an arrest at that moment, is that correct?

THE WITNESS: Correct.

MR. KUNSTLER: Did anybody in that group strike you?

THE WITNESS: No, they did not.

MR. KUNSTLER: Did anybody in that group throw anything at you?

THE WITNESS: I don't recall them throwing. They may have.

MR. KUNSTLER: And when you last had contact with Lowenthal and Hayden, did you tell them you would arrest them the next day?

THE WITNESS: Before we released Lowenthal and Hayden to the crowd, we informed them that they would be arrested by us at the next convenient time.

MR. KUNSTLER: Now that brings us to Monday, August 26. There came a time when you saw Tom Hayden and Wolf Lowenthal?

THE WITNESS: Correct. They were in a group of people who were southeast of the field house.

MR. KUNSTLER: Did you find yourself in the center of this group again as you had the night before?

THE WITNESS: Yes.

MR. KUNSTLER: Now when you went to arrest Mr. Hayden or Mr. Lowenthal, the two of you, did Mr. Hayden or Mr. Lowenthal tell the crowd, "Help, get these coppers, keep them from arresting us," or anything similar to what you had heard the night before?

THE WITNESS: No, nothing like the night before. They just informed the crowd that they were being arrested.

MR. KUNSTLER: Did you explain when you were in the middle of this group with Mr. Hayden and Mr. Lowenthal why you were arresting them?

THE WITNESS: I believe we told them obstructing a police officer, resisting arrest, and I don't know if it was disorderly conduct in there too.

MR. KUNSTLER: But it is true, is it not, Officer, that these arrests that you were making there were for activities that occurred on another day, is that correct?

THE WITNESS. Correct.

MR. KUNSTLER: Did they offer any resistance at any time from the time you walked up to them and said, you are under arrest, and the time you took them and put them in the squadrol?

THE WITNESS: No, they did not.

MR. KUNSTLER: Detective Riggio, you had testified, as I recall, that Mr. Froines had demanded to know why you were arresting Lowenthal and Hayden. Then at that moment, as I remember, you indicated that Mr. Froines said something, demanding that you release the two men, or. as you put it, I think, "all hell would break loose in the city," is that correct?

THE WITNESS: Correct.

MR. KUNSTLER: You continued with the arrest, did you not?

THE WITNESS: Correct.

MR. KUNSI'LER: Did all hell break loose in the city, to your knowledge?

THE WITNESS: My opinion, yes.

MR. KUNSTLER: Your opinion was all hell broke loose because of these arrests?

THE WITNESS: Yes.

MR. KUNSTLER: Were you somewhere where all hell broke loose after these arrests?

THE WITNESS: I was in the police building when the march occurred at the police building and I could observe what was occurring in the street.

MR. KUNSTLER: And that is what you call "all hell breaking loose?"

THE WITNESS: That is what I call "all hell breaking loose."

MR. KUNSTLER: Describe "all hell breaking loose."

THE WITNESS: The tie-up in the traffic around the police building, the fact that the police building had to be secured by police personnel at the entrance to the building, and the amount of people who were chanting and screaming and shouting outside the police building.

MR. KUNSTLER: That is what you characterize as "all hell breaking loose," is that correct?

THE WITNESS: That is what I do, yes.

MR.. KUNSTLER: You are smiling when you say that. Is there any reason for that smile?

THE WITNESS: No reason for my smile.

MR. KUNSTLER: Did you see the marchers throw anything at the policemen?

THE WITNESS: I did not observe that long.

MR. KUNSTLER: How long did you observe?

THE WITNESS: A matter of a minute.

MR. KUNSTLER: It was in that minute that you made the determination that all hell had broken loose?

THE WITNESS. Correct.

MR. KUNSTLER: In your definition people marching on the sidewalk, crossing the street, shouting something which you could hear from the thirteenth floor, this was a definition of "all hell breaking loose" in Chicago?

THE WITNESS: Correct.

MR. KUNSTLER: And all of this, do you attribute to Mr. Froines' remarks in the park?

THE WITNESS: In my opinion, yes.

MR. KUNSTLER: You think he instigated all of that?

THE WITNESS: That is my opinion, yes.

MR. KUNSTLER: Detective Riggio, did you ever tell the FBI about the incident, forgetting Mr. Froines' name, did you tell them that an unknown male said these words to you in Lincoln Park?

THE WITNESS: Yes, I did.

MR. KUNSTLER: I will show you D-34, which is a report labeled FBI report on September 25, 1968. I ask you whether it in any way refreshes your recollection as to whether you told them about this incident by looking through the documents themselves?

THE WITNESS: I did tell them about this incident, yes. I don't have to look at the documents.

MR. KUNSTLER: There is no question in your mind that you told them?

THE WITNESS: I believe I did, yes.

MR. KUNSTLER: Now does any mention of that appear in any of those reports?

THE WITNESS: These are not my statements.

MR. FORAN: Object, your Honor.

THE COURT: I sustain the objection.

MR. KUNSTLER: After you had gone to the police station with Hayden and Lowenthal, did you go back to 407 South Dearborn to pick up Rennie Davis again?

THE WITNESS: I believe we went by there, yes.

MR. KUNSTLER: Did you finally find them again?

THE WITNESS: Yes, I did, shortly after midnight of the twenty-sixth.

MR. KUNSTLER: After you saw Davis, what did you do?

THE WITNESS: I fell into step behind Mr. Davis.

MR. KUNSTLER: Behind Mr. Davis. Where did Mr. Bell fall in step?

THE WITNESS: Behind Mr. Hayden.

MR. KUNSTLER: Now you have testified, I believe, there was a crowd of people in the vicinity, is that correct?

THE WITNESS: Correct.

MR. KUNSTLER: Is it your testimony that the crowd in some way interfered with the arrest of Mr. Hayden?

THE WITNESS: The crowd was not permitted to get to Officer Bell or Tom Hayden.

MR. KUNSTLER: And when you say the crowd was not permitted, what did the police officers say to the crowd?

THE WITNESS: The police officers told the crowd to go back along with me, and we held them back from going toward the incident that was occurring.

MR. KUNSTLER: When you say "held back." did you seize people? Did you grab them?

THE WITNESS: Grabbed people, pushed them, just kept people from running past.

MR. KUNSTLER: How many did you grab?

THE WITNESS: Oh, Mr. Davis and a few others.

MR. KUNSTLER: You grabbed Mr. Davis?

THE WITNESS: I didn't say I grabbed Mr. Davis. I held Mr. Davis from going back. I stopped Mr. Davis from going back.

MR. KUNSTLER: Where was Mr. Hayden?

THE WITNESS: Mr. Hayden was laying in the street toward the southwest corner of Michigan and Balbo Drive.

MR. KUNSTLER: How did Mr. Hayden get to the ground?

THE WITNESS: Mr. Hayden fell to the ground.

MR. KUNSTLER: Is it what you would call going limp?

THE WITNESS: I would call it that, yes.

MR. KUNSTLER: Mr. Hayden wasn't offering any resistance, was he?

THE WITNESS: Yes, he was, sir, by pulling away from Officer Bell.

MR. KUNSTLER: Do you recall seeing Officer Bell punch Mr. Hayden to the ground?

THE WITNESS: Officer Bell did not punch Mr. Hayden to the ground.

MR. KUNSTLER: Now, with Mr. Hayden on the ground, did the crowd throw anything at you?

THE WITNESS: Nothing struck me, sir.

MR. KUNSTLER: You weren't hit with any fists, were you?

THE WITNESS: No, I don't recall being hit.

MR. KUNSTLER: You weren't hit with any stones or sticks?

THE WITNESS: No, I was not.

MR. KUNSTLER: Brass knuckles?

THE WITNESS: I was not.

MR. KUNSTLER: I have no further questions.

THE COURT: With that I think we can recess for the day.

October, 15, 1969

MR. DELLINGER: Mr. Hoffman. we are observing the moratorium.

THE COURT: I am Judge Hoffman, sir.

MR. DELLINGER: I believe in equality, sir, so I prefer to call people Mr. or by their first name.

THE COURT: Sit down. The clerk is about to call my cases.

MR. DELLINGER: I wanted to explain to you we are reading the names of the war dead.

THE MARSHAL: Sit down.

MR. DELLINGER: We were just reading the names of the dead from both sides.

THE MARSHAL: Sit down.

THE CLERK: No. 69 CR 180. United States of America vs. David T. Dellinger, et al. Case on trial.

MR. KUNSTLER: Your Honor, just one preliminary application this morning. The defendants who were not permitted by your Honor to be absent today or to have a court recess for the Vietnam moratorium brought in an American flag and an NLF Flag which they placed on the counsel table to commemorate the dead Americans and the dead Vietnamese in this long and brutal war that has been going on. The marshal removed those from the table. First he took the NLF Flag after directing me to order the client to have it removed which I refused to do, and then he removed it himself, and then subsequently he removed the American flag.

THE COURT: We have an American flag in the corner. Haven't you seen it during the three-and-a-half weeks you have been here?

MR. KUNSTLER: Yes, but we wanted the juxtaposition, your Honor, of the two flags together in one place.

THE COURT: Mr. Kunstler, let me interrupt you to say that whatever decoration there is in the Courtroom will be furnished by the Government and I think things look all right in this courtroom.

MR. KUNSTLER: Your Honor, I am applying for permission to have both flags on this Vietnam Moratorium Day.

THE COURT: That permission will be denied. That is a table for the defendants and their lawyers and it is not to be decorated. There is no decoration on the Government's table.

MR. KUNSTLER: That is the Government's wish, your Honor. We don't tell them what to do or what not to do.

THE COURT: But I tell everybody what to do as far as the decorations of this courtroom are concerned and we are not going to have the North Vietnamese flag on the table, sir.

Your motion for flags to he placed on the table, flags of any nation, is denied, and at the same time I point out standing in the courtroom--and it has been here since this building was opened--is an American flag.

ABBIE HOFFMAN: We don't consider this table a part of the court and we want to furnish it in our own way.

THE MARSHAL: Sit down.

THE COURT: I will ask you to sit down.

Bring in the jury, Mr. Marshal.

(jury enters)

MR. DELLINGER: We would like to propose

MR. SCHULTZ: If the Court please--

MR. FORAN: Your Honor. If the Court please, may the marshal take that man into custody?

MR. DELLINGER: A moment of silence--

MR. SCHULTZ: Your Honor, this man--

THE COURT: Mr. Marshal. take out the jury.

(jury excused)

MR. DELLINGER: We only wanted a moment of silence.

MR. FORAN: Your Honor, this man has announced this on the elevator coming up here that he was intending to do this.

MR. DELLINGER: I did not. I would have been glad to, but I did not.

MR. FORAN: Your Honor, I object to this man speaking out in court.

THE COURT: You needn't object. I forbid him to disrupt the proceedings. I note for the record that his name is--

MR. DELLINGER: David Dellinger is my name.

THE COURT: You needn't interrupt my sentence for me.

MR. DELLINGER: You have been interrupting ours. I thought I might finish that sentence.

THE COURT: The name of this man who has attempted to disrupt the proceedings in this court is David Dellinger and the record will clearly indicate that, Miss Reporter, and I direct him and all of the others not to repeat such occurrences.

MR. KUNSTLER: Your Honor, I just want to object to Mr. Foran yelling in the presence of the jury. Your Honor has admonished counsel many times on the defense side for yelling, but particularly when the jury was halfway out the door.

MR. FORAN: Your Honor, that is outrageous. This man is a mouthpiece. Look at him, wearing an arm band like his clients, your Honor. Any lawyer comes into a courtroom and has no respect for the Court and acts in conjunction with that kind of conduct before the Court, your Honor, the Government protests his attitude and would like to move the Court to make note of his conduct before this court.

THE COURT: Note has been duly made on the record.

MR. KUNSTLER: Your Honor, I think that the temper and the tone of voice and the expression on Mr. Foran's face speaks more than any picture could tell.

THE COURT: Mr. Kunstler--

MR. FORAN: Of my contempt for Mr. Kunstler, your Honor.

MR. KUNSTLER: To call me a mouthpiece, and for your Honor not to open his mouth and say that is not to be done in your court, I think that violates the sanctity of this court. That is a word that your Honor knows is contemptuous and contumacious.

THE COURT: Don't tell me what I know.

MR. KUNSTLER: I am wearing an armband in memoriam to the dead, your Honor, which is no disgrace in this country.

I want him admonished, your Honor. I request you to do that. The word "mouthpiece" is a contemptuous term.

THE COURT: Did you say you want to admonish me?

MR. KUNSTLER: No, I want you to admonish him.

THE COURT: Let the record show I do not admonish the United States Attorney because he was properly representing his client, the United States of America.

MR. KUNSTLER: To call another attorney a mouthpiece and a disgrace for wearing a black armband--

THE COURT: To place the flag of an enemy country--

MR. KUNSTLER: No, your Honor, there is no declared war.

MR. HAYDEN: Are you at war with Vietnam?

THE COURT: Any country--

Let that appear on the record also.

Bring in the jury. I don't want--

MR. KUNSTLER: Are you turning down my request after this disgraceful episode? You are not going to say anything?

THE COURT: I not only turn it down, I ignore it.

MR. KUNSTLER: That speaks louder than words, too, your Honor.

THE COURT: And let that appear of record, the last words of Mr. Kunstler, and, Miss Reporter, be very careful to have them on the record.

(jury enters)

THE COURT: I say good morning again, ladies and gentlemen of the jury. Will the witness please resume the stand?

MR. WEINGLASS: Now, it was your assignment to watch Mr. Davis?

THE WITNESS: Correct.

MR. WEINGLASS: Wasn't it also your assignment to threaten Mr. Davis, to tell him to get out of town?

THE WITNESS: That is incorrect, sir.

MR. WEINGLASS: You never threatened him?

THE WITNESS: I don't recall threatening Mr. Davis.

MR. WEINGLASS: You don't recall? But it is possible, isn't it?

THE WITNESS: I did not threaten Mr. Davis or tell Mr. Davis or Mr. Hayden to get out of town.

MR. WEINGLASS: You are positive of that?

THE WITNESS: I am fairly positive of that, yes.

MR. WEINGLASS: Fairly positive? Could you explain to the jury why, when I asked you that just a minute ago, you said you couldn't recall.

THE WITNESS: I already explained that, sir. I can't recall because I didn't make the statement.

MR. WEINGLASS: Isn't it a fact that you were armed and you had a weapon?

THE WITNESS: Naturally, sir.

MR. WEINGLASS: That you struck Mr. Davis on occasion?

THE WITNESS: No, I never struck Mr. Davis.

MR. WEINGLASS: You told him he had better get out of town or he would be killed?

THE WITNESS: No, sir, I never said that.

MR. WEINGLASS: Wasn't the purpose of your mission to drive these two young men out of town so they wouldn't have their peaceful demonstration?

THE WITNESS: No, sir, that was not the purpose of my mission.

MR. WEINGLASS: Didn't you discontinue on Tuesday when you found out that they couldn't be driven out of town, or Mr. Davis was doing nothing wrong?

THE WITNESS: No, sir, that is not true.

MR. WEINGLASS: Nothing further.

Irwin Bock's Testimony (police officer)

MR. SCHULTZ: Please state your name.

THE WITNESS: Irwin Bock.

MR. SCHULTZ: Your occupation, please.

THE WITNESS: Chicago police officer.

MR. SCHULTZ: Where are you presently assigned?

THE WITNESS: I am assigned to the subversive unit.

MR. SCHULTZ: Have you ever worn a Chicago police uniform?

THE WITNESS: No sir, I have not.

MR. SCHULTZ: Since becoming a Chicago policeman, have you joined any organizations?

THE WITNESS: Yes, I have. I joined the Veterans for Peace here in Chicago. I am at present a member of the executive committee of that organization. I am on the executive board of the Chicago Peace Council.

MR. SCHULTZ: Mr. Bock, are you or have you been since you became a member of the Chicago Police Department a member of any other organization?

THE WITNESS: Yes, sir, I am at present on the steering committee of the New Mobilization.

MR. SCHULTZ: While a member of these organizations that you have just related to the Court and to the jury, were you in your undercover capacity as a Chicago police officer?

THE WITNESS: Yes, sir, I was..

MR. SCHULTZ: Do you recall, Mr. Bock, the next time you saw the defendant Rennie Davis?

THE WITNESS: Yes, sir, three days later, on August 4, at a meeting at the Moraine Hotel in Highland Park.

MR. SCHULTZ: Were any other defendants present?

THE WITNESS: Dave Dellinger and Tom Hayden. Dave Dellinger spoke first at the meeting. He welcomed the people. He said that "a lot of you have come from the far ends of the country. We haven't come here to disrupt the Democratic Convention, nor have we come here to support any candidate to that convention." He then introduced Rennie Davis as the coordinator of the actions for Chicago.

Davis said to the people that on August 24 movement centers would open up throughout the Chicago area. He said on the following day, August 25, that there would be a huge picket held in the Loop area. He said that we would test the police on this day to see what reaction they would have toward the demonstrators, to see whether or not they took a hard stand or a soft stand. Davis said that on August 29 a rally would be held in the Grant Park area at the Bandshell and from this rally a mill-in would take place in the Loop. The mill-in would be set up so that it would close down such places as banks, draft boards, Federal buildings, police headquarters. Davis said the Loop would be closed on that day.

MR. SCHULTZ: After Davis finished speaking, what, if anything occurred, please?

THE WITNESS: Dave Dellinger adjourned the meeting or the morning session and said we should have lunch. The majority of the people left the meeting hall in the hotel and went toward the beach area.

MR. SCHULTZ: Specifically where on the beach area did you go with your lunch?

THE WITNESS: I joined a group of people close to where Rennie Davis and Tom Hayden were standing.

MR. SCHULTZ: Did you have occasion to overbear anything that the defendants Davis and Hayden were saying?

THE WITNESS: Yes, sir. Rennie Davis said that the demonstrators could use the snake dance as they do in Japan to break police lines. Tom Hayden replied to Davis and said, "Yes, we can do that," or "That's great, but the demonstrators need something else to use against the police." He said, "We have the formula for Mace and if we place this in the squirt-type bottle such as a Windex bottle or an atomizer-type bottle, the demonstrators then could use that against the police."

MR. SCHULTZ: Did you hear any more of the conversation?

THE WITNESS: No, sir, I did not.

MR. SCHULTZ: Now, Mr. Bock, when is the next time you saw either Davis, Dellinger, or Hayden?

THE WITNESS: That was August 9. Rennie Davis was at the National Mobilization office, Abbie Hoffman, Tom Hayden, and Lee Weiner, a David Baker-I believe Steve Buff and Richard Bosciano were also present, and there were about ten other people.

MR. SCHULTZ: Do you recall anybody else being present at that meeting, any other defendants?

THE WITNESS: A John Froines was present also.

MR. FROINES: Why didn't he say Dellinger?

MR. SCHULTZ: Do you recall if any other defendant was present?

THE WITNESS: Dave Dellinger was also at that meeting.

THE WITNESS: Hayden said that he, Rennie Davis, and Abbie Hoffman had been making plans for diversionary tactics to take place while the main march was going to the Amphitheatre. These diversionary tactics were the breaking of windows, pulling of fire alarm boxes, the setting of small fires, and that they had two purposes, Davis said the first purpose was to divide the police in such a way that it would take the entire police force to either watch the demonstrators or put down the disturbances.

He said that this would necessitate the calling of the police away from the Amphitheatre and would allow the demonstrators to go to the Amphitheatre and confront the war makers.

Tom Hayden said that if the South and West Sides would rise Lip as they did in the April riots in Chicago here, the city would have a lot of trouble on their hands. Abbie Hoffman turned to Hayden and said, "it would be like another Chicago Fire." Davis then introduced a David Baker, who he said had been active during the Detroit riots in a militant capacity. He said that Baker's group Would be coming to Chicago to aid in the training of the National Mobilization marshals.

Abbie Hoffman said that the Yippies would aid in the diversionary tactics on August 28 and that he wanted the National Mobilization marshals to aid the Yippies on August 25 in defense of Lincoln Park.

MR. SCHULTZ: Mr. Bock, calling your attention to August 13, 1968, in the early afternoon, do you recall where you were?

THE WITNESS: Yes, sir, I do. I was at the south end of Lincoln Park near the field house.

MR. SCHULTZ: Did you see any of the defendants there at that time?

THE WITNESS: Yes, sir, I did. Rennie Davis, Tom Hayden, and Lee Weiner.

MR. SCHULTZ: Did you observe anything occur in the presence of the defendants Hayden, Davis and Weiner and in the presence of yourself?

THE WITNESS: Yes, sir. David Baker instructed the people present in the snake dance.

MR. SCHULTZ: What, if anything, occurred, please?

THE WITNESS: The people practiced the snake dance as Baker had instructed it and Tom Hayden, Rennie Davis and Lee Weiner took part in that practice both as a demonstrator and in a leadership role in the snake dance.

MR. SCHULTZ: Did you take part in the snake dance?

THE WITNESS: Yes, sir, I did. . . .

MR. SCHULTZ: Now, calling your attention to Wednesday, August 21, in the early afternoon, with what defendant or defendants did you have a conversation?

THE WITNESS: I talked with Lee Weiner. Weiner told me of a marshals' meeting that was to take place at the offices of the National Mobilization at four o'clock that afternoon.

MR. SCHULTZ: Did you go to that meeting?

THE WITNESS: Yes, sir, I did.

MR. SCHULTZ: Who was present at the meeting?

THE WITNESS: Rennie Davis, John Froines, Lee Weiner, and about fifteen marshals that were to participate during the Democratic Convention.

MR. SCHULTZ: Was there a conversation at that meeting?

THE WITNESS: Rennie Davis said, "We have several alternatives that we can do on August 28 in relation to the march that had been announced."
He said, "First of all we could have the march as we had announced."
   He said, "Secondly, we could have a rally take place in the Grant Park area, with a confrontation.
   "The last alternative is to hold a rally and then take over some buildings in the Loop area."
   He said, "This could be accomplished by giving speeches during the time of that rally to incite the crowd for such a takeover." He illustrated a takeover such as the one that took place at Columbia, physically blocking the entrances and exits so no one could enter or leave. He said, "The people would be arrested in such a situation rather than just merely dispersed."
   He then suggested three buildings for possible discussion. One was the Federal Building, one was the Pick-Congress and the other was the Conrad Hilton.
   Lee Weiner said at this point that this was too important to discuss here and that we ought to discuss this at his apartment later that evening.

MR. SCHULTZ: You say Weiner said this?

THE WITNESS: I beg your pardon, it was John Froines.

MR. SCHULTZ: If the Court please, I would ask the Court again if he would direct the marshals to direct the defendants and their lawyers to stop laughing out loud as they just did. Mr. Kunstler was probably more guilty of it than any of the defendants.

THE COURT: I direct the marshal to go over there to the defendants' table and request them as we have done repeatedly in the past not to laugh loudly during this trial. This is a trial in the United States District Court. It is not a vaudeville theatre.

MR. KUNSTLER: But, your Honor, we are human beings, too. You can't make automatons out of us, or robots; we are human beings and we laugh occasionally, and if it comes irrepressibly, I don't really see how that really becomes a court matter.

MR. SCHULTZ: Mr. Kunstler is laughing so he can influence the jury with the impression that this is absurd. That is why he is laughing aloud because he--
   If Mr. Dellinger would stop talking when we are addressing the Court

MR. DELLINGER: I am trying to tell something to my lawyer. It is absurd. It is--he is a vaudeville actor.

THE COURT: You have made your observation, Sir.

MR. SCHULTZ: May I proceed, your Honor?

After that meeting at the offices of the National Mobilization Committee, where did you go, please?

THE WITNESS: We adjourned the meeting and I went to eat dinner.

MR. SCHULTZ: After you ate dinner, where did you go?

THE WITNESS: I met John Froines, Richard Bosciano, and Steve Buff and drove them out to the meeting.

MR. SCHULTZ: Mr. Bock, please relate the conversation that occurred that evening.

THE WITNESS: Lee Weiner said that we should have a march anyway without a permit since this would provoke an arrest situation. He said he could see the headlines the next day saying "100,000 Demonstrators Arrested Confronting the Democratic Convention."

He said, however, he favored Rennie Davis' last point personally. He said there could be a rally held in Grant Park at the Bandshell, speeches could be given to incite the crowd on the takeover of a building in the Loop area.

He said that the Conrad Hilton would be the best building--for various reasons.

He said that because of the size of the Conrad Hilton, it would be better only if we took over one floor of the Hilton, and he said the fifteenth floor would be best.

Lee Weiner said we probably would get help from within.

John Froines said that such a takeover would be like Columbia, the physical stopping of anybody coming or going in that building. He said it would receive the necessary publicity since the cameras and the press and TV were already situated there.

He said that he and Lee Weiner would report to Rennie Davis the following day the decision of the marshals that evening. . . .

MR. SCHULTZ: Mr. Bock, when we finished yesterday we were at Monday night, August 26, 1968, at Lincoln Park. You were at the fieldhouse area and you saw Davis, Weiner, Froines and Rubin standing together with some other people. Would you relate what conversation occurred when you approached this group, please, at about seven o'clock on the evening of Monday, August 26?

THE WITNESS: Rennie Davis said that the people reacted well to Tom Hayden's arrest and that they stood up well to the police at the statue.

He said, "We should have a wall-to-wall sit-in in front of the Conrad Hilton. When the police come to break these people up, that they would break into small bands and go directly into the Loop causing disturbances. They could break windows, pull fire alarm boxes, stone police cars, break street lights."

Mr. Rubin then said that they ought to do these things and they ought to do one more. He said they could start fires in the Loop.

Mr. Froines then said that the demonstrators would need things to use against the police. He said that they could purchase ammonia from many stores in the city and if they placed this ammonia into small bottles or something that would break. they could throw this at the police. He said by adding soap or soap chips to the ammonia, it would prolong the effects of the ammonia on the police officers or National Guard.

Lee Weiner said that they could let the air out of tires at the stop lights or stop signs in the Loop, jam up the traffic.

A Walter Gross said that it would be faster if we just slashed the tires and then Lee Weiner agreed and said it would.

MR. SCHULTZ: Did you see any of the defendants later on that night, that Monday night?

THE WITNESS: No sir, I did not.

MR. SCHULTZ: All right, now, calling your attention to the next day, which is Thursday, the twenty-ninth of August, in the morning, do you recall where you went, please?

THE WITNESS: I went across the street from the Conrad Hilton into Grant Park.

MR. SCHULTZ: And did you see any of the defendants in Grant Park when you arrived there, please?

THE WITNESS: Yes, sir. John Froines and Lee Weiner.

MR. SCHULTZ: Would you relate what occurred, please, on arriving with the group?

THE WITNESS: On arriving, I noticed that Wolfe Lowenthal's arm was bandaged and in a sling, and a companion of his had bandages on also. He told me that he had injured his arm last night in the street.

Weiner said we should have had some cocktails last night. Craig Shimabukuro asked Weiner whether he meant Molotov cocktails or not. He said he did. "They're easy to make. All it takes is gasoline, sand, rags, and bottles."

Weiner said a good mobile tactic would be to pick a target in the Loop area and bomb that target. He said a better diversionary tactic would be the bombing of the underground garage. "Because of the size of the underground garage, it would take an enormous amount of police to protect that area and to search it."

He said or when it was bombed, that it would also take an enormous amount of fire equipment to put any fires out down there. Weiner then asked me if I could obtain the bottles necessary to make the Molotov cocktails. I told him I would. Weiner said that he and Craig Shimabukuro would then obtain the other materials necessary to make the Molotov cocktails, and that we were to meet back in Grant Park one hour from the time we left after the meeting.

At this point. a gentleman came by with a camera, and Lee Weiner said, "That guy just took our pictures. Let's split."

MR. SCHULTZ: After this conversation was over, where did you go, please?

THE WITNESS: I went to phone mv control officer. . . .

MR. SCHULTZ: And after you finished playing baseball, what occurred, please?

THE WITNESS: By now a large group of people had come to the picnic and I saw Tom Hayden, Rennie Davis, Lee Weiner and John Froines with other people seated close to the house.

MR. SCHULTZ: Relate, please, the convention that occurred when you arrived at this group.

THE WITNESS: Just as I arrived. a man in a business suit and holding a pad asked Rennie Davis and Tom Hayden a question, "What has the National Mobilization gained from the demonstrations during the Democratic Convention?"

Rennie Davis answered first and he said that we had won America and that the American people now are on the side of the peace movement.

Tom Hayden said that this was the first step toward the revolution and that the second step would be coming soon.

MR. SCHULTZ: Then what occurred, please?

THE WITNESS: Lee Weiner said that the police had arrested Craig Shimabukuro in the underground garage last night. He said that had the police awaited five more minutes, they would have caught him with the necessary materials in his car to make the Molotov cocktails. Weiner said that there must be a police agent high in the staff of the National Mobilization.

John Froines agreed with Weiner, saying there is someone high in the staff of the National Mobilization who is a police agent. Tom Hayden said that he would like to get his hands on that s.o.b. Froines said that "I would like to get my licks in on him, too."

John Froines said the next time the National Mobilization plans anything they will have enough things to use against the police and National Guard so that he wouldn't have to use his own identification to buy the butyric acid which was used earlier that week.

MR. SCHULTZ: At that point, what, if anything, did you do?

THE WITNESS: I made an excuse that I had to work and left the area.

MR. SCHULTZ: No further questions on direct, your Honor.

Closing Argument

Closing Argument for the Defendants by William Kuntsler

MR. KUNSTLER: Ladies and Gentlemen of the jury:

This is the last voice that you will hear from the defense. We have no rebuttal. This Government has the last word.

In an introductory fashion I would just like to state that only you will judge this case as far as the facts go. This is your solemn responsibility and it is an awesome one.

After you have heard Mr. Schultz and Mr. Weinglass, there must be lots of questions running in your minds. You have seen the same scenes described by two different people. You have heard different interpretations of those scenes by two different people. But you are the ones that draw the final inference. You will be the ultimate arbiters of the fate of these seven men.

In deciding this case we are relying upon your oath of office and that you will decide it only on the facts, not on whether you like the lawyers or don't like the lawyers. We are really quite unimportant. Whether you like the judge or don't like the judge, that is unimportant, too. Whether you like the defendants or don't like the defendants

THE COURT: I am glad you didn't say I was unimportant.

MR. KUNSTLER: No. The likes or dislikes are unimportant.

And I can say that it is not whether you like the defendants or don't like the defendants. You may detest all of the defendants, for all I know; you may love all of them, I don't know. It is unimportant. It shouldn't interfere with your decision, it shouldn't come into it. And this is hard to do.

You have seen a long defense here. There have been harsh things said in this court, and harsh things to look at from your jury box. You have seen a man bound and gagged. You have heard lots of things which are probably all not pleasant. Some of them have been humorous. Some have been bitter. Some may have been downright boring, and I imagine many were. Those things really shouldn't influence your decision. You have an oath to decide the facts and to decide them divorced of any personal considerations of your own, and I remind you that if you don't do that, you will be living a lie the rest of your life, and only you will be living with that lie.

Now, I don't think it has been any secret to you that the defendants have some questions as to whether they are receiving a fair trial. That has been raised many times.

MR. FORAN: Your Honor, I object to this.

THE COURT: I sustain the objection.

MR. KUNSTLER: They stand here indicted under a new statute. In fact, the conspiracy, which is Count I, starts the day after the President signed the law.

MR. FORAN: Your Honor, I object to that. The law is for the Court to determine, not for counsel to determine.

THE COURT: I sustain the objection.

MR. KUNSTLER: Your Honor, I am not going into the law. They have a right to know when it was passed.

THE COURT: I don't want my responsibility usurped by you.

MR. KUNSTLER: I want you to know, first that these defendants had a constitutional right to travel. They have a constitutional right to dissent and to agitate for dissent. No one would deny that, not Mr. Foran, and not I, or anyone else.

MR. KUNSTLER: Just some fifty years ago, I think almost exactly, in a criminal court building here in Chicago, Clarence Darrow said this:

"When a new truth comes upon the earth, or a great idea necessary for mankind is born, where does it come from? Not from the police force, or the prosecuting attorneys, or the judges, or the lawyers, or the doctors. Not there. It comes from the despised and the outcasts, and it comes perhaps from jails and prisons. It comes from men who have dared to be rebels and think their thoughts, and their faith has been the faith of rebels.

"What do you suppose would have happened to the working men except for these rebels all the way down through history? Think of the complacent cowardly people who never raise their voices against the powers that be. If there had been only these, you gentlemen of the jury would be hewers of wood and drawers of water. You gentlemen would have been slaves. You gentlemen owe whatever you have and whatever you hope to these brave rebels who dared to think, and dared to speak, and dared to act."

This was Clarence Darrow fifty years ago in another case.

You don't have to look for rebels in other countries. You can just look at the history of this country.

You will recall that there was a great demonstration that took place around the Custom House in Boston in 1770. It was a demonstration of the people of Boston against the people who were enforcing the Sugar Act, the Stamp Act, the Quartering of Troops Act. And they picketed at one place where it was important to be, at the Custom House where the customs were collected.

You remember the testimony in this case. Superintendent Rochford said, "Go up to Lincoln Park, go to the Bandshell, go anywhere you want, but don't go to the Amphitheatre."

That was like telling the Boston patriots, "Go anywhere You want, but don't go to the Custom House," because it was at the Custom House and it was at the Amphitheatre that the protesters wanted to show that something was terribly and totally wrong. They wanted to show it at the place it was important, and so the seeming compliance of the City in saying n "Go anywhere you want throughout the city. Go to Jackson Park. Go to Lincoln Park," has no meaning. That is an excuse for preventing a demonstration at the single place that had meaning, which was the Amphitheatre.

The Custom House in Boston was the scene of evil and so the patriots demonstrated. They ran into a Chicago. You know what happened. The British soldiers shot them down and killed five of them, including one black man, Crispus Attucks, who was the first man to die, by the way, in the American revolution. They were shot down in the street by the British for demonstrating at the Custom House.

You will remember that after the Boston Massacre which was the name the Colonies gave to it. all sorts of things happened in the Colonies. There were all sorts of demonstrations--

MR. FORAN: Your Honor, I have sat here quite a while and I object to this. This is not a history lecture. The purpose of summation is to sum up the facts of the case and I object to this.

THE COURT: I do sustain the objection. Unless you get down to evidence, I will direct you to discontinue this lecture on history. We are not dealing with history.

MR. KUNSTLER: But to understand the overriding issues as well, your Honor-

THE COURT: I will not permit any more of these historical references and I direct you to discontinue them, sir.

MR. KUNSTLER: I do so under protest, your Honor. I will get down, because the judge has prevented me from going into material that I wanted to--

MR. FORAN: Your Honor, I object to that comment.

THE COURT: I have not prevented you. I have ruled properly as a matter of law. The law prevents you from doing it, sir.

MR. KUNSTLER: I will get down to the evidence in this case. I am going to confine my remarks to showing you how the Government stoops to conquer in this case.

The prosecution recognized early that if you were to see thirty-three police officers in uniform take the stand that you would realize how much of the case depends on law enforcement officers. So they strip the uniforms from those witnesses, and you notice you began to see almost an absence of uniforms. Even the Deputy Police Chief came without a uniform.

Mr. Schultz said, "Look at our witnesses. They don't argue with the judge. They are bright and alert. They sit there and they answer clearly."

They answered like automatons––one after the other, robots took the stand. "Did you see any missiles?"

"A barrage."

Everybody saw a barrage of missiles.

"What were the demonstrators doing?"

"Screaming. Indescribably loud."

"What were they screaming?"

"Profanities of all sorts."

I call your attention to James Murray. That is the reporter, and this is the one they got caught with. This is the one that slipped up. James Murray, who is a friend of the police, who thinks the police are the steadying force in Chicago. This man came to the stand, and he wanted you to rise up when you heard "Viet Cong flags," this undeclared war we are fighting against an undeclared enemy. He wanted you to think that the march from Grant Park into the center of Chicago in front of the Conrad Hilton was a march run by the Viet Cong, or have the Viet Cong flags so infuriate you that you would feel against these demonstrators that they were less than human beings. The only problem is that he never saw any Viet-Cong flags. First of all, there were none, and I call your attention to the movies, and if you see one Viet Cong flag in those two hours of movies at Michigan and Balbo, you can call me a liar and convict my clients.

Mr. Murray, under whatever instructions were given to him, or under his own desire to help the Police Department, saw them. I asked him a simple question: describe them. Remember what he said? "They are black." Then he heard laughter in the courtroom because there isn't a person in the room that thinks the Viet Cong flag is a black flag. He heard a twitter in the courtroom. He said, "No, they are red."

Then he heard a little more laughter.

Then I said, "Are they all red?"

He said, "No, they have some sort of a symbol on them."

"What is the symbol?"

"I can't remember."

When you look at the pictures, you won't even see any black flags at Michigan and Balbo. You will see some red flags, two of them, I believe, and I might say to you that a red flag was the flag under which General Washington fought at the Battle of Brandywine, a flag made for him by the nuns of Bethlehem.

I think after what Murray said you can disregard his testimony. He was a clear liar on the stand. He did a lot of things they wanted him to do. He wanted people to say things that you could hear, that would make you think these demonstrators were violent people. He had some really rough ones in there. He had, "The Hump Sucks," "Daley Sucks the Hump"—pretty rough expressions. He didn't have "Peace Now." He didn't hear that. He didn't give you any others. Oh, I think he had "Charge. The street is ours. Let's go."

That is what he wanted you to hear. He was as accurate about that as he was about the Viet Cong flag, and remember his testimony about the whiffle balls. One injured his leg. Others he picked up. Where were those whiffle balls in this courtroom?

You know what a whiffle ball is. It is something you can hardly throw. Why didn't the Government let you see the whiffle ball? They didn't let you see it because it can't be thrown. They didn't let you see it because the nails are shiny. I got a glimpse of it. Why didn't you see it? They want you to see a photograph so you can see that the nails don't drop out on the photograph. We never saw any of these weapons. That is enough for Mr. Murray. I have, I think, wasted more time than he is worth on Mr. Murray.

Now, I have one witness to discuss with you who is extremely important and gets us into the alleged attack on the Grant Park underground garage.

This is the most serious plan that you have had. This is more serious than attacking the pigs, as they tried to pin onto the Yippies and the National Mobe. This is to bomb. This is frightening, this concept of bombing an underground garage, probably the most frightening concept that you can imagine.

By the way, Grant Park garage is impossible to bomb with Molotov cocktails. It is pure concrete garage. You won't find a stick of wood in it, if you go there. But, put that aside for the moment. In a mythical tale. it doesn't matter that buildings won't burn.

February 13, 1970

In judging the nonexistence of this so-called plot, you must remember the following things.

Lieutenant Healy in his vigil, supposedly, in the garage, never saw anything in anybody's hands, not in Shimabukuro's, whom he says he saw come into the garage, not in Lee Weiner's hands, whom he said he saw come into the garage, or any of the other four or five people whom he said he saw come into the garage. These people that he said he saw come into the garage were looking, he said, in two cars. What were they looking into cars for? You can ask that question. Does that testimony make any sense, that they come in empty-handed into a garage, these people who you are supposed to believe were going to fire bomb the underground garage?

Just keep that in mind when you consider this fairy tale when you are in the jury room.

Secondly, in considering it you have the testimony of Lieutenant Healy, who never saw Lee Wiener before. You remember he said "I never saw him before. I had looked at some pictures they had shown me."

But he never had seen him and he stands in a stairwell behind a closed door looking through a one-foot-by-one-foot opening in that door with chicken wire across it and a double layer of glass for three to four seconds, he said, and he could identify what he said was Lee Wiener in three to four seconds across what he said was thirty to forty yards away.

MR. FORAN: Your Honor, I object to "three or four seconds." It was five minutes.

MR. KUNSTLER: No, sir. The testimony reads, your Honor, that he identified him after three or four seconds and if Mr. Foran will look--

MR. FORAN: Then he looked at him for five minutes.

MR. KUNSTLER: He identified him after three or four seconds.

THE COURT: Do you have the transcript there?

MR. FORAN: Your Honor, I would accept that. He identified him immediately but he was looking at him for five minutes.

MR. KUNSTLER: I just think you ought to consider that in judging, Lieutenant Healy's question. This officer was not called before the grand jury investigating that very thing. And I think you can judge the importance of that man's testimony on whether he ever did tell the United States Attorney anything about this in September of 1968.

I submit he didn't because it didn't happen. It never happened. This is a simple fabrication. The simple truth of the matter is that there never was any such plot and you can prove it to yourselves. Nothing was ever found, there is no visible proof of this at all. No bottles. No rags. No sand. No gasoline. It was supposed to be a diversionary tactic, Mr. Schultz told you in his summation. This was a diversionary tactic. Diversionary to what? This was Thursday night.

If you will recall, the two marches to the Amphitheatre that got as far as 16th and 18th streets on Michigan had occurred earlier. The only thing that was left was the Downers Grove picnic. It was a diversionary operation to divert attention from the picnic at Downers Grove. It was diversionary to nothing. The incident lives only in conversations, the two conversations supposedly overheard by Frapolly and Bock, who are the undercover agents who were characterized, I thought, so aptly by Mr. Weinglass.

Now just a few more remarks. One, I want to tell you that as jurors, as I have already told you, you have a difficult task. But you also have the obligation if you believe that these seven men are not guilty to stand on that and it doesn't matter that other jurors feel the other way. If you honestly and truly believe it, you must stand and you must not compromise on that stand.

MR. FORAN: Your Honor, I object to that. Your Honor will instruct the jury what their obligations are.

THE COURT: I sustain the objection. You are getting into my part of the job.

MR. KUNSTLER: What you do in that jury room, no one can question you on. It is up to you. You don't have to answer as to it to anybody and you must stand firm if you believe either way and not

MR. FORAN: Your Honor, I object to that.

THE COURT: I sustain the objection. I told you not to talk about that, Mr. Kunstler.

MR. KUNSTLER: I think I have a right to do it.

THE COURT: You haven't a right when the Court tells you not to and it is a matter of law that is peculiarly my function. You may not tell the jury what the law is.

MR. KUNSTLER: Before I come to my final conclusion, I want to thank you both for myself, for Mr. Weinglass, and for our clients for your attention. It has been an ordeal for you, I know. We are sorry that it had to be so. But we are grateful that you have listened. We know you will weigh, free of any prejudice on any level, because if you didn't, then the jury system would be destroyed and would have no meaning whatsoever. We are living in extremely troubled times, as Mr. Weinglass pointed out. An intolerable war abroad has divided and dismayed us all. Racism at home and poverty at home are both causes of despair and discouragement. In a so-called affluent society, we have people starving, and people who can't even begin to approximate the decent life.

These are rough problems, terrible problems, and as has been said by everybody in this country, they are so enormous that they stagger the imagination. But they don't go away by destroying their critics. They don't vanish by sending men to jail. They never did and they never will.

To use these problems by attempting to destroy those who protest against them is probably the most indecent thing that we can do. You can crucify a Jesus, you can poison a Socrates, you can hand John Brown or Nathan Hale, you can kill a Che Guevara, you can jail a Eugene Debs or a Bobby Seale. You can assassinate John Kennedy or a Martin Luther King, but the problems remain. The solutions are essentially made by continuing and perpetuating with every breath you have the right of men to think, the right of men to speak boldly and unafraid, the right to be masters of their souls, the right to live free and to die free. The hangman's rope never solved a single problem except that of one man.

I think if this case does nothing else, perhaps it will bring into focus that again we are in that moment of history when a courtroom becomes the proving ground of whether we do live free and whether we do die free. You are in that position now. Suddenly all importance has shifted to you—shifted to you as I guess in the last analysis it should go, and it is really your responsibility, I think, to see that men remain able to think, to speak boldly and unafraid, to be masters of their souls, and to live and die free. And perhaps if you do what is right, perhaps Allen Ginsberg will never have to write again as he did in "Howl," "I saw the best minds of my generation destroyed by madness," perhaps Judy Collins will never have to stand in any Courtroom again and say as she did, "When will they ever learn? When will they ever learn?"

Closing Arguments on Behalf of the Government by Thomas

MR. FORAN: May it please the Court, counsel, ladies and gentlemen of the jury: The recognition of the truth, which is your job, is a very strange thing. There is a real difference between intellectualism and intelligence. Intellectualism leaves out something that intelligence often had and what it really is is a kind of a part of the human spirit. You know many men will be highly intellectual and yet they will have absolutely terrible judgment.

When you stop and think of it. among the twelve of you there is certainly somewhere in excess of four hundred years of human intelligence and instinct, and that is a lot, and that is important. . . .

Much of the concept of the assault by the defendants on the Government's case is: Would anybody do some of these wild things? Most people wouldn't. But those defendants would.

Some of the things that the Government's witnesses testified that some of these defendants did were pretty wild things, and it would be hard to believe that most people, most decent people, would ever do anything like it. Is it so hard to believe that these men would do it?

Has any one of you, for instance, noticed how in the last few days as we reach the end of the case and it comes before for decision, the sudden quieting in the courtroom, the sudden respect, the sudden decency that we see in this courtroom? For that, are we to forget the four-and-a-half months of what we saw?

The defendants in this case—first of all, they kind of argued in a very strange way that there was no violence planned by these defendants at the Democratic Convention.

Since they have no evidence that violence wasn't planned, the way they argue it is

that they say Bock, Frapolly, and Oklepek and Pierson lied. They state that they lied categorically. They said, "Because Bock, Frapolly, Pierson, and Oklepek were undercover agents for the police or newspapers, and therefore, they cannot be honest men.

Now how dare anybody argue that kind of a gross statement? Some of the bravest and the best men of all the world, certainly in law enforcement, have made their contributions while they were undercover. That statement is a libel and a slander on every FBI agent, every Federal narcotics agent, every single solitary policeman who goes out alone and unprotected into some dangerous area of society to try to find out information that is helpful to his government. It is a slander on every military intelligence man, every Navy intelligence man who does the same thing.

There is something that is very interesting, and I bet you haven't noticed it.

The August 9 meeting, you remember that meeting was at Mobilization headquarters. There was a lot of talk and a lot of planning at that meeting. Frapolly, Bock, and Oklepek were all there. So were Dellinger, Davis, Hayden, Weiner, Froines, and Hoffman.

All three of the Government witnesses testified that the march routes to the Amphitheatre were discussed. All agreed that the dangers of the march routes were discussed. All agreed that mill-ins in the Loop were planned during that week: disruptions, blocking cars driving down the street, smashing windows, shut the Loop down, generally make havoc in the Loop area, setting small fires—and, by the way, it all happened.

All of those things that I just mentioned happened on Wednesday of Convention week, and all of them happened in the downtown area right at Michigan and Balbo.

You know, they were saying, "What did they plan that happened?" Well, everything. That was a pretty good shot on the first big meeting.

In addition to the defendants, who else was there at that meeting? Bosciano, Radford, Baker, Steve Buff, and about eight other people. Where are they? If Bock and Frapolly and Oklepek were lying, why weren't they in here testifying that something else was said at that meeting, or that Davis was telling the truth about what he said was said at that meeting. Where are they?

Buff took the witness stand, and they didn't even ask him about the meeting. They didn't even ask him.

The reason that none of the friends and pals of these defendants that were at those meetings didn't come in here and testify or, if they did, ignored the meetings, was because Bock, Frapolly and Oklepek were telling the truth, and if they talked about those meetings on the witness stand, they would have no choice, they would either have to back Bock and Frapolly and Oklepek or they would have to lie. They were at those meetings planning and organizing for the violence that they were going to instigate and incite in Chicago.

And when all that organizing and planning was completed, the time to start the execution of the plan had arrived.

The first thing they had to do is they had to keep this crowd of people getting excited, getting into trouble, but not so much trouble that they would run into a mass arrest situation before Wednesday because they needed the crowd on Wednesday if they were going to have their big confrontation.

And so what they decided--and stop and think of it, remember at the beginning of this case they were calling them all by diminutive names, Rennie and Abbie and Jerry, trying to pretend they were young kids. These are highly sophisticated, highly educated men, every one of them. They are not kids. Davis, the youngest one, took the witness stand. He is twenty-nine. These are highly sophisticated, educated men and they are evil men.

(laughter)

THE COURT: Mr. Marshal.

MR. FORAN: What they have in mind they need to be sophisticated for and they need to be highly educated for because what they have in mind is what Davis told you he had in mind. It is no judgment of mine. Davis told ' you from that witness stand after two-and-a-half days of the toughest cross-examination I was ever involved in because he was so smart and so clever and so alert, but at last he told you "Revolution. Insurrection." And he told you--I am not--you heard it right from the witness stand.

And so these sophisticated men decided that the first thing that they had to do was to test the police. They had to find out what they could do, where they would be stepping too far, you know, where they would run into trouble.

So the first march they had on Sunday they sent the whole--most of them went down opposite the Hilton Hotel. They had an orderly legal march, legal picketing, and there was absolutely no trouble.

Remember Davis back at that August 9 meeting, "We'll lure the McCarthy kids and other young people with music and sex and try to hold the park." And all of this was done the first night. The first night they carried out that plan. But to carry out the big plan they had to generate more heat the next day so that by Wednesday the psychological training ground of this crowd and the psychological torture of the police, that combination would have reached the proper mix for what they had in mind for Wednesday night.

Say you are in the park after 11:00 p.m., and the law says you are supposed to go; a policeman says, "Leave." You say, "Hell, no." He has only two choices, doesn't he? He either has to walk away from you and not enforce the law, or he has to use whatever physical force is necessary to make you leave.

So, he reaches down-say he takes you by the arm. Then what do you do? You scream, "Let me alone! Let me alone! Police brutality!" And you start wrestling around. Then he had again only two choices. Either he had to physically subdue you right there on the spot, or he had to get help in order to carry you out.

MR. KUNSTLER: There is no evidence of that at all, your Honor. Mr. Foran is making up a story here. I object, your Honor.

THE COURT: I overrule your objection. You may continue, sir.

MR. FORAN: If the police get tough and wrongfully--and it is wrong for a policeman to say, "This man is not going to go," so he cracks him, that is wrong. He shouldn't do that. But say he does it, which they do, policemen do that, then the crowd takes that as total justification to attack the police with rocks and bottles. and to say, "We are defending ourselves."

The technique is simple, and it can fit any situation, and you have seen it fit situations in this courtroom.

Somebody violates the regulation of this courtroom, and the marshal asks him to leave, and he won't, so he takes him by the arm, "Aaaaccchhh! Dirty rotten marshal!" And that had happened, and that is the way it is done, and it is done. You know, this is done in complicated situations and in simple situations.

Monday night in Lincoln Park as the curfew approached, there was Rubin, "Arm your-selves with anything you can. Now is the time to make our stand." Earlier, he had been doing the same thing. That is the night they built the barricade, just like they planned on August 9.

It was a rough night in the park. There was gas. Davis is there on the bullhorn. He is shouting encouragement to the crowd to "Fight the pigs" and "Hold the park," commit-ting a criminal act, by the way, inciting a crowd. He had just left his cohort, Hayden, downtown. who had been arrested near the Hilton . . . .

Rubin, as usual, was in the park on Tuesday. He gives a speech to the crowd telling them to take this country away from the people who run it. "Take to the streets in small groups," just as he told Pierson that the Viet Cong had done, and he finished up his revolution exhortation with, "See you in the streets."

These are criminal acts. They are urging people to violence.

Seale followed on the podium with a wild speech telling the crowd to "Get their pieces and barbecue that pork." And we are supposed to wonder, you know, it doesn't mean what it means. That is what the argument is. "It doesn't mean what it means." Of course, you know what it means. "You get your gun and you kill a policeman." That is what is means. It is as obvious as anything from the context of the speech. You heard the whole speech. To say anything else is ridiculous. It is calling black white.

Up at the park, again, Tuesday night, over and over again, the police were saying, "Clear the park. Clear the park." Finally, at 12:30 A.M., the police moved forward again, and again they were met with a hail of missiles. This time, Froines was right up in the front line, throwing rocks and stones himself.

The police really let them have it with tear gas that night. They had a dispenser, and there was a lot of gas, and the crowd got out quickly. I don't know, maybe that is a better way, but I don't know. There was a lot of gas. It is a temporary bad feeling, but at least nobody gets hurt. Maybe it is a better way.

The battle plan that had been talked about by Davis on August 9, was almost ready. Young people had been moved into the park. They fought and resisted the police.

And now the time had come to start shifting the scene down to the downtown area, and just as they planned, the Hilton area was going to be the focus of the next action.

The crowd was pretty heated and pretty militant, and it gad been whipped up really in Lincoln Park, starting way back on August 13 with all of these things, wit at crazy snake dancing, and with the skirmish lines. To be trained in karate is something because karate is a vicious thing. If you are any good at it, you can kill somebody with it. It is a vicious way to fight.

The police had been taunted and insulted and attacked until the weak ones among them, and there are plenty of weak policemen, were losing their professionalism. and they were ripe to be driven into joining some of these participants in rioting.

And then they have that meeting in Mobilization headquarters the next morning where they set it up with a kind of--well, it is a combination of "the massive action with the cutting edge of resistance." They used it successfully at the Pentagon and they were now going to transfer it into the practicalities of Chicago.

Dellinger, Davis, Hayden, Froines, Weiner and Rubin all leave to do their various jobs.

The meeting started at the Bandshell. Dellinger was running the public show up on the stage and Davis was giving instructions to his marshals out behind that refreshment stand, those marshals who, as Froines said, were a lot better street fighters than they ever were what marshals are supposed to be.

He says "Disperse the police. Reduce their effectiveness."

Others of the militant group were seen preparing their vicious, filthy weapons-- bags of urine, pointed sticks, sharpening tiles.

The mood of those militants in that crowd was shown real quickly when that flag came down to half-mast. When that flag came down and those six policemen went in to arrest the man, they were grossly attacked by that crowd.

And the honesty of the defense is pointed out most clearly by the argument of counsel that they were throwing their lunches at the police and that these were picnickers throwing lunches at the police. These weren't picnickers unless those picnickers eat rocks and bottles for lunch.

Rubin in his volatile way had been caught up in the excitement and he was in there pitching, "Kill the pigs. Kill the pigs."

But Dellinger and Davis were a lot cooler than that. They let them continue for a while. It went on for about fifteen minutes and then they cooled it down because it was still daylight and things were--you know, it wasn't quite ready yet. And that's when Davis got hit. Look at this picture in the jury room. He's got a cut on his head and he's bleeding some and he's smiling and he looks very alert and he doesn't look like he's going to fall unconscious to me.

The thing that you have got to recognize is that you have to tie the Bandshell back to that meeting Wednesday morning. Exactly what was planned at that meeting Wednesday morning happened at the Bandshell.

A diversionary march was set up by Dellinger. Another action was set up by Dellinger. As I said earlier, I think like a ventriloquist he used Tom Neumann. Neumann's name had been talked about that morning at that meeting at the Mobilization office as one of the speakers. Neumann was one of the men. The plan was made there at that meeting.

You can gather a whole bunch of people, most of them don't want to riot, but maybe want to protest, maybe want to get in on the act, maybe want to have some fun, maybe want to fight policemen. You gather enough people together, and you have some people who are dedicated to causing public disorder for serious purposes. You don't need a big crowd. And that is what these people always try to do. They tried to shift it off on all youth. They are talking about our children.

There are millions of kids who, naturally, if we could only remember how it is—you know, you resent authority, you are impatient for change, you want to fix things up. Maybe you are very sensitive and you feel the horrors of racism which is a real cancer in the American character, there is no question about that. You feel a terrible frustration of a terribly difficult war that maybe as a young kid you are going to have to serve in. Sure, you don't like things like that.

There is another thing about a kid, if we all remember, that you have an attraction to evil. Evil is exciting and evil is interesting, and plenty of kids have a fascination for it. It is knowledge of kids like that that these sophisticated, educated psychology majors know about. They know about kids, and they know how to draw the kids together and maneuver them, and use them to accomplish their purposes. Kids in the 60s, you know, are disillusioned. There is no question about that. They feel that John Kennedy went, Bobby Kennedy went, Martin Luther King went—they were all killed—and the kids do feel that the lights have gone out in Camelot, the banners are furled, and the parade is over.

These guys take advantage of them. They take advantage of it personally, intentionally, evilly, and to corrupt those kids, and they use them, and they use them for their purposes and for their intents. And you know, what are their purposes and intents?

Well, they tell you, these men tell you this, and this is what troubles me, that some of the things you can really taste.

What is their intent? And this is their own words: "To disrupt. To pin delegates in the Convention hall. To clog streets. To force the use of troops. To have actions so militant the Guard will have to be used. To have war in the streets until there is peace in Vietnam. To intimidate the establishment so much it will smash the city. Thousands and thousands of people perform disruptive actions in Chicago. Tear this City apart. Fuck up the Convention. Send them out. We'll start the revolution now. Do they want to fight? The United States is an outlaw nation which had broken all the rules so peace demonstrators can break all the rules. Violate all the laws. Go to jail. Disrupt the United States Government in every way that you can. See you in Chicago."

And these men would have you believe that the issue in this case is whether or not they really wanted permits.

Public authority is supposed to stand handcuffed and mute in the face of people like that and say, "We will let you police yourselves"? How Would public authority feel if they let that park be full of young kids through that Convention with no policemen, with no one watching them? What about the rape and the bad trips and worse that public authority would be responsible for if it had?

They tried to give us this bunk that they wanted to talk about racism and the war and they wanted a counter-convention. They didn't do anything but look for a confrontation with the police. What they looked for was a fight, and all that permits had to do with it was where was the fight going to be, and that's all.

And they are sophisticated and they are smart and they are well-educated. And they are as evil as they can be. . . .

Riots are an intolerable threat to every American and those who lead others to defy the law must feel the full force of the law." You know who said that? Senator Bob Kennedy said that, who they tried to adopt.

"In a government of law and not of men, no man, no mob, however unruly or boisterous, is entitled to defy the law."

Do you know who said that? John Kennedy.

The lights in that Camelot kids believe in needn't go out. The banners can snap in the spring breeze. The parade will never be over if people will remember, and I go back to this quote, what Thomas Jefferson said, "Obedience to the law is the major part of patriotism." These seven men have been proven guilty beyond any doubt. They didn't attack the planning they were charged with. They did not say it didn't happen. The are guilty beyond any doubt at all of the charges contained in the indictments against them.

You people are obligated by your oath to fulfill your obligation without fear, favor, or sympathy. Do your duty.

Verdict

February 18, 1970

THE COURT: I understand, gentlement, that the jury has brought in a verdict.

Is the jury here? Have you brought the jury here?

THE MARSHAL: Your Honor, the jury hs reached a verdict.

MR. SCHULTZ: Your Honroe, before the jury is brought in, may I make a statement? May I address the Court please?

THE COURT: You certainly may.

MR. SCHULTZ: Your Honor, considering what has gone on in this courtroom before, we would ask your Honor to have the court cleared of all spectators except the press. I have the authority for it if your Honor requires it.

THE COURT: Oh I have done it often before in the trial of jury cases.

I want to ask you a question, Mr. Schultz, before I call on Mr. Kunstler. I see there are a number of ladies. I can identify some one or two as members of the press. You think my rule of exclusion hre should apply to the wives of the defendants?

MR. SCHULTZ: Yes, your Honor, in fact, the wives of the defendants have been probably more contumacious than any others.

THE COURT: You may reply, Mr. Kunstler.

MR. KUNSTLER: Your Honro, we would want to voic the strongers possible objection to the application by the Government. To clear the courtroom at what is probably the most significant part of the trial, the rendering of a verdict, of the friends and relatives of the defendants is to deny them a public trial. The verdict of this jury should not be received in secret with or without the press being here. I think this is making a star chamber proceeding out of this procedure.

There have been many claims made by the defendants about this trial, that it has not been a fair trial, that it has been a trial which has been dictated by an almost indecent effort to comvict them, and we have made this contention, as your Honor knows, against you and against the prosecution.

This is the last possible motion that the Government can make in this case and the defense is hoping that with this last motion, that your Honro will at long last deny a motion made by the prosecution and not let these men stand here alone in the courtroom that has essentially been their home for five months. I beg and implore you to deny this motion of the Government.

THE COURT: I will decide to enter this order. The following remain: of course, the defendants and those who have sat at the Government's table throughout this trial. The ladies and gentlement of the press, all media.

Now all of the parties here other than those I have mentioned are directed to leave the courtroom.

A SPECTATOR (ANITA HOFFMAN): The ten of you will be avenged. They will dance on your grave, Julie, and the grave of the pig empire.

A VOICE: They are demonstrating all over the country for you.

MR SCHULTZ:: I just might point out for the record that we have in the hallway now the same kind of screaming we had in the courtroom.

MR. DELLINGER: That's my thirteen year old daughter they're beating on.

MR. HOFFMAN: Why don't you bring your wife in, Dick, to watch it?

MR. DELLINGER: You ought to be a proud man

MR. HOFFMAN: She would like to hear it.

THE COURT: Mr. Marshal, will you please bring in the jury?

(jury enters)

THE COURT: Good morning ladies and gentlemen of the jury.

I am informed by the United States Marshall that you have reached a verdict or some verdicts.

Is that true? Is there a forewoman or foreman?

THE FOREMAN: A foreman.

THE COURT: Would you hand the verdicts to the marshal, please, and, Mr. Marshal, will you hand them to the clerk?

I direct the clerk to read the verdicts.

THE CLERK: "We, the jury find the defendant David T. Dellinger guilty as charged in Count II of the indictment and not guilty as charged in Count I."

"We, the jury find the defendant Rennard D. Davis guilty as charged in Count III of the indictment and not guilty as charged in Count I."

"We, the jury find the defendant Thomas E. Hayden guilty as charged in Count IV of the indictment and not guilty as charged in Count I."

"We, the jury find the defendant Abbott H. Hoffman guilty as charged in Count V of the indictment and not guilty as charged in Count I."

"We, the jury find the defendant Jerry C. Rubin guilty as charged in Count VI of the indictment and not guilty as charged in Count I."

"We, the jury find the defendant Lee Weiner not guilty as charged in the indictment."

"We, the jury find the defendant John R. Froines not guilty as charged in the indictment."

Signed by Edward F. Kratzke, Foreman, and eleven other jurors.

THE COURT: Thank you ladies and gentlemen.

I wish I were eloquent enough to express my appreciation to you for your several months of service in this case, one of the most difficult I ever tried, one of the longest, and I know you had a great responsibility also.

I express to you in behalf of everybody concerned our deep and appreciative thanks for your service.

You are excused now.

Sentence

February 20, 1970

THE COURT: I now proceed with the imposition of sentence.

MR. KUNSTLER: Your Honor, we were not informed on Wednesday that sentence would occur today.

THE COURT: There is no obligation of a Court to notify you of every step it takes.

MR. KUNSTLER: Well, it is wrong, your Honor, both morally and I think legally.

THE COURT: If you are telling me I am morally wrong in this case, you might add to your difficulty. Be careful of your language, sir. I know you don't frighten very easily.

MR. KUNSTLER: The defendants had no way of knowing they are going to be sentenced today. Their families are not even present, which would seem to me in common decency would be permitted.

THE COURT: The reason they were kept out is my life was threatened by one of the members of the family. I was told they would dance on my grave in one of the hearings here within the last week.

MR. KUNSTLER: Your Honor, are you serious?

THE COURT: Yes, I am, sir.

MR. KUNSTLER: Well, your Honor, I have no answer for that then.

THE COURT: I am not a law enforcement officer.

MR. KUNSTLER: It is your life.

THE COURT: I deny your motion to defer sentencing.

MR. KUNSTLER: I think my other applications, your Honor, can await sentencing. I have several other applications.

THE COURT: All right, I will hear from you first then with respect to the defendant David T. Dellinger.

MR. KUNSTLER: Your Honor, I think for all of the defendants, Mr. Weinglass and I are going to make no statement. The defendants will speak for themselves.

THE COURT: All right, Mr. Dellinger, you have the right to speak in your own behalf.

MR. DELLINGER: I would like to make four brief points.

First, I think that every judge should be required to spend time in prison before sentencing other people there so that he might become aware of the degrading antihuman conditions that persist not only in Cook County Jail but in the prisons generally of this country.

I feel more compassion for you, sit, than I do any hostility. I feel that you are a man who has had too much power over the lives of too many people for too many years. You are doing, and undoubtedly feeling correct and righteous, as often happens when people do the most abominable things. . . .

My second point is whatever happens to us, however unjustified, will be slight compared to what has happened already to the Vietnamese people, to the black people in this country, to the criminals with whom we are now spending our days in the Cook County jail.

I must have already lived longer than the normal life expectancy of a black person born when I was born, or born now. I must have already lived longer, twenty years longer, than the normal life expectancy in the underdeveloped countries which this country is trying to profiteer from and keep under its domain and control.

Thirdly, I want to say that sending us to prison, any punishment the Government can impose upon us, will not solve the problem of this country rampant racism, will not solve the problem of economic injustice, it will not solve the problem of the foreign policy and the attacks upon the underdeveloped people of the world.

The Government has misread the times in which we live, just like there was a time when it was possible to keep young people, women, black people, Mexican-American, anti-war people, people who believe in truth and justice and really believe in democracy, which it is going to be possible to keep them quiet or suppress them.

Finally, all the way through this I have been ambivalent in my attitude toward you because there is something spunky about you that one has to admire, however misguided and intolerant I believe you are. All the way through the trial, sort of without consciousness or almost against my own will I keep comparing you to George III of England, perhaps because you are trying to hold back the tide of history although you will not succeed, perhaps because you are trying to stem and forestall a second American revolution. . . .

I only wish that we were all not just more eloquent, I wish we were smarter, more dedicated, more united. I wish we could work together. I wish we could reach out to the Forans and the Schultzes and the Hoffmans, and convince them of the necessity of this revolution.

I think I shall sleep better and happier with a greater sense of fulfillment in whatever jails I am in for the next however many years than if I had compromised, if I had pretended the problems were any less real than they are, or if I had sat here passively in the courthouse while justice was being throttled and the truth was being denied. . . .

THE COURT: Mr. Davis, would you like to speak in your own behalf? You have that right.

MR. DAVIS: I do not think that it is a time to appeal to you or to appeal the system that is about to put me away. I think that what moves a government that increasingly is controlled by a police mentality is action. It is not a time for words; it is a time that demands action.

And since I did not get a jury of my peers, I look to the jury that is in the streets. My jury will be in the streets tomorrow all across the country and the verdict from my jury will keep coming for the next long five years that you are about to give me in prison.

When I come out of prison it will be to move next door to Tom Foran. I am going to be the boy next door to Tom Foran and the boy next door, the boy that could have been a judge, could have been a prosecutor, could have been a college professor, is going to move next door to organize his kids into the revolution. We are going to turn the sons and daughters of the ruling class in this country into Viet Cong.

THE COURT: Mr. Hayden, you have the right to speak in your own behalf.

MR. HAYDEN: I have very little that I want to say because I don't have very much respect for this kind of freedom of speech. This is the kind of freedom of speech that I think the Government now wants to restrict us to, freedom to speak in empty rooms in front of prosecutors, a few feet from your jail cell.

We have known all along what the intent of the Government has been. We knew that before we set foot in the streets of Chicago. We knew that before we set foot on the streets of Chicago. We knew that before the famous events of August 28, 1968. If those events didn't happen, the Government would have had to invent them as I think it did for much of its evidence in this case, but because they were bound to put us away.

They have failed. Oh, they are going to get rid of us, but they made us in the first place. We would hardly be notorious characters if they had left us alone in the streets of Chicago last year, but instead we became the architects, the masterminds, and the geniuses of a conspiracy to overthrow the government. We were invented. We were chosen by the Government to serve as scape goats for all that they wanted to prevent happening in the 1970s.

I have sat there in the Cook County Jail with people who can't make bond, with people who have bum raps, with people who are nowhere, people who are the nothings of society, people who say to me, "You guys burned your draft cards. I would like to burn my birth certificate so they can never find me again."

I sit there and watch television, and I hear Mr. Foran say the system works. this trial proves the system works.

Mr. Foran, I would love to see a television cameraman come into Cook County jail and show the people how the system is working. Maybe you could televise us sitting around the table with the roaches running over our wrists while we watch somebody on television, a constitutional expert explaining how the jury verdict demonstrates once again the vitality of the American system of justice.

If you didn't want to make us martyrs, why did you do it? If you wanted to keep it cool, why didn't you give us a permit? You know if you had given us a permit, you know that by doing this to us it speed sup the end for the people who do it to us.

And you know that if this prosecution had never been undertaken, it would have been better for those in power. It would have left them in power a little longer. You know that by doing this to us it speeds up the end for the people who do it to us.

You don't believe it but we have to do this. We have no choice. We had no choice in Chicago. We had no choice in this trial. The people always do what they have to do. Every person who is born now and every person under thirty now feels an imperative to do the kind of things that we are doing. They may not act on them immediately, but they feel the same imperative from the streets. Some day they are going to proclaim the that imperative from the bench and from the courthouse. It's only a matter of time. You can give us time. You are going to give us time. But it is only a matter of time.

THE COURT: Mr. Hoffman, the law gives you the right to speak in your own behalf. I will hear from you if you have anything to say.

MR. HOFFMAN: Thank you.

I feel like I have spent fifteen years watching John Daly shows about history. You Are There. It is sort of like taking LSD, which I recommend to you, Judge. I know a good dealer in Florida. I could fix you up.

Mr. Foran says that we are evil men, and I suppose that is sort of a compliment. He says that we are unpatriotic? I don't know, that has kind of a jingoistic ring. I suppose I am not patriotic.

But he says we are un-American. I don't feel un-American. I feel very American. I said it is not that the Yippies hate America. It is that they feel that the American Dream has been betrayed. That has been my attitude.

I know those guys on the wall. I know them better than you, I feel. I know Adams. I mean, I know all the Adams. They grew up twenty miles from my home in Massachusetts. I played with Sam Adams on the Concord Bridge. I was there when Paul Revere rode right up on his motorcycle and said, "The pigs are coming, the pigs are coming. Right into Lexington." I was there. I know the Adams. Sam Adams was an evil man.

Thomas Jefferson. Thomas Jefferson called for a revolution every ten years. Thomas Jefferson had an agrarian reform program that made Mao Tse Tung look like a liberal. I know Thomas Jefferson.

Hamilton: Well, I didn't dig the Federalists. Maybe he deserved to have his brains blown out.

Washington? Washington grew pot. He called it hemp. It was called hemp them. He probably was a pot head.

Abraham Lincoln? There is another one. In 1861 Abraham Lincoln in his inaugural address said, and I quote "When the people shall grow weary of their constitutional right to amend the government, they shall exert their revolutionary right to dismember and overthrow that government."

If Abraham Lincoln had given that speech in Lincoln Park, he would be on trial right here in this courtroom, because that is an inciteful speech. That is a speech intended to create a riot.

I don't even know what a riot is. I thought a riot was fun. Riot means you laugh, ha, ha. That is a riot. they call it a riot.

I didn't want to be that serious. I was supposed to be funny. I tried to be, I mean, but it was sad last night. I am not made to be a martyr. I tried to sign up a few years, but I went down there. They ran out of nails. What was I going to do? So I ended up being funny.

It wasn't funny last night sitting in a prison cell, a 5 x 8 room, with not light in the room. I could have written a whole book last night. Nothing. No light in the room. Bedbugs all over. They bite. I haven't eaten in six days. I'm not on a hunger strike; you can call it that. It's just that the food stinks and I can't take it.

Well, we said it was like Alice in Wonderland coming in, now I feel like Alice in 1984, because I have lived through the winter of injustice in this trial.

And it's fitting that if you went to the South and fought for voter registration and got arrested and beaten eleven or twelve times on those dusty roads for no bread, it's only fitting that you be arrested and tried under the civil rights act. That's the way it works.

Just want to say one more thing.

People-- I guess that is what we are charged with-- when they decide to go from one state of mind to another state of mind, when they decide to fly that route, I hope they go youth fare no matter what their age.

I will see you in Florida, Julie.

THE COURT: The next defendant, Mr. Rubin, do you desire to speak in your own behalf? You have that privilege.

MR. RUBIN: Well, five months are over. Look at the courtroom, fluorescent lighting. We sat for five months in swivel chairs. The press, the marshals, the judge, now it is over.

This is one of the proudest moments of my life. This one of the happiest moments of my life, if you can dig what I mean. I am happy because I am in touch with myself, because I know who I am. I am happy because I am associated with Rennie, Tom, Dave, Abby and myself. That makes me very happy.

This is my life. I used to look like this. I use to look like this, Judge. See? *(displaying picture)*

I was a reporter for a newspaper. Most everybody around this table once looked like this, and we all believed in the American system, believed in the court system, believed in the election system, believed that the country had some things wrong with it, and we tried to change it.

I'm being sentenced to five years not for what I did in Chicago-- I did nothing in Chicago. I am going to jail because I am part of a historical movement and because of my life, the things I am trying to do, because, as Abbie said, we don't want to be-- we don't want to have a piece of the pie.

We don't just want to be part of the American way of life. We don't want to live in the suburbs. We don't want to have college degrees. We don't want to stand before the judge and say, "Yes, we respect you judge, no matter what happens." We don't want that. We are moved by something else. We are moved by a firm belief in ourselves.

And you are sentencing us for being ourselves. That's our crime: being ourselves. Because we don't look like this anymore. That's our crime/

Judge, I want to give you a copy of my book. I want you to read it on your vacation in Florida, because this is why I am on trial. I inscribed it. I made two little inscriptions. One says, "Dear Julius, the demonstrations in Chicago in 1968 were the first steps in the revolution. What happened in the courtroom is the second step." Then I decided to add another note, and that was: "Julius, You radicalized more young people than we ever could. You're the country's top Yippie." I hope you will take it and read it.

What you are doing out there is creating millions of revolutionaries. Julius Hoffman, you have done more to destroy the court system in this country than any of us could have done. All we did was go to Chicago and the police system exposed itself as totalitarian.

And I am glad we exposed the court system because in millions of courthouses across this country blacks are being shuttled from the streets to the jails and nobody knows about it. They are forgotten men. There ain't a whole corps of press people sitting and watching. They don't care. You see what we have done is, we have exposed that. Maybe now people will be interested in what happens in the courthouse down the street because of what happened here. Maybe now people will be interested.

This is the happiest moment of my law.

THE DEFENDANTS: Right on.

THE COURT: I call on the Government to reply to the remarks of the defendants and each of them.

MR. FORAN: The Government has no comment on their remarks, your Honor, I think the evidence in this case speaks for itself/

THE COURT: Mr. Clerk, the defendant David T. Dellinger will be committed to the custody of the Attorney General of the United States or his authorized representative for imprisonment for a term of five years. Further, the defendant Dellinger will be fined the sum of $5,000 and costs of prosecution, the defendant to stand committed until the fine and costs have been paid. That sentence of five years will be concurrent with the sentence the court imposed for contempt of court previously. The two sentences will run concurrently.

Mr. Clerk, the defendant Rennard C. Davis will be committed to the custody of the Attorney General of the Untied States for a term of five years. Further a fine of-- a fine will be imposed against Mr. Davis in the sum of $5,000 and costs of prosecution.

The defendant Thomas C. Hayden will be committed to the custody of the Attorney General of the United States for a term of five years. Further a fine of $5,000 and costs of prosecution will be imposed.

The defendant Abbott H. Hoffman will be committed to the custody of the Attorney General of the United States for imprisonment for a term of five years. Further a fine of $5,000 and costs--

MR. HOFFMAN: Five thousand dollars, Judge? Could you make that three-fifty?

THE COURT: -$5,000 and--

MR. HOFFMAN: How about three and a half?

THE COURT: -and costs will be imposed, costs of prosecution will be imposed.

The defendant Jerry C. Rubin will be committed to the custody of the Attorney General of the United States for a term of five years. Further there will be a fine of $5,000 and cost of prosecution will be imposed.

Not only on the record in this case, covering a period of four months or longer, but from the defendants made here today, the Court finds that the defendants are clearly dangerous persons to be at large. Therefore the commitments here will be without bail.

THE COURT: Does the defense have any observations?

MR. KUNSTLER: In conclusion, your Honor, speaking both for Mr. Weinglass and myself, we didn't need to hear our clients speak today to understand how much they meant to us but, after listening to them a few moments ago we know that what they have said here has more meaning and will be longer remembered than any words said by us or by you.

We feel that if you could even begin to understand that simple fact, then their triumph would have been as overwhelming today as is our belief--

MR. KUNSTLER: —as inevitable—

THE COURT: I gave you an opportunity to speak at the very beginning. You said counsel did not desire to speak.

MR. KUNSTLER: Your Honor, couldn't I say my last words without you cutting me off?

THE COURT: You said you didn't want to speak.

MR. KUNSTLER: Your Honor, I just said a moment ago we had a concluding remark. Your Honor has succeeded perhaps, in sullying it, and I think maybe that is the way the case should end, as it began.

ABBIE HOFFMAN: We love our lawyers.

THE COURT: Mr. Marshal, the court will be in recess.

CPSIA information can be obtained
at www.ICGtesting.com
Printed in the USA
FSHW022329021221
86652FS